2016
mom

SIMPLY NIGELLA

ALSO BY NIGELLA LAWSON

HOW TO EAT
The Pleasures and Principles of Good Food

HOW TO BE A DOMESTIC GODDESS
Baking and the Art of Comfort Cooking

NIGELLA BITES

NIGELLA FRESH

FEAST
Food to Celebrate Life

NIGELLA EXPRESS
Good Food Fast

NIGELLA CHRISTMAS
Food, Family, Friends, Festivities

NIGELLA KITCHEN
Recipes from the Heart of the Home

NIGELLISSIMA
Easy Italian-Inspired Recipes

SIMPLY NIGELLA

NIGELLA LAWSON

Photographs by KEIKO OIKAWA

FLATIRON
BOOKS
NEW YORK

www.flatironbooks.com

Design and Art Direction: Caz Hildebrand and Camille Blais
Cooking Assistant: Hettie Potter
Editorial Assistant: Zoe Wales
Home Economics Advisers: Caroline Stearns and Yasmin Othman
Props: Linda Berlin
Layout/Typesetting: Julie Martin
Index: Vicki Robinson
U.S. Production Manager: Adriana Coada

The Library of Congress Cataloging-in-Publication Data is available upon request.

ISBN 978-1-250-07375-4 (hardcover)
ISBN 978-1-250-09012-6 (signed edition)
ISBN 978-1-250-07376-1 (e-book)

Our books may be purchased in bulk for promotional, educational or business use.
Please contact your local bookseller or Macmillan Corporate and Premium Sales Department
at (800)221-7945 x 5442 or by email at MacmillanSpecialMarkets@macmillan.com

First U.S. Edition: November 2015

10 9 8 7 6 5 4 3 2 1

For Mimi and Bruno

CONTENTS

INTRODUCTION

It is a commonplace to talk of cooking as being therapeutic – and there are times when that is the case – but for me cooking stems from an engagement with life, which in itself combines hopefulness with playfulness. These gifts restored to me, this book began to emerge.

Of course, even when I felt I couldn't cook, or didn't have a kitchen of my own, I still needed to bring food to the table, and I am grateful for this. If cooking isn't hinged on necessity, it loses its context, and purpose. I cook to give pleasure, to myself and others, but first it is about sustaining life, and only then about forging a life.

We make worlds for ourselves all the time; for me, the locus has always been the kitchen. And while there have been times in my life when cooking has created a safe place, and a vital space where I could lose myself in creative concentration, all of which have been documented in my previous books, with this book it has been different. I first had to cook myself strong. Now, you will never hear me talking about "healthy" food. I loathe the term, but not as much as I am disgusted by the contemporary mantra of "clean eating." In *How To Eat*, written so long ago, I wrote: "What I hate is the new-age voodoo about eating, the notion that foods are either harmful or healing, that a good diet makes a good person and that that person is necessarily lean, limber, toned and fit... Such a view seems to me in danger of fusing Nazism (with its ideological cult of physical perfection) and Puritanism (with its horror of the flesh and belief in salvation through denial)."

The Clean-Eating brigade seems an embodiment of all my fears. Food is not dirty, the pleasures of the flesh are essential to life and, however we eat, we are not guaranteed immortality or immunity from loss. We cannot control life by controlling what we eat. But how we cook and, indeed, how we eat does give us – as much as anything can – mastery over ourselves.

The food in this book is what I've been cooking for myself and, although the impetus was certainly to seek out food that made me feel physically strong, I have always believed that food you cook for yourself is essentially good for you. This is not just because real ingredients are better for you than fake foods, but because the act of cooking for yourself is in itself a supremely positive act, an act of kindness. And while I have read much about mindful eating, I have not found much, if anything, on mindful cooking. When I cook, I am absorbed in the simple rituals of chopping, stirring, tasting, losing myself in the world of flavor, sensation, and straightforward practicalities.

And as I progressed, this book became fused with the joyful realities of making a new home. It makes me smile to see the colors of my kitchen, and the house I have created around myself, reflected in the colors of this book. But, of course, it also necessarily tells the broader story of how I live: how I feed my friends and family, the aesthetic pleasure I derive from food, and my belief that what and how we cook can make our lives easier, make us feel better and more alive, and connect us to ourselves, to others, and the world.

A NOTE ON INGREDIENTS AND UTENSILS

The editor who commissioned my first book told me that he always thought of *How To Eat* as the "Pea, Marsala, and Rhubarb Cookbook." And it's true that I am a person of enthusiasms, and go through bouts of extreme reliance on certain ingredients. This is manifested in *Simply Nigella* by the fulsome use of cold-pressed coconut oil, ginger, chiles, and lime: I can't seem to cook without reaching for one of these in my kitchen right now. My books are nothing if not a diary of how I eat, and how I cook, so whatever my current passions are will always be reflected in their pages.

Sometimes the ingredients I require you to buy are not those stocked in every supermarket, but they are always easily available online, and I do ensure that any recherché ingredient gets proper use. I do not want to go shopping unnecessarily, and nor – I presume – do you. Much as I enjoy the ritual of cooking, I do feel it can be good to break out of one's normal routine and repertoire, even if it means adding to the clutter already in my kitchen cupboards. And I do want to stress that if I suggest a foray to, for example, an Asian supermarket – or its online equivalent – it is because the requisite ingredients there tend to be much cheaper, and of much higher quality, than the versions stocked in a local supermarket. A list of stockists for such ingredients can be found on **www.nigella.com/books/simply-nigella/stockists**. Rest assured, this refers to just a handful of recipes.

I have referred to short grain brown rice a number of times in these pages: this is different from regular brown rice, as it takes less time to cook, and absorbs liquid differently.

I have mentioned caramelized garlic in a number of recipes, and have always given instructions on how to make a batch using a very hot oven, but it makes sense to bake the garlic head when you already have something in the oven, and you can simply bake it for longer at a lower temperature at the same time. Thus, 45 minutes in a 425°F oven translates to 2 hours at 325°F, or you can find some mid-point in between. At all times in the kitchen, you need to make your recipes work for you, not the other way around.

Ginger is required to be peeled and grated in many recipes in this book. The easiest way to peel ginger is to use the tip of a teaspoon, and a fine microplane grater is the best tool for grating ginger, as well as mincing garlic and zesting citrus fruit.

Coconut oil is specified as cold-pressed, and this is sometimes labeled as "raw" or "extra-virgin"; it is distinct from deodorized or refined types. Coconut oil is solid until the temperature reaches 76°F, at which point it liquifies.

Eggs are always extra large, and preferably free-range organic.

When baking, all ingredients – unless otherwise specified – should be at room temperature before you start.

Where appropriate, I have mentioned when a recipe is either dairy- or gluten-free, but only where one might expect it to contain dairy or gluten (such as the baking recipes). They are also indicated by colored dots – green for dairy-free, pink for gluten-free – in the index.

I prefer sea salt flakes when I cook or eat, and the measurements given are not interchangeable with fine salt. If you are replacing them with fine salt, half the amount is required.

Where no freezing or make-ahead tip is given alongside a recipe, neither is recommended.

Flour cup measures are scooped and leveled and brown sugar cup measures are firmly packed unless otherwise stated.

Many recipes suggest using cast iron skillets (although alternatives are always given too). Treated well, and seasoned properly, they are the most effective non-stick frying pans, and can be used in the oven as well as on the stove. They also last a lifetime, while pans with a non-stick coating need to be replaced regularly. Mine are very basic and inexpensive, but they serve me well, and I find both the ancient ore they are forged from, and their steady heft, reassuring. Through them, I feel I am linked to a long line of cooks down the ages. The heavy-based Dutch ovens I use in many recipes are enameled cast iron and come with a tight-fitting lid; if you are using something less robust then the cooking times may need to be adjusted. A more luxurious and relatively new-fangled addition to the cast ironware in my kitchen is a slow cooker. As with all cast iron, it retains the heat well and evenly, and avoids any problem of hot spots. Moreover, the pot part can be used in the oven and on the stove.

I often give measurements for pans used in a recipe: except for baking pans, which are specific, these are just to offer guidance.

I use a conventional electric oven; if you are using a fan or convection oven, consult the manual to adjust temperature.

QUICK AND CALM

QUICK AND CALM

There is a tendency which I deplore among those of us who write about food, even as I sometimes am lured into its trap, to make nervous apologies for any activity in the kitchen. We stress how little effort a recipe demands, vaunting the scant amount of time we require you to be in the kitchen. And yes, the recipes in this chapter are simple, they are quick, they are reassuringly undemanding. And yet, I cannot apologize for time spent in the kitchen: it is where I want to be.

There are recipes elsewhere that feed larger groups of people, and for different sorts of occasions; here, my focus is on a quick supper, mostly for two (though you can scale up or down, as needed) and the dishes I've chosen are those that make me feel good at the end of a busy day. But I need to feel good not just when I'm at the table eating, and afterward, but also before, as I'm planted by my stove, decompressing and letting my mind go or, rather, letting it move from a fizzing brain, to my hands. I don't want to be cooking anything that challenges me, but I want to be cooking; if the recipe's right, the activity soothes rather than stresses.

Of course, none of us can truly say that cooking is always what we want to be doing at the end of a long day, but "much depends on dinner," and a day feels disconcertingly out of kilter to me if I haven't eaten well at the end of it. The recipes that follow are how I ensure a calm evening, a good dinner and make me feel that there is nowhere I would rather be than in the moment, and in my kitchen.

A riff on a Caesar salad

There are those who hold the view that a classic recipe is just that: a dish that's earned its status because it, enduringly, works, and to fiddle with it is an act of desecration. It's not a dishonorable stance, but I think it essentially flawed. The classics, in food as in literature, are the very forms that can withstand and, indeed, spawn a plethora of interpretations.

I have subverted the Caesar Salad before. In *How To Eat*, I replaced the traditional croutons with some mini-cubes of potatoes, roasted till crunchy, and tossed – still hot – into the salad, and often still make it thus. My new, heat-blasted version here is a greater deviation and, for me, it's the perfect supper after a long working day, or a fine lunch on a leisurely Saturday. For those missing the crouton element, I suggest a large croûte, in the form of a piece of toast, brushed with extra-virgin olive oil, to munch alongside.

SERVES 2

1 romaine heart

2 tablespoons regular olive oil

1 clove garlic, peeled and finely grated or minced

4 anchovy fillets (the sort packed in oil), finely chopped

zest and juice of ½ unwaxed lemon, plus ½ lemon to serve

2 tablespoons vegetable oil

2 eggs

Parmesan to shave over

○ Preheat the oven to 425°F.

○ Cut the romaine heart in half lengthways and lay both halves on a small baking or aluminum foil pan, cut-side up. Mix the olive oil, minced garlic, and chopped anchovies in a bowl, and spoon over the lettuce. Put the pan in the oven to cook for 10 minutes, then add the finely grated lemon zest and the juice and put back in the oven for another 5 minutes until wilted and slightly charred at the edges.

○ In a small cast iron or heavy-based, non-stick frying pan that is just big enough to fry 2 eggs – I use an 8 inches in diameter one – pour in the vegetable oil. When hot, crack in 1 egg, followed by the other, and fry until the whites are cooked through but the yolks are still runny.

○ Put a romaine half on each serving plate and top with a fried egg. Using a vegetable peeler, shave strips of Parmesan over each plate, adding ¼ lemon, too, in case more is needed to squeeze over.

Brocamole

I have borrowed the name – and inspiration for this recipe – from *mon cher confrère*, Ludo Lefebvre, and it is, as you've probably surmised, a broccolified guacamole (though his recipe contains no avocado). I don't feel too bad about pinching his title: it did, after all, come from his book *Ludo Bites*...

While the recipe is an obvious contender for a chip-and-dip arrangement when friends are over, I make it mostly for a quiet sofa-side supper, to be spread on sourdough toast or dipped into with crudités, or both. I make no apology for not eating all meals at the table. Some days just call for a slob-out on the sofa, but for me the food needs to be something that pulls me out of shattered collapse. This is such a recipe.

While it makes a lot, it does keep well (strangely, considering it has avocado in it) and also gives you a fantastic packed lunch for the next day, either with some raw vegetables to dip into it, or used as a sauce for cold soba – or indeed any other – noodles, in which case I add some toasted pumpkin seeds and toss them through the dressed noodles.

1 head broccoli (crown, not leggy broccolini)	small bunch cilantro
½ cup vegetable oil	1 fresh green chile
1 tablespoon extra-virgin olive oil	juice of 2 limes
1 ripe avocado	sea salt flakes or kosher salt, to taste
2 scallions, trimmed and roughly chopped	

- Trim the florets from the head of broccoli, and cook them in a big saucepan of salted boiling water for about 3 minutes (until crisp-tender).

- Drain and plunge straight into ice-cold water. Once the broccoli is cold, drain very well and tip into a food processor, adding the oils as you process to a thick purée.

- Halve the avocado, remove the pit and then spoon the flesh into the processor. Add the scallions, too, along with most of the cilantro. If you don't want this too fiery, seed the chile, then roughly chop it and add, along with half of the lime juice, and purée again.

- Taste to see if you want more lime juice – I generally find 1½ limes optimal, but it depends on their juiciness – and add salt to taste.

- Serve in a bowl, sprinkled with the remaining cilantro, ready to be dipped into or spread onto toast.

MAKE AHEAD NOTE	STORE NOTE
Can be made up to 6 hours ahead. Cover with plastic wrap or parchment paper and refrigerate until needed.	Leftovers can be stored, covered, in refrigerator for up to 2 days.

Feta and avocado salad with red onions, pomegranate, and nigella seeds

My sister, Horatia, often puts hunks of feta on a plate, sprinkles with nigella seeds (family solidarity), douses in olive oil, and serves them alongside some flatbread with drinks. As you can, too. But I have parlayed this into a simple supper, as piquant as it is pretty. Since feta is the main ingredient here, it really does make a difference if you can get hold of chunky fresh feta from a deli or a Middle-Eastern store, but this still works with good-quality feta in packages. A bowl of baby spinach salad on the side is, along with puffy – rather than crisp – Turkish flatbread (or *pide*), my favorite accompaniment.

Steeping the onion in vinegar – an old trick of mine, which many of you may recognize – not only takes away the acrid rasp of raw onion, but also turns the red strips to a lambent crimson or, further, a positive puce if left to steep long enough. Two hours is optimum: longer is even better, and it does keep. If time is short, 20 minutes should be enough, in which case double the amount of vinegar, letting the onion drown rather than bathe in it.

Should nigella seeds (called *kalonji* in Indian cooking, where they are used a lot) elude you, and you have to leave them out, I promise I won't be offended. Black mustard seeds are a more-than-acceptable substitute here; or you can drop the spice element altogether. A good quality Greek extra-virgin olive oil is my anointing olive oil of choice, and it goes perfectly here, strong and true, despite the geo-political discordancy.

SERVES 2

½ red onion, peeled

2 tablespoons red wine vinegar

8 ounces feta cheese

½ teaspoon nigella or black mustard seeds

1 ripe avocado

2 tablespoons pomegranate seeds

1–2 tablespoons extra-virgin olive oil (see Intro)

○ Slice the red onion into fine half-moons and put this delicate tangle into a small, non-metallic bowl, pour the vinegar over this, and make sure all of the onion is submerged. Cover with plastic wrap and leave to steep (see Intro).

○ When the vinegar's done its trick and the onion strips are lit up like shards of a stained-glass window designed by Schiaparelli, get on with the rest of the salad.

○ Get out 2 plates, and divide the feta between them, breaking it up into uneven chunks. Sprinkle it with the nigella or black mustard seeds.

○ Peel and remove the pit from the avocado, then cut the flesh into long, thin, gondola-shaped slices, and arrange around the feta. Scatter with pomegranate seeds and trickle with a green gleam of extra-virgin olive oil. Serve with the onions, lifted from their steeping juice and draped over the plate.

MAKE AHEAD NOTE

The pickled onions can be made up to 1 week ahead. Put into a non-metallic container, cover, and store in refrigerator until needed.

Halloumi with quick sweet chili sauce

When I described halloumi once as "salt-flavored Polystyrene," people thought I was being derogatory. Nothing could have been further from the truth. There is something so compelling about this squeaky cheese, and my refrigerator is stocked with it at all times. Most regularly I treat it as vegetarian bacon, dry-fried in a hot pan then dolloped with a peeled, soft-boiled egg (I'd rather peel an egg, even when it's hurty-hot, than poach one). But the idea for this recipe came to me one evening when I felt the need to counter the siren call of the halloumi's saltiness with some sweet-and-heat.

I use a copper pixie-pan for the quick sauce — which takes all of 4 minutes — but if you don't have one, just make more and keep it afterward in a sealed jar, heating up what you need on further occasions.

3 fresh red chiles

2 tablespoons honey

1 lime, halved

1 x 8-ounce block halloumi cheese

TO SERVE:

salad leaves of your choice

extra-virgin olive oil to taste

° Slice 2 of the chiles, leaving the seeds in, then seed the third and chop it into a fine dice (this is for full-on fieriness; you may seed more cautiously if you wish) and add to a small saucepan – ideally, the sort sold as a butter-melting pan – along with the honey, and squeeze in 1 teaspoon of lime juice from one half of the lime. Put the pan on the smallest ring on the stove and bring to a bubble, then turn the heat down low, and let it foam away for 4 minutes. Stir frequently and do not leave the pan unattended, otherwise it will foam over the stove. Remove from the heat.

° Before you turn to the halloumi, arrange a few salad leaves on 2 plates, and pour as much or as little oil over them as you want. Cut the un-juiced half of the lime into wedges, and put one on each plate if so wished.

° Slice the halloumi block into 8 pieces, and heat a cast iron skillet or heavy-based frying pan. When it's hot, add the slices and cook them – without any oil in the pan – for 30–60 seconds until they are tiger-striped underneath, then turn the slices over and cook until the underside is patchily bronzed, too.

° Remove the halloumi to the salad-lined plates and spoon the lipstick-red pieces of chile in their honeyed glaze over the cheese. Eat immediately. Not hard to do.

STORE NOTE

Transfer cooled leftover chili sauce to a jar, then seal and store in refrigerator for up to 2 weeks.

Roast radicchio with blue cheese

I have always held that what is true in the kitchen holds equally true out of the kitchen, but it occurs to me that there is one salient exception. In life, bitterness ("like drinking poison and expecting the other person to die" as I believe Carrie Fisher put it, though attribution is vexed) is to be avoided at all costs, but when it comes to eating, it is one of the greatest goods. As a mindset, I have never seen the allure of bitterness or been even momentarily tempted to succumb to it; in the kitchen, I am in its thrall. If you feel the same way, then you should definitely have the James Beard Award-winning *Bitter* by Jennifer McLagan in your library. Those of you who are yet to be convinced, try this recipe first. Consider it an entry-level introduction, and one of the easiest, most elegant suppers I know. A few steamed baby white potatoes bolster it perfectly, their waxy sweetness providing a creamy foil to the muted pungency of the bitter leaves and blue cheese, though I love it as it is, or with the bitterness-boost provided by a tangle of watercress.

My favorite radicchio is not the round sort from Chioggia but the ultra-bitter, less tender-leaved, zeppelin-shaped Treviso Precoce. But it has a much shorter season (more costly, too), and the round radicchio, in all its plump Episcopal splendor, is not to be disparaged.

SERVES 2

1 large round radicchio or 2 Treviso Precoce, if possible	2 ounces Gorgonzola Piccante or other blue cheese
1 tablespoon regular olive oil	2 tablespoons pine nuts
good grinding of pepper	1 tablespoon chopped fresh chives
1½ teaspoons balsamic vinegar	watercress, to serve (optional)

○ Preheat the oven to 425°F.

○ If using the round radicchio, slice into quarters from bottom to tip (try to keep the quartered heads in whole pieces if you can). If you're using the long Treviso Precoce, then just halve them.

○ Arrange them on a foil pan or a small, shallow baking pan lined with foil. Drizzle with the oil, grind some pepper over them, then sprinkle with the vinegar. Finally, crumble the cheese on top, or add blobs of it if the cheese is creamy, and then transfer to the hot oven to cook for 10 minutes.

- While the radicchio's in the oven, heat a small, heavy-based frying pan and toast the pine nuts by tossing them in the hot dry pan until they have colored. Remove to a cold plate.

- Transfer the wilted, no-longer-crimson, but bronze-tipped radicchio with its molten pockets of cheese to a couple of plates, lined with watercress if so desired. Scatter with the toasted pine nuts and the chopped fresh chives.

Cauliflower and cashew nut curry

You know I am never knowingly undercatered, and therefore are probably not surprised that I am suggesting turning a whole cauliflower into a curry for just 2 people. In my defense, I should say that I once made this for 4 people, and nearly hyperventilated as I saw the first 2 fill up their plates, and feared how meager the portions would be for the 2 of us remaining. Besides, you cannot in all seriousness suggest that a quarter of a cauliflower is really enough for one person's supper: this is not a vegetable accompaniment; it is the main event. Yes, I know that it would be enough from a nutritional point of view, but blame my atavistic refugee mentality: I just can't do it. I feel part of the security I derive from cooking is knowing that there will be leftovers for later.

My suggestion would be to serve this just as it is, but with some pillowy naan bread warmed up in the oven for dippage as you eat. But if you want to, by all means rustle up some rice or – let me be a middle-class cliché – quinoa. This is, anyway, what you could term a Multi-Culti Curry: it shamelessly fuses Thai and Indian flavors (and you could indeed use an Indian curry paste in place of the Thai one here) but with honorable intent, and to most pleasing effect. I am a Londoner, after all, and a clashingly cosmopolitan kitchen comes naturally to me. I trust it causes no consternation beyond.

SERVES 2

1 medium-sized head cauliflower

2–3 teaspoons sea salt flakes or kosher salt, or to taste

2 bay leaves

1 tablespoon cold-pressed coconut oil

2 scallions, thinly sliced

2 teaspoons finely chopped fresh ginger

seeds from 3 cardamom pods

1 teaspoon cumin seeds

1 tablespoon finely chopped cilantro stalks

¼ cup Thai red curry paste (see Intro)

1 x 14-ounce can coconut milk

²/₃ cup cashew nuts

1 lime, halved

small handful chopped fresh cilantro

naan or flatbreads, to serve (optional)

- Put a saucepan of water on to boil for the cauliflower. Cut said cauliflower into florets. Once the pan's boiling, add 2 teaspoons of sea salt flakes and the bay leaves, and cook the florets for 4–5 minutes or until they're cooked, but only just.

- While the cauliflower is bubbling away, heat the coconut oil in a wok – or pan into which all the ingredients will fit – that comes with a lid, and then add the scallions, the chopped ginger, the cardamom and cumin seeds, and the finely chopped cilantro stalks. Stir over a medium heat for 1 minute or so.

- Add the curry paste, stirring again before adding the coconut milk. Stir well, and bring to a bubble.

- Once the cauliflower florets have had their 5 minutes' boiling, check they are tender, drain, and add to your wok or pan. Stir into the sauce and taste to see if you want to add the remaining salt; I always do. Then put on the lid, and simmer for another 10 minutes or so: you want the cauliflower to be tender, well-covered, and soused by the sauce. This would be a good time to start warming the naan (if that's what you're having).

- Meanwhile, heat a small, heavy-based frying pan and toast the cashews until they have colored. Stir half of them into the cauliflower pan, and tip the other half onto a cold saucer or plate for now.

- Taste the sauce again to see if you want to squeeze in some lime, and check the seasoning at the same time, then ladle the cauliflower and sauce onto 2 waiting plates. Scatter with the reserved cashews, sprinkle with the chopped cilantro, and add a lime wedge to each plate.

STORE NOTE

Cool leftovers, then cover and refrigerate within 2 hours of making. Will keep in refrigerator for up to 3 days. Reheat gently in a saucepan, or in short blasts in a microwave, until piping hot.

Shrimp and avocado lettuce wraps

I've taken what are essentially the shrimp and avocado tacos I've eaten whenever on the West Coast, and replaced the tortillas with lettuce leaves and subdued the traditional *pico de gallo* (the classic Mexican salsa of tomatoes, onion, jalapeños, and cilantro) by substituting the raw yellow onion with a modest amount of chopped scallion. Still, it's plenty fiery enough; it's just that I don't like raw onion much. If you do, bung it in.

I love the softness of the lettuce wraps, but nothing's to stop you reverting to tortilla mode. Alas, the shrimp I get here come frozen not fresh, but I simply take out what I need from the freezer in the morning and leave to thaw in the refrigerator during the day, which means I have the speediest supper when needed urgently, as I find it so often is, come the evening.

I like the scorch I get from using a cast iron skillet, but if you're using a heavy-based frying pan, put it over a slightly lower heat with the oil already in the pan.

SERVES 2

1 teaspoon cold-pressed coconut oil or regular olive oil

8 raw shell-off jumbo shrimp, thawed if frozen

zest and juice of 1 lime, preferably unwaxed

2 ripe tomatoes (3–4 ounces total)

1 scallion

1 fresh jalapeño pepper

¼ cup chopped fresh cilantro

salt to taste

1 Boston or Bibb lettuce

1 ripe avocado

○ Heat a cast iron skillet (if you're using one) and add the oil (otherwise just warm the oil in a heavy-based frying pan). When it's sizzling, add the shrimp and stir-fry until just cooked through. Using – for ease – a fine microplane, if you have one, grate the zest of the lime over the shrimp and add a squeeze of lime juice, then stir and transfer to a plate for the moment.

○ Seed and finely chop the tomatoes and drop into a small bowl. Thinly slice the white part of the scallion, and add to the tomatoes. Seed (or not, if you want this properly hot, as I do) and finely chop the jalapeño and drop this into the bowl, too. Stir in the chopped cilantro and squeeze 1½ teaspoons of lime juice over this, then mix gently and add salt to taste.

○ Get out a couple of plates. Tear 2 leaves – whole – from the lettuce and sit one on top of another to make a receptacle, then repeat 3 more times, so that each plate has 2 double-layer lettuce wraps on it. Slice each shrimp in half lengthways – as if you were trying to open out each shrimp like a book and then cutting down the spine – and divide between the lettuce wraps. Peel, pit, and slice the avocado, and divide the pieces between the 4 shrimp-filled lettuce cups. Spoon some of the salsa over the shrimp and avocado slices, but do leave some in the bowl to spoon over as you, messily, eat.

Salmon, avocado, watercress, and pumpkin seed salad

This is a regular lunch or supper at *casa mia*, as anyone who follows me on Twitter or Instagram will recognize. I sometimes poach the salmon and keep it in the refrigerator (see Make Ahead Note, overleaf), just so that I can make it even faster when the need hits. It's quick work anyway, so this is more of an aside than a piece of advice. Although you can always swiftly make a *salade tiède* by flaking the salmon onto the leaves while it's still warm.

I like to use wild Alaskan salmon, which accounts for the vivid hue here. It doesn't have an exceedingly strong taste – I always feel it's as if the salmon is frozen while still alive, the waters must be so cold – but nor does it have that spooky flabbiness of farmed salmon. And it isn't anywhere near as expensive as wild Scottish salmon, desirable and wholly delicious as that is.

If you have half an avocado that needs using up, you can put it to excellent use here, as you don't really need a whole one if this is to feed only two of you.

2 wild Alaskan salmon fillets (approx. 8 ounces total)

2 scallions, trimmed

1 teaspoon black peppercorns

2½ teaspoons lime juice

2 teaspoons sea salt flakes or kosher salt

FOR THE SALAD:

3 tablespoons pumpkin seeds

4 ounces watercress

1 teaspoon organic raw apple cider vinegar

1 small ripe avocado

1 tablespoon extra-virgin olive oil

1 teaspoon sea salt flakes or kosher salt, or to taste

- Put the salmon fillets in a small frying pan (I use one with an 8-inch diameter) and cover with cold water from the tap. Add the scallions and peppercorns, squeeze in the lime juice and sprinkle in the salt, then bring to a boil, uncovered. When the pan is bubbling, turn the fillets over, then remove the pan from the heat and leave to stand for 7 minutes. Then take the fillets out of the liquid and leave to cool completely, which could take up to 1 hour. Once cool, the salmon will be cooked through, with its flesh desirably tender and coral inside.

- While the salmon's cooling, make a start on the salad. Toast the pumpkin seeds by tossing them in a dry, heavy-based frying pan on the stove. They will start jumping a little, and will darken and get a smokier taste. It doesn't take long to toast them, so don't leave the pan and, indeed, keep giving it a quick swirl. Then transfer to a cold plate.

- When you're ready to unite salmon with salad, put the watercress into a large shallow bowl (or split between 2 bowls), sprinkle with the vinegar, and toss. Now add the salmon, removing the skin and tearing the fish into bite-sized pieces or shreddy bits, as you wish.

- Halve the avocado and remove the pit, then spoon the flesh out onto the salmon and watercress, or cut it into slices if you prefer. Drizzle the oil over the salad, sprinkle with the salt and half of the toasted pumpkin seeds, and toss gently to mix. Scatter the remaining pumpkin seeds on top, and eat.

MAKE AHEAD NOTE

The salmon can be cooked up to 3 days ahead. Cool for up to 1 hour, then cover and refrigerate until needed.

Miso salmon

In *How To Eat*, I had a recipe for miso-steeped salmon that was very different from this, and in fact was my adaptation, more suited to our shores, of the Nobu black cod with miso that had just hit America and, so many years on, is still a fixed entry in the lexicon of would-be fashionable menus. This version is altogether simpler and quicker, and also lighter and sprightlier. Although I make this as an effortlessly exquisite supper for 2, you can see how easy it would be to up the numbers and make it when you have friends for supper. Were I cooking for more of a crowd, I'd advise you to make the Broccoli Two Ways (**p.230**) to go with it. As it is, I prefer to steam some baby bok choy, simply dressed with a few drops of Asian sesame oil. Some leggy broccolini would work equally well.

1 tablespoon sweet white miso

1 tablespoon lime juice

1 tablespoon soy sauce

1 tablespoon fish sauce

1 clove garlic, peeled and finely grated or minced

2 salmon fillets or steaks (8 ounces total)

1 fresh red chile, seeded and thinly sliced

- Preheat the oven to 425°F.

- Place a resealable bag in a measuring cup, folding the edges over the top of the cup to make it easy to fill, then spoon in the white miso. Add the lime juice, soy sauce, fish sauce, and grated or minced garlic to the bag, and then seal and massage the contents to create a smooth, paste-like marinade.

- Open up the bag, slip in the salmon fillets, then seal it again and squidge it so that the fillets are covered with the marinade. Now lay the bag flat, leaving the salmon to steep for 15 minutes at room temperature.

- Line a shallow baking pan with aluminum foil, then fish out your salmon from the bag, shaking off the marinade, and place, flattest-side down, on the foil.

- Place the pan in the oven and cook the salmon for 7–10 minutes, depending on the thickness of your fish. You want it cooked through, but still juicy and coral within.

- When they're cooked, transfer the fillets to a couple of warmed plates, then scatter with the chile strips, dividing them between each fillet.

Indian-spiced cod

According to Rex, my excellent fishmonger, there is plenty of sustainable cod around the English coast of Cornwall, and so I use it with an easy conscience here. Its price compared, say, to pollock or hake, certainly makes it a treat, but then so does its luscious, firm, silky-fleshed taste. This recipe will accommodate any thick fillets of firm white fish and, indeed, would work (from a cooking point of view) with salmon, too. If you are using cod, ask your fishmonger to cut from the loin, not the tail. And I urge you to go to a fishmonger if you can. It makes me feel much more assured about the fish I am using, in the first instance, and if we stop going to fishmongers, they will die out, which I do not want to see happen. Furthermore, it can be a mistake to presume that a supermarket will always be the cheaper choice.

I think of this as an Indian-inspired take on the British dish of cod and mushy peas; my accompaniment of choice being the Quick Coconutty Dal on **p.234**, though feel free to serve with a simple salad if you prefer. And if you have your eye on the Pink-Pickled Eggs on **p.268**, then these would be splendid here too.

Similarly, if you want to use Greek yogurt rather than coconut milk yogurt, which I adore, and extravagantly use whenever I can, please do (it's certainly less expensive), but in that case you will need only 1 teaspoon of lime juice along with the grated zest of the whole lime.

3 tablespoons coconut milk yogurt

zest and juice of 1 lime, preferably unwaxed

1 teaspoon garam masala

½ teaspoon hot chili powder

½ teaspoon ground turmeric

1 teaspoon fine sea salt

4 teaspoons yellow mustard seeds

¼ teaspoon ground mace

2 skinless cod loin fillets (approx. 14 ounces total)

TO SERVE:

lime wedges and either crushed pink peppercorns or crushed red pepper flakes from a jar

○ Preheat your oven to 400°F. If you're making the dal on **p.234** to eat alongside, get started on that before the fish. Put the yogurt into a shallow dish, such as a small oblong Pyrex dish, then grate in – using a fine microplane preferably – the zest of the lime and squeeze in all the juice.

○ Whisk in the garam masala, chili powder, turmeric, salt, mustard seeds, and mace.

○ Coat each cod fillet in the spiced yogurt mixture, turning carefully to cover each one as evenly and thickly as you can.

○ Sit the fillets on a small, shallow baking pan and roast in the oven for 15 minutes. Check after this time that they are cooked through. The thickness of the fish will vary so it may need longer; you just need to check that the flesh is no longer glassy.

○ Transfer to 2 waiting plates, add some lime wedges, and put some gently crushed pink peppercorns (or crushed red pepper flakes) nearby for tableside sprinkling, if so wished. Serve with a salad or the Quick Coconutty Dal.

Jackson Pollock

I'm sorry, but I just couldn't help myself. And while my little joke doesn't work should you use other firm white fish, the recipe does, so please use whatever fish you prefer. But there have been huge efforts to encourage the British to eat our local pollock over recent years, though for some reason the name was seen to put people off. For a while, comic though this sounds, a British supermarket rebranded pollock as "colin," though I can't believe that it helped matters much, and is slightly confusing given that *colin*, when not the man's name, is the French for hake (north of the Loire, that is; they call it *merlu* in the south). The chargrilled peppers in oil that I use here (and elsewhere in this book) are mixed, chopped, oil-steeped ones, but oil-packed roasted peppers will work just as well.

SERVES 2

2 skinless pollock fillets (8–10 ounces total)

8 ounces spinach

¾ cup parsley leaves

1½ teaspoons sea salt flakes or kosher salt

zest and juice of ½ unwaxed lemon

3 tablespoons vegetable oil

1 tablespoon extra-virgin olive oil

2 teaspoons cold water (if needed)

1 cup roughly chopped roasted red peppers in their oil (or mixed colors if available)

1 clove garlic, peeled and finely grated or minced

- Preheat the oven to 400°F. Take the fish fillets out of the refrigerator. Tip the spinach leaves into a colander and rinse under the cold tap to clean, then shake the colander in the sink, pushing down on the spinach, to get rid of excess water.

- Start by making the green sauce. You can use either a bowl and a stick blender, or the small bowl of a food processor. Blitz a cup and a half of the spinach with the parsley, ½ a teaspoon of sea salt flakes, the finely grated lemon zest and juice, and the vegetable oil until you start to have an emulsified sauce. Add the extra-virgin olive oil, and blitz again, then taste for seasoning and add the cold water if the sauce needs thinning: it needs to have a certain amount of runniness for the artistic effect we have planned.

- Tip the roasted red peppers, and their oil, into a small oven pan – I use a shallow one measuring 10 x 12 inches with a lip of 1¾ inches. Add the grated garlic and sprinkle with ½ a teaspoon of sea salt flakes and stir to mix. Sit the pollock fillets on top and bake in the oven for 5–7 minutes, until the fish is cooked through.

- While the fish is in the oven, heat up a wok or large saucepan (with a lid), and add the rest of the spinach along with the remaining salt, put on the lid, and let the spinach wilt; this shouldn't take more than 2 minutes.

- Check the fish is cooked and, when it is, take the pan out of the oven. Get out a large plate, and add the wilted spinach in dollops, using a slotted spoon, so that you're not making everything too watery. Now add the fish fillets, cutting each in half first, and – again using a slotted spoon – the roasted red peppers, arranging them around the fish and spinach, letting some chunks land on top, then dribble a little of the peppers' orange oil over the fish.

- Spoon and streak the green sauce over as you wish; by all means, consult the picture here – or indeed an art book – for guidance.

Mackerel with ginger, soy, and lime

I do delight in mackerel. Part of the pleasure, for me, is derived from the beauty of its blue-silver-gold-glinting skin with those almost otherworldly striations, but that doesn't mean I cook it for aesthetic reasons alone.

The sharp and feisty marinade here is the perfect foil to the mackerel's rich flesh, and if the marinating process means you don't get that crunchy, crisp skin, it's a trade-off I'm willing to make. Actually, if you grill this on a barbecue, at nuclear heat, for a mere-if-melting moment (after a yawningly long time a-heating) you may indeed get that Japanese-restaurant crispness, but a hot oven provides a tenderness so absorbingly complete, and without any frenzied interruption to the calmness of the occasion, that I can't suggest any better way to proceed than below.

I like to serve a little sushi ginger alongside, either out of a package or, better still, made from the startlingly simple recipe on **p.266**. And a quick stir-fry of shredded Brussels sprouts works for me, too. Just heat a wok, add 2 teaspoons of vegetable oil and when it's sizzling, grate in (or mince and add) a clove of garlic and add 1 teaspoon of sesame seeds, stir, then quickly toss in about 6 ounces Brussels sprouts, thinly sliced with a sharp knife, and stir-fry for 2–3 minutes. Finally, throw in a teaspoon of sea salt flakes or kosher salt mixed in a shot glass of water, and a spritz of lime, and stir-fry for 30 seconds to a minute, before seasoning to taste, and you're done. But nothing would be wrong in simply serving a crisp and astringently dressed salad alongside, instead.

zest of 1 lime, preferably unwaxed, and 2 teaspoons juice

2 tablespoons soy sauce

1 tablespoon grated fresh ginger

1 teaspoon maple syrup

drop Asian sesame oil

4 mackerel fillets

○ Preheat the oven to 425°F.

○ Finely grate the zest of the lime (you'll need some of the juice later) and set this aside in a little bowl covered with plastic wrap for the time being.

○ Take out a resealable bag and put in all the marinade ingredients – 2 teaspoons of lime juice, the soy sauce, ginger, maple syrup, and drop of sesame oil – then squish it around, before adding the mackerel fillets. Seal the bag, and give it another gentle squidge or two, then leave it flat for 10 minutes. Now would be the time to start slicing the Brussels sprouts, should you be wanting to eat them alongside (see Intro).

○ Line a small, shallow baking pan – into which the fillets will fit neatly – with aluminum foil, and tip in the fillets, marinade and all, then turn the mackerel skin-side up before putting into the hot oven to roast for 10 minutes. Check, obviously, to see if the fish is cooked through before serving. If it needs only a tiny bit longer, just take the pan out of the oven and let it sit on a heatproof surface for a few more minutes.

○ Get out a couple of plates and put 2 fillets on each, sprinkling most of the reserved lime zest over them. Add your vegetable accompaniment of choice, sprinkling the rest of the grated lime zest over that, and tuck in, adding sushi ginger as you go, should that make you happy. It makes me happy.

Spiced and fried haddock with broccoli purée

This recipe could hardly be easier, and requires no complication, nor any effort to keep it simple. Good fish, lightly dredged in spiced flour then flash-fried, is an old-fashioned pleasure, and one to be savored. Here I use gluten-free flour in preference to regular all-purpose flour to coat the fish. I had wanted the slight grittiness of rice flour, but had none in the house, and gluten-free flour (which I did have) contains rice flour and worked fabulously. Obviously, you can use all-purpose flour if you wish. And while the verdiglorious accompaniment may look like old-time British mushy peas, it is, in fact, broccoli, blitzed with a stick blender. I use frozen broccoli simply because I find that, cooked in this way, the taste is – counterintuitively – fresher and needs no more added to it than a little salt and pepper to taste, along with the mildest, yet emphatically creamy, hit of coconut. If you cringe at the idea of coconuttiness, however delicate, then use butter or a really good extra-virgin olive oil instead.

SERVES 2

FOR THE BROCCOLI PURÉE:

1 pound (approx. 4½ cups) frozen broccoli florets

1–2 tablespoons cold-pressed coconut oil or butter or extra-virgin olive oil

salt and pepper to taste

FOR THE SPICED HADDOCK:

3 tablespoons gluten-free or all-purpose flour

1 teaspoon ground ginger

1 teaspoon paprika

1 teaspoon fine sea salt

2 haddock fillets, skin on (approx. 12 ounces total)

1 tablespoon vegetable oil

TO SERVE:

½ lemon, cut into wedges

○ Put a saucepan of water on for the broccoli, and when it comes to a boil, salt to taste and cook the frozen broccoli florets (unthawed) for 10 minutes from the time the water comes back to a boil, or until it's tender enough to be puréed. Drain and return to the pan, along with 1 tablespoonful of cold-pressed coconut oil, and set about it with your stick blender, adding salt and pepper and a further tablespoon of oil to taste. Put the lid on and leave while you fry the fish, which is the work of moments.

○ Get out a plate in which the fish fillets can lie flat, and in it mix the flour, spices, and salt, then dredge the fish on both sides, so that the fillets are well coated. Place a cast iron skillet or a heavy-based, non-stick frying pan – into which the fillets will fit neatly – on the stove top. In the case of the cast iron skillet, heat it before adding the vegetable oil; if using a non-stick frying pan, add the oil first.

○ When the oil is hot, put both fillets in the pan, skin-side down, and cook for 3 minutes. Turn them over and cook for another 1½ minutes, or until the fish is just cooked through. These timings are based on fillets that are – as you can see – square-ish and quite thick. If yours are thinner, 2 minutes skin-side down, followed by 1 minute on the other side, should do it.

○ Once the fish is cooked, transfer to a plate lined with paper towels while you dollop the broccoli purée onto 2 dinner plates. Add the haddock fillets, crisp-skin-side-up, and eat with calm relish, and possibly a spritz of lemon.

Steamed branzino with ginger and soy

While branzino is undeniably a luxury, this recipe makes frugal use of it. I buy
1 wild branzino fillet, and cut it in half so that it feeds 2. I should admit, though, that
the impetus here is not so much thrift, as concern about fitting the branzino into the
steamer. And when I say steamer, I rig up a makeshift one by bringing water to boil
in my wok (which comes with a lid) and sitting a round wire cake-cooling rack on
top of it. The prepared fish goes on a heatproof plate, the plate goes on the rack,
the lid goes on, and it's as simple as that. Obviously, if you own a steamer, then
it will be even simpler. (And I suppose you could cook the fish, with its flavorings,
wrapped in a piece of lightly greased aluminum foil in a 400°F oven for 5 minutes,
or until just cooked through.) This fish is so delicate, and so lightly but beautifully
sauced – and its flavors, while gentle, are confident and resonant.

Alongside, I like a simple, undressed salad made of ½ an English cucumber, halved,
seeded, then cut into juliennes or fine batons, along with 4–6 radishes (depending
on their size) cut into tiny red-tipped matchsticks, all tossed together. It would also be
perfect with some wilted spinach on the side.

SERVES 2

1-inch piece fresh ginger, peeled	1 teaspoon Asian sesame oil
1 skinless branzino fillet (approx. 8 ounces)	cilantro, to serve
1 tablespoon soy sauce	

○ Put a steamer on to boil. Make the cucumber and radish salad, and see Intro if
  you're going down that recommended route. Cut the peeled ginger into very thin
  slices across, then cut each slice into thin strips. Now cut the branzino in two,
  across, so that you have a pair of shorter fillets.

○ Get out a heatproof plate, with a lip, that will fit into the steamer (see Intro) and is
  also big enough for the 2 fillets. Sprinkle the plate with half of the ginger strips, sit
  the fish on top, and then add the rest of the ginger strips. Mix the soy sauce and
  sesame oil together and spoon over the fish. Sit the plate on the steamer rack, cover
  and steam for 5 minutes, or until the fillets are just cooked through.

○ Divide the salad between 2 plates, then carefully transfer a fillet to each plate,
  pouring the scant but scented sauce over the fish, and making sure you get every
  bit of ginger, too. Sprinkle with a few cilantro leaves and eat immediately, savoring
  each exquisite mouthful.

Deviled roe on toast

I love soft roe on toast. My mother often used to make it on a Saturday night – after the statutory chicken at lunch – and the contrast between the soft gaminess of the roe and the butteriness of the toast, and that essential, sharp squeeze of lemon, fills me not with a nostalgia for my childhood but for a taste that is now so rare, it feels as if it is about to slip into a historical archive or the exclusive province of the British gentleman's club (or upmarket restaurants that aspire to that ungenerous estate).

For those too young to have grown up with them, I have to tell you that soft roe is the sperm of the herring. I see no place for squeamishness on the issue, but I know that many of you might not feel the same way. Your loss. And while so many fish are in declining numbers, the seas are awash with herring roe. Toward the end of the year, a third of a male herring's body weight is roe; this is because herrings mate by spraying their roe (the female has hard roe, with a granular rather than soft texture) into the sea. But enough of this now.

Herring roe may be a little more difficult to come by in America, but speak to your fishmonger. If he cleans his fish in the store he should be able to reserve some for you if you order ahead, or may even have some frozen. This is essentially an after-dinner savory, which I like best eaten on its own. If you know what I'm talking about, you won't need further encouragement. If you don't, then please give it a go: this is such a lovely little supper for two.

1 tablespoon cornstarch	drop regular olive oil
½ teaspoon cayenne pepper	2 fat slices good bread (I like white sourdough)
½ teaspoon ground mace	juice of ½ lemon
8 ounces soft herring roe	smoked sea salt flakes or regular sea salt flakes, to sprinkle over
1 tablespoon unsalted butter, plus more for the toast	1 teaspoon finely chopped fresh chives (or other herb of your choice) to sprinkle over

- Mix the cornstarch, cayenne, and mace in a resealable bag. Tear off a double sheet of paper towels, lay it flat, and put the herring roe on top, then get another piece, place it on top, and gently pat down to remove excess liquid. Now add the roe to the flour and spice mix in the resealable bag, seal, and shake gently so that all the pieces are covered.

- In a small cast iron skillet (I use one of 8 inches in diameter) or heavy-based, non-stick frying pan, melt the tablespoonful of butter and drop of oil, and when bubbling, add the herring roe and cook for 2–3 minutes, turning gently a few times, so that it is cooked through and bronzed in parts, but still keeping its shape.

- Meanwhile, put the bread in the toaster, and butter (generously for me) when ready.

- When the roe is cooked, spritz in the lemon juice, pushing the roe gently in the pan with a wooden spatula or whatever utensil you favor, then top the waiting pieces of buttered toast with the contents of the pan. Sprinkle with smoked sea salt flakes, should you be lucky enough to have some, or use regular sea salt flakes, and then scatter with the chopped chives. When I was a child, we ate this with a knife and fork, but now I like to cut the roe-topped toast in half and eat by hand.

Crunchy chicken cutlets

Chicken cutlets are to Americans – give or take – what the British describe as escalopes, and such is my alliteration addiction, I had to go for this nomenclature. I could have called them Cornflake Crunchy Chicken Cutlets as the crisp coating is provided not by bread crumbs, but by cornflakes. This is particularly handy if you want a gluten-free crunch, though do check the cornflake packaging to be sure. In theory, cornflakes should by their very nature be gluten-free but, because of cross-contamination issues in factories, that isn't always the case. If this isn't an issue, then use any cornflakes you like.

You can buy chicken escalopes already beaten, but otherwise just buy a couple of chicken breasts and, one at a time, place them on a cutting board lined with plastic wrap, cover the chicken with another layer of plastic wrap, and bash the living daylights out of them with a rolling pin. This is a gratifying way to de-stress at the end of a long day.

Once flattened, each breast provides a generously portioned escalope (you could use just one chicken breast and halve it across before bashing) but I like the expansiveness of a plateful of crunchy cutlet, and all I'd suggest you'd eat alongside is a handful of arugula, dotted with some halved cherry tomatoes, dressed simply. That's to say, I sprinkle a few sea salt flakes over the salad-lined plates, then squeeze some lemon juice on top, followed by a glug of excellent olive oil.

SERVES 2

2 chicken escalopes or breast fillets (8–10 ounces total), preferably organic

¼ cup Dijon mustard

1 clove garlic, peeled and finely grated or minced

½ teaspoon ground cinnamon

1 egg

3 cups cornflakes

1½ teaspoons pimentón picante or paprika

2 tablespoons vegetable oil

cherry tomatoes and arugula or salad leaves of your choice, to serve

1 lemon, cut into wedges

° Take the chicken out of the refrigerator so that it isn't too cold by the time you get frying. If you are using filleted chicken breasts, rather than escalopes, then proceed as described in the Intro.

° Get out a shallow dish that, preferably, you can get both escalopes in, and spoon in the mustard and the garlic. Add the cinnamon and egg and whisk to combine. Put the escalopes in, turn them, and leave to sit in the mixture while you prepare the "crumbs."

° Put the cornflakes into a bowl and crush them by hand. This, sadly, is not as brutal as it sounds: merely break them up with your fingers to get coarsely crushed flakes, but not dust. Add the pimentón or paprika and use a fork to mix in.

° Dredge the egg-and-mustard-soaked escalopes, one by one, in the cornflake crumbs, so that they are well covered, and then transfer to a wire rack for 5–10 minutes so they can dry out.

° Heat the oil in a cast iron skillet or heavy-based frying pan in which the chicken pieces will fit neatly and, when hot, fry for 3 minutes on the first side, then turn them over carefully and give them another 3 minutes, by which time the chicken should be cooked through in the middle, though do check. Remove to waiting plates, already strewn with tomatoes and arugula or salad leaves of your choice.

MAKE AHEAD NOTE

Coat escalopes, then put on a baking sheet lined with parchment paper, and freeze. Once solid, transfer to a resealable bag and freeze for up to 3 months. Cook directly from frozen, adding 1–2 minutes to the cooking time, and ensure cutlets are cooked through before serving.

Spiced chicken escalopes with watercress, fennel, and radish salad

When it comes to chicken, I am most decidedly a thigh rather than a breast woman, so trust me when I say that I am very happily using the white meat in preference to the dark here.

The vinegary, robustly spiced marinade may take an initial leap of faith. But jump: jump now. It tangily tenderizes meat that is so often dry when cooked, and the warmth of the spicing makes this a richly filling supper, while not detracting at all from its lightness. This is why I suggest using 1 breast portion to make 2 escalopes, which makes it a thrifty choice at the same time. And it is oh-so-speedy to cook.

The salad that nestles alongside is the perfect accompaniment: the watercress and radishes peppery, the fennel fragrant. And this salad is worth bringing out on other occasions, too. Ideally, the fennel and radishes should be sliced wafer-thin with a mandoline, but I'm far too clumsy to be safe with one and, besides, this is home, not restaurant food, and all the better for it.

1 chicken breast, preferably organic	4–6 radishes
1 tablespoon rice vinegar	2 handfuls watercress
2 teaspoons vegetable oil	½ teaspoon sea salt flakes
½ teaspoon ground turmeric	1–1½ tablespoons extra-virgin olive oil
1 teaspoon ground ginger	2 teaspoons cold-pressed coconut oil or regular olive oil or vegetable oil
¼ teaspoon cayenne pepper	
1 small bulb fennel	1 lime, to serve

○ Line a cutting board with plastic wrap, though do not cut off the piece from the roll quite yet. On another cutting board, cut the chicken breast in half across, and put half on top of the plastic wrapped board, then cover with more of the plastic wrap and tear off from the roll. With a rolling pin, bash the chicken until it's as thin as a veal escalope. Remove, then repeat this process with the as-yet-unbashed piece of chicken breast.

○ Put the vinegar, vegetable oil, turmeric, ginger, and cayenne into a resealable bag, add the chicken escalopes, then seal and leave on a plate to marinate for 10 minutes.

○ While the chicken marinates, halve the fennel, cut out the core, and cut each half into thin slices, then slice the radishes as thin as you can without stressing or cutting yourself. Put the watercress into a large bowl with the fennel and radishes, add the salt and the extra-virgin olive oil, and toss lightly – I use my hands for this – to combine. I don't add vinegar here, but there will be lime to squeeze over if you feel the salad needs it once you're eating. Arrange the lightly dressed salad on a serving platter or divide between 2 dinner plates.

○ Heat the 2 teaspoons of coconut (or other) oil in a cast iron skillet or a heavy-based, non-stick frying pan that will take both pieces of chicken, and when hot, add the escalopes and cook for 2 minutes on each side. You will need to cut into a thicker part to check they're cooked through, before removing to the platter. Halve the lime, and squeeze the juice from one half over the escalopes, then cut the remaining half into 2 wedges and put one on each person's plate.

Strapatsada

This is a Greek recipe given to me by Alex Andreou (of Squid and Orzo (**p.141**) and Old Rag Pie (**p.318**) fame). Actually, strictly speaking it's Italian, or of Italian derivation: *strapazzare* meaning, in the context of eggs, "to scramble." And really that's what this is: eggs scrambled with tomatoes. I have long since dropped my "no red with egg" rule – my Eggs in Purgatory from *Nigellissima* saw to that – but eating this makes me regret ever having voiced such an opinion in the first place.

True, I was initially hesitant about this, as the notion of tomatoes mixed into scrambled eggs didn't seem appealing. But the thing is, it doesn't quite taste like that. This is what cooking is all about: what the ingredients do together in the pan, not what they sound like on the page. A simple alchemy.

This is the sort of supper you need when you get home and the refrigerator is bare, or you're too tired to cook. And it's just the thing for those nights when you come home late, possibly a little worse for wear, or even not. Please don't wait for exhaustion or excessive alcohol consumption to make this.

Now, were you to be blessed with wonderful tomatoes, the sort you'd get in Greece, I would add another couple and dispense with the tomato paste element. And I give you the choice of basil or thyme, as the strapatsada is wonderful with either, but I'd tend to use the former in summer and the latter in winter. I am reliably informed that the cheese you would eat with it is Xynotyro, but since there's no way I have of getting my hands on that in my neighborhood, I go for manchego or percorino as the closest substitutes available locally. What you want is a sharp and salty cheese that will crumble and melt a little, if that helps.

8 small (not cherry) tomatoes (10–12 ounces total)

3 tablespoons regular olive oil

1 tablespoon tomato paste

pinch salt

pinch sugar

2 large eggs

1 ounce Xynotyro cheese, or sharp, salty, crumbly cheese such as manchego or pecorino

small handful basil leaves or leaves stripped from few sprigs thyme

4 slices good bread, such as sourdough, or whatever you like

○ Cut the tomatoes in half – a Greek person would now cut out the cores; this English person is too lazy – and then cut them into rough chunks.

○ Warm the oil in a heavy-based frying pan (I use a cast iron skillet of 10 inches in diameter, heating the pan before adding the oil) and tumble in the chunks of tomato. Cook, stirring every now and again, for about 5 minutes, by which time the tomatoes will have started to break down into the oil and be oozing oranginess. If you want your bread toasted, now's the time.

○ Add the tomato paste, salt, and sugar, and cook for another 5 minutes, by which time the tomato skins will be coming away from the flesh. Crack in the eggs and then stir, just as if you were scrambling them, until they are creamy, which is hardly any time at all (obviously, if you like your scrambled eggs set, cook the egg and tomato mixture here for longer).

○ Take the pan off the heat, crumble or grate the salty cheese over the mixture, and sprinkle with the basil or thyme leaves. Dollop some on your toast, or just eat straight from the pan using bread as your cutlery. For the record, I have one helping on toast, and another with just the bread. There's enough for 4 slices of bread here, but if you're eating solo and can't finish it all (really?), then know that this is also fabulous cold.

STORE NOTE

Leftovers can be refrigerated for up to 2 days.

BOWLFOOD

BOWLFOOD

If I could, I'd eat everything out of a bowl. For me "bowlfood" is a simple shorthand for food that is simultaneously soothing, bolstering, undemanding, and sustaining. I'm not talking about comfort food in the traditional sense, with its implications of nostalgia, the nursery, and indiscriminate stodge. And I'm certainly not talking about comfort eating, which I've always held to be the greatest misnomer. Rather, *discomfort* eating is what that term always implies to me, with its random, rushed, unassuageable hungers – eating, dislocated from appetite, as a means of self-persecution, holds no comfort for me. But bowlfood is comfort eating in a more innocent sense and, yes, perhaps infantile, too. Just as babies are weaned with foods that provide an unchanging taste and texture, repeated from spoonful to spoonful, so I derive succor from the food I eat out of a bowl, with fork or spoon, each mouthful satisfyingly the same as the one before. And there are lazy days when even chewing is too much, and then I turn gratefully to the solace of soup. But the bowls of noodles I slurp, the shepherd's pie or meatballs I spoon gratefully into my mouth, are neither bland and numbing – as comfort food tends to imply – nor about offering some edible antidote to life's miseries or disappointments, but rather a glad and calm celebration of the simple ritual of eating, and the quiet joys of both food and existence alike. Om!

Ramen

This is one of my favorite solo suppers. I have made it for the family, but then, what with the multiplied chopping, prepping, and dishing up, a certain frantic note can be introduced into the proceedings. For the same reason, although my photographer here, Keiko, admonished me gently, telling me that no Japanese person makes ramen at home, I find the chaos and noise at noodle joints is not what I want when I'm in the mood for ramen, and so I sacrifice authenticity for pleasure. But I felt that I was sacrificing a little too much authenticity for Keiko's comfort when I told her that I liked my ramen with soba noodles. This was a step too far, and so I tried to ingratiate myself with her by using the noodles she picked out of my Carb Cupboard (I have such a thing), but I do love soba noodles in my ramen, and am afraid will persist in this incorrect habit.

I found fresh dashi, a Japanese broth infused with seaweed and bonito fish, in a pouch, at my local supermarket, but otherwise there are plenty of instant dashi granules or cubes around and if I haven't got any, I just use vegetable bouillon. The flavor from the dried shiitake mushroom is so beautiful, that any light broth is a good choice. Speaking of which, if I have time, I use 4 dried whole shiitake mushrooms and soak them for a couple of hours after the 15 minutes' bubbling – indeed, I sometimes get them soaking at breakfast so that the flavors deepen all day and I'm ramen'd up in no time at all in the evening. But I am not that organized often enough, in which case I use dried ready-sliced shiitake, see method, and suggest you do, too. When I'm ramen-ready, I want no one or nothing to hold me up.

¼ cup dried ready-sliced shiitake mushrooms (see Intro)

1-inch piece fresh ginger, peeled and cut into fine matchsticks

2 cups cold dashi or vegetable broth

2–3 ounces instant ramen noodles or soba noodles

1 egg

3 baby bok choy

2 radishes

2 teaspoons sweet white miso

½ teaspoon soy sauce, or to taste

drop Asian sesame oil

1 scallion (green part only), thinly sliced

¼ teaspoon crushed red pepper flakes

- Put the dried shiitake in a saucepan that has a tight-fitting lid. Add the ginger matchsticks and pour in the cold dashi, bring to a boil, then clamp on the lid, lower the heat, and let it simmer for 15 minutes.

- Meanwhile, put a saucepan of water on for the noodles; these take hardly any time. So, toward the end of the broth's 15 minutes' simmering time, cook the noodles following the package instructions, then drain and refresh under a cold running tap and leave in the strainer or colander. Fill the saucepan with water again, bring to a boil, add the egg, and simmer for 6½ minutes, by which time the yolk will be set around the edge, but still have a bit of ooze in the middle.

- While the broth's simmering, trim the ends of the baby bok choy, tear off the leaves, and separate the stems into one pile and the leaves into another. Quarter the radishes, lengthways. When the broth's had its 15 minutes, bring it to a rolling boil, and add the bok choy stems and the quartered radishes. Let it come back to a boil, then add the bok choy leaves and turn off the heat. Now add the miso and soy sauce and a drop of sesame oil, and put the lid back on.

- When the egg is ready, pour out the boiling water, then run cold water from the tap into the pan until the egg has cooled enough to peel.

- Put the drained noodles into a bowl and pour the broth and vegetables over them. Cut the egg in half lengthways, then add both halves to the soup. (And yes, I know the bowl you see here only has one half.) Sprinkle the sliced scallion and crushed red pepper flakes over the top, and eat yourself into Zen bliss.

Thai noodles with cinnamon and shrimp

I have been alive a long time and, at least when it comes to eating, have spent that time wisely and well. So, it's not often that I eat something that tastes so different from anything I've come across before. But this is such a dish. A gorgeous and mesmerically talented chef called, so perfectly, Tum, cooked it when I was on vacation in Thailand last year, and I made him cook it again and again, and then finally asked him if I could video his making it, so I could try and recreate it at home.

I was apprehensive about doing so, not least because I was frightened of facing up to my inadequate camera work and the lesser ingredients found at home. And yet, even with frozen shrimp, the substitution of regular celery for the Chinese celery (which is all leaf, no stalk to speak of, and stronger-tasting) and a less-experienced hand at the wok, the very first mouthful brought back the magical enchantment of its taste in Thailand.

You do need to buy leafy celery, and even though the stalks don't get a look-in, you chop the slender stems to which the leaves are attached and add them to the wok along with the other flavorings at the very beginning.

Apart from having to make geographically enforced changes, I have stuck to Tum's recipe, including the ready-ground pepper and chicken broth concentrate (actually, he used chicken powder). I just had to share this spectacularly unfamiliar but compelling recipe with you. I hope you will be as bowled over by it as I was.

1 tablespoon vegetable oil

2 cloves garlic, peeled and roughly chopped

1-inch piece fresh ginger, peeled and cut into fine matchsticks

1 star anise

½ long or 1 short stick cinnamon, broken into shards

2–3 leafy stems at the top of 1 celery stalk (see Intro), stems cut into short lengths, leaves roughly chopped

1½ tablespoons light soy sauce

1 tablespoon dark soy sauce

1 tablespoon oyster sauce

¼ teaspoon ground white pepper

7 tablespoons cold water

1 teaspoon chicken broth concentrate

1 tablespoon ketjap manis, or 1 tablespoon dark soy sauce mixed with 1 tablespoon dark brown sugar

10 raw shell-off jumbo shrimp, thawed if frozen

3 ounces mung bean (glass) noodles or rice vermicelli, soaked and drained as per package instructions

fat pinch ground cinnamon

fat pinch ground cloves

- On a high heat, heat the oil in a large wok. Add the garlic, ginger, star anise, cinnamon, and the sliced leafy stems of celery, and cook, stirring, for 1 minute.

- Stir in both soy sauces and leave to simmer for 30 seconds, then stir in the oyster sauce and ground pepper.

- Add the water, followed by the chicken broth concentrate and the ketjap manis (or the mixture of dark soy sauce with soft brown sugar), stir until everything's well combined, and bring to a boil.

- Now add the shrimp, immersing them in the liquid. Simmer until the shrimp are cooked through.

- Finally, add the drained noodles and stir well – I find a couple of pasta forks, one in each hand, best for this – so that everything is combined, and most of the dark liquid is absorbed. Add the pinches of ground cinnamon and cloves, stir again, and if you're not serving straight from the wok, decant into a serving bowl, and sprinkle with the reserved chopped celery leaves.

STORE NOTE

Cool leftovers, then cover and refrigerate within 2 hours of making. Will keep for up to 2 days. Delicious cold.

Thai steamed clams

This is another recipe from my Thai vacation, although I had to recreate it from taste memory rather than from any actual record. I have, knowingly, made some changes, as the original uses a chili paste and also had a scanter broth. But I keep good-quality, authentic Thai curry pastes in the house at all times, and I wanted the delicate sweetness of the coconut water, even though it's out of a carton. And I greedily wanted more of the richly flavored but light broth: it is quite lovely just to bring the bowl of aromatic clam liquor to your lips once you've eaten the clams; besides, Chef Tum made this as part of a huge feast, but I eat it just as it is, for supper, enjoying the trance-inducing ritual of picking out the sweet flesh of the clams. You can, of course, make an accompanying bowl of jasmine rice (which takes about 10–15 minutes) and eat the broth-soused rice as a second course, after a delicate appetizer of steamed clams.

For me, the scent of Thai basil is crucial here. But I suppose if I hadn't eaten it in situ, with Thai basil, I would be perfectly happy with some chopped fresh cilantro in its stead.

SERVES 2–4

2 pounds manila clams	1 teaspoon lime juice
2 teaspoons Thai red curry paste	handful Thai basil leaves or cilantro
½ cup coconut water	

° Tip the clams into a large bowl, cover with cold water, and leave to soak for 15 minutes. At the end of the 15 minutes, drain the clams, discarding any that remain open.

° Get out a wok with a lid, and spoon in the Thai curry paste, then pour in the coconut water, add the lime juice, and stir or whisk to mix. Now turn on the heat and, when the coral-tinted liquid comes to a bubble, tip in the clams and cover with the lid. They should take about 5 minutes to cook – by which time they should be gaping and open, revealing plump golden flesh within – but shake the pan sporadically to make sure the clams move about in the liquid so that they steam equally.

° Transfer to a large bowl, discarding any clams that have stayed closed. Distribute most of the gorgeously scented Thai basil leaves throughout the bowl and either serve from this bowl or decant into individual bowls, scattering a few extra leaves on top, and making sure that each of you has an empty bowl for the shells, too.

Thai turkey meatballs

This is not a souvenir from my holiday, but an adaptation of a wonderful supper I ate at an American friend's house. It is Thai only so far as it uses green Thai curry paste and related ingredients, but I have no reason to believe there are even turkeys in Thailand, let alone turkey meatballs. In other words, it isn't Thai at all, but it tastes so good and is so easy to make, that I go with it willingly. I do, however, use authentic Thai curry paste and coconut milk, both of which are inestimably better and much cheaper from online Thai food shops than they are from the supermarket. And ever since I saw the amount of chicken powder they go through in Thailand, I unapologetically use chicken broth made from concentrate. Not that I have ever felt bad about using bouillon cubes or concentrate, actually. Maybe that's bravado. I do feel a bit sheepish about it, but I refuse to pretend to be more virtuous and less lazy than I am.

Speaking of laziness, please don't be put off by a bit of meatball-rolling – the thought is worse than the deed. In fact, I find it immensely gratifying and soothing work, absorbing without being challenging. Think of it as a mindfulness exercise, if you like. I could write a whole book about mindfulness in the kitchen. But another time, maybe…

One final note: I like to eat this straight out of a bowl, but I do sometimes serve flat rice noodles alongside or, rather, nestling underneath, too.

4 zucchini (approx. 1½ pounds)

1 pound ground turkey

3 scallions

1 clove garlic, peeled and finely grated
or minced

1-inch piece fresh ginger, peeled and
finely grated (1½ teaspoons)

small bunch fresh cilantro, chopped

1 teaspoon crushed red pepper flakes

zest and juice of 1 lime, preferably unwaxed

1 teaspoon sea salt flakes or kosher salt, plus more
to taste

2 teaspoons vegetable oil

3 tablespoons Thai green curry paste, or to taste

1 x 14-ounce can coconut milk

2 cups chicken broth

3 tablespoons fish sauce

12 ounces sugar snap peas

TO SERVE:

small handful Thai basil leaves

2–3 limes, cut into wedges

- To make the meatballs, take one of the zucchini (approx. 6 ounces) and trim the ends. Using a vegetable peeler, remove some of the skin in stripes, and then coarsely grate the zucchini onto a piece of paper towel: I recommend you use a coarse box cheese grater here; if the grater's too fine, the zucchini will just turn to mush. Press as much water as you can out of the grated zucchini.

- Put the grated zucchini, and any excess liquid now squeezed out of it, into a big bowl, and add the ground turkey, breaking it up as you tip it in.

- Trim the scallions and halve lengthways, then finely chop them, putting the white part in with your turkey and reserving the green part for later.

- Add the garlic and ginger, then add 2 tablespoons of the chopped cilantro, along with the crushed red pepper flakes, lime zest, and salt.

- Using a fork or your hands (the latter being my preference), mix the meatball mixture thoroughly but lightly. If you handle it too much, you will make heavy, dense meatballs, which you don't want. Once the mixture's gently combined, shape into small meatballs, using a heaping teaspoonful as a guide. You should get about 30 meatballs, provided you don't start making ever bigger ones as you go, which is easily done.

- Heat the oil in a large Dutch oven or pan (with a lid), and fry the chopped green part of the scallion briefly, just turning it in the hot pan. Now add the Thai green curry paste, and then use the cream from the top of the coconut milk, whisking it into the paste over the heat.

- Pour in the rest of the coconut milk, along with the chicken broth and fish sauce, and let it come to a boil.

○ Peel the rest of the zucchini in stripes as before, then halve them lengthways, quarter them in the same way, and slice into (roughly) ½-inch pieces. Add these to the bubbling pan, then gently drop in the meatballs, letting them fall in circles as you work around the pan from the outer edge inward, and leaving them unprodded, as they will be very tender and easy to break up.

○ Wait for the pan to come to a bubble again, then clamp on the lid, turn down the heat, and leave to simmer for 20 minutes. Check that the zucchini are tender and the meatballs are cooked through, before stirring in the sugar snap peas and the juice of the zested lime. Check the seasoning, and adjust as you wish.

○ Take off the heat and scatter with Thai basil (if you have some) or just sprinkle with a little more of the chopped cilantro. And I like to chop some limes into wedges and bring to the table for people to spritz over as they eat.

MAKE AHEAD NOTE	FREEZE NOTE
The meatballs and sauce can be made 1 day ahead. Cool, cover, and refrigerate within 2 hours of making. Reheat gently until piping hot, being careful not to break up the meatballs.	The cooked and cooled meatballs and sauce can be frozen, in an airtight container, for up to 3 months. Thaw overnight in refrigerator before reheating as in Make Ahead Note.

Black rice noodles with ginger and chili

I can't get enough of spicy noodles, and this is another example that breathes its seductive fire into my soul. I concede that the ingredients list is long, but I like to do a comprehensive shop at the Asian supermarket, and this means I have everything at hand when the mood strikes, which is often. I know I've gone a little fancy with the black rice noodles, but I saw these – along with green tea noodles and a panoply of other flavors – and just had to buy them. If you can get the black rice noodles, they do have a certain hardiness which means you can leave leftovers to get cold and then pack them up for a mean box lunch the next day. But soba noodles, or any other noodles of your choice, can be substituted without loss of face or flavor.

SERVES 1–2

2 tablespoons chopped raw blanched peanuts

1 fat clove garlic, peeled and finely chopped

2½-inch piece fresh ginger, peeled and finely chopped

1 teaspoon vegetable oil

2 teaspoons Asian sesame oil

2 tablespoons soy sauce

2 tablespoons Chinese (Shaoxing) rice wine

1½ tablespoons hot sauce, such as Sriracha

2 tablespoons cold water

8 ounces black rice noodles (see Intro)

2 scallions, trimmed

2 tablespoons chopped fresh cilantro, plus some whole leaves to put on top

- Toast the peanuts in a dry frying pan until golden, then tip onto a plate to cool.

- Put the garlic and ginger in a cold heavy-based pan with the vegetable and sesame oils, heat them gently, then increase the heat a little and give the pan a minute's sizzling – not letting anything burn – and take off the heat.

- Now, carefully – as the hot oil could spit – add the soy sauce, Chinese rice wine, hot sauce, and the 2 tablespoons of cold water. Put back on the heat and bring to a bubble, then immediately take off the heat and pour into a large bowl to cool.

- Cook or soak the noodles in boiling water, until they are tender, or following the package instructions, then refresh under cold water, drain, and toss with the sauce.

- Cut each scallion into 3 pieces and then shred lengthways into strips, adding to the noodles, along with the chopped cilantro and most of the toasted peanuts.

- Divide the cold dressed noodles between 2 small bowls, and top each with a few cilantro leaves and the rest of the nuts.

Chinese-inspired chicken noodle soup

Actually, there are dual inspirations for this soup, for it is really a version of My Mother's Praised Chicken from *Kitchen* infused with Chinese flavors. What you end up with is the sort of soup you want to eat in bowls held up inelegantly close to your mouth so that you are in easy slurping distance. I am embarrassed to say that I can't use chopsticks, unless they're the children's sort held together with a piece of card and an elastic band, but this soup really makes me want to learn.

I always recommend organic chicken (or organic meat generally) but I am mindful of the fact that not everyone can afford the luxury. Even so, if you use an intensively farmed chicken here (and lack of taste is only one concern), you just won't get a flavorsome enough soup, in which case add some bouillon cubes or concentrate to the water.

I've given an exuberant list of ingredients for sprinkling on at the end, as I love that final fling of flavor. And though I haven't added them here, should you be making a fresh foray to an Asian food store to make this, and you see Chinese flowering chives about, they would be a real treat, and are so beautiful. Despite the Asian inspiration for the soup's flavor, I make a steep geographical about-turn and use golden nests (one per person) of an egg-enriched tagliolini for the noodle element, though I do also love this with those very thin mung bean or rice vermicelli. In fact, I just can't think of a bad way of eating this: even noodle-less, and thus rather not living up to its title, this is bliss in a bowl.

3 leeks, cleaned and trimmed

3 carrots, peeled and trimmed

3 stalks celery, trimmed

3-inch piece fresh ginger, peeled and finely grated

1 small or medium chicken, preferably organic

1 tablespoon vegetable oil

½ cup Chinese (Shaoxing) rice wine

tied stalks from bunch of cilantro, plus leaves to serve (see right)

2½ quarts cold water

2 teaspoons sea salt flakes or kosher salt

1 teaspoon Szechuan pepper or crushed red pepper flakes

2 tablespoons soy sauce, plus more to serve

2 fat cloves garlic, peeled and finely grated or minced

zest and juice of 1 lime, preferably unwaxed

10 ounces baby bok choy, tatsoi, choi sum, or other greens of choice

4 ounces radishes

2 ounces dried fine egg noodles or vermicelli per person

salt for noodle water to taste

½ teaspoon Asian sesame oil, plus more to serve (see below)

TO SERVE:

Asian sesame oil

2 (or more to taste) fresh red chiles, seeded and finely diced (optional)

leaves from bunch of cilantro (see left)

finely chopped chives (optional)

○ Slice each trimmed leek in half lengthways, and cut into ½-inch slices. Set aside. Cut the carrots into 1½-inch lengths and quarter each log lengthways. Chop the celery into ½-inch slices, reserving any leaves to add to the soup at the end. Grate the ginger onto a plate for the time being. I use a fine microplane grater and get 4–5 teaspoons of fiery pulp out of this. Don't wash up the grater yet, as you'll need it for the garlic and lime later.

○ Now, with your vegetables prepped, untruss your chicken, cut off (but do not discard) the ankle part of the leg (I find kitchen scissors more than adequate to the task), and put the chicken, breast-side down, on a cutting board, then press down until you hear the breastbone crack – perhaps I shouldn't like this as much as I do – and the chicken is slightly flattened. Wash your hands, and then warm the tablespoon of vegetable oil in a pan that comes with a lid and that's big enough to take all the ingredients comfortably; I use a saucepan of 12 inches in diameter, 5 inches deep, which is a tight, but good, fit.

○ When the oil is hot, put the chicken in, breast-side down, and leave to brown for 3 minutes; the heat should not be too high for this or it'll start burning. Turn the chicken the other way up, then turn up the heat to high and chuck in the rice wine. While it's bubbling, throw in the chicken ankle pieces along with the tied cilantro stalks, sliced carrots, and celery.

○ Pour in the water, then add the sea salt flakes, Szechuan pepper (or crushed red pepper flakes), soy sauce, and finely grated ginger. Add the garlic, then grate in the zest of the lime, and squeeze in the juice of half of it. Let this come to a boil.

○ Once it's bubbling, clamp on the lid, turn the heat to low, and let it simmer, covered, for 1 hour. Once the hour is up, take the lid off, then turn up the heat and bring it back to a boil again, and, once it is, add the leeks you sliced earlier. Cover partially with the lid and cook for 10 minutes, then let the broth simmer uncovered and confidently for another 10 minutes. This is to let the broth strengthen a bit. Then turn off the heat altogether, though keep the pan on the stove, clamp the lid back on, and leave for at least 20 minutes and up to 1 hour. While this is going on, I'd put a saucepan of water on to boil the noodles later, and salt it when it comes to a boil.

○ When you want to eat, remove the chicken to a board: it may be falling to pieces, but so much the better. Remove the chicken skin (I discard it, as for me there's no joy in chicken skin unless it's crisp), then take the meat off the bone and shred it. And by the way, should you not use up all the chicken for the soup, know that it is magnificent – flavorsome and tender – in a salad or sandwich the next day.

○ Chop the stems of the greens you're using, and put the leaves into a separate pile. Quarter the radishes top to tail. Bring the pan of soup back to a boil, add the stalks of the greens and the quartered radishes, and let it come back to a boil once more. At the same time, add the noodles to the pan of boiling salted water, and cook them (if you're using the fine noodles or vermicelli they shouldn't take more than 2–3 minutes).

○ Add the leafy parts of the greens to the bubbling soup and drain the noodles. Put the noodles and shredded chicken into your serving bowls. Taste the soup for seasoning, and add more salt (or soy) and the juice of the remaining half of lime, if you think it needs it. When satisfied, ladle the fragrant broth, with its vegetables, on top of the chicken and noodles, add a drop of sesame oil to each bowl, then sprinkle with chopped chiles, cilantro, or chives, as you wish. Bring the bottles of soy sauce and sesame oil, and some more of the chopped chiles and herbs to the table for people to add as they eat. Warning: don't burn your mouth; this smells so good, I'm afraid it's easy to be dangerously impatient and eat while the soup's still scaldingly hot.

STORE NOTE	FREEZE NOTE
Transfer leftover cooked chicken to a container, cover, and chill within 1 hour. It will keep in refrigerator for up to 3 days.	The cooked and cooled chicken can be frozen, in airtight containers or resealable bags, for up to 2 months. Thaw overnight in refrigerator before using.

Drunken noodles

The general explanation given for why Thai drunken noodles are so called is that they have enough crushed red pepper in them to shake you out of even the worst hangover. The only difficulty here – prepared though I am to believe it – is that making a traditional *pad kee mao* is not an undertaking I'd recommend while worse for wear. So this is my simplified version. I've cut to the chase – no meat, fish, or veggies, just highly seasoned, searingly hot noodles.

Not that you need to be hung-over to eat them. Why give yourself all that pain, in order to get to the pleasure? Mind you, I say that as someone for whom a glass and a half of white wine is too much, though I could cope with a beer, so cold it hurts, while going for the blissful burn of these addictively hot noodles.

Anyway, I make them so often when in serenely sober Bowlfood Mood. Most of the ingredients come from the store cupboard, and the finished dish is in front of you in 10 minutes. I find these hot noodles hard to beat, and they do really blow your head off: if you want less of a fiery fright, then halve the red pepper flakes. To start with, at least…

SERVES 2, OR A VERY DRINK-SOAKED OR GREEDY 1

6 ounces dried flat rice noodles (the pad thai sort)	1 clove garlic, peeled and finely grated or minced
2 tablespoons cold water	1 lime, preferably unwaxed
1 tablespoon oyster sauce	½ teaspoon crushed red pepper flakes
1 teaspoon Asian sesame oil	¼ cup soy sauce
2 teaspoons vegetable oil	handful chopped fresh cilantro
1-inch piece fresh ginger, peeled and finely grated (2 teaspoons)	

- Soak the rice noodles in hot water for 8 minutes, or following the package instructions, then drain and refresh under a cold running tap.

- Put the 2 tablespoons of water into a cup and stir in the oyster sauce, then set aside for a moment.

- Put the oils in a wok, turn on the heat, and add the ginger and garlic, and grate in the zest of the lime – I use a coarse microplane grater here, only because it's faster than a fine one. Sprinkle in the red pepper flakes. Stir well, then tip in the soaked, drained rice noodles and stir them – I find this easier with an implement in each hand – quickly in the hotly seasoned oil.

Add the watered-down oyster sauce, the juice of ½ the lime, and the soy sauce, then transfer to a waiting bowl (or bowls) and toss with the chopped cilantro. Keep the bottle of soy sauce and the remaining ½ lime close at hand, should you need either of them as you eat. I am such a pyrophile, I like to keep some extra red pepper flakes at hand, too.

Rice bowl with ginger, radish, and avocado

A rice bowl is a wondrous thing, but often – despite the simplicity of its title – a rather cluttered and complicated one. Here, I have pared it back, to make a gorgeously seasoned rice bowl, with nothing more than a few seeds, herbs, and radishes stirred through it, and an avocado to top it. It's a simple take on an inspiringly expansive idea. So please use this as a starting point only. It's very much a non-recipe recipe, and every time I make it, I add something different, depending on what's at hand.

The only constant is the rice. I cannot get enough of short grain brown rice – so much more nubbly and delicious than regular whole grain rice or white rice – but I find it doesn't cook quite like rice does normally. That's to say, usually the unswerving rule when cooking rice is 1 part rice to 2 parts water. I have found that with short grain brown rice it is 1 part rice to 1½ parts water (despite what it says on the package). And even though I've given a measurement for the ginger, in reality, I just shave off slices with the vegetable peeler until I feel I have enough.

Raw radishes are my usual go-to, but I had some cold leftover roasted radishes, so that's what you see in the picture. If you want to have them hot, just roast halved radishes, cut-side down, with a little oil in a hot oven (about 425°F) for 10 minutes.

SERVES 2

¾ cup short grain brown rice

1 cup cold water

2-inch piece fresh ginger, peeled

4–6 radishes

1½ tablespoons tamari or soy sauce

1 teaspoon organic raw apple cider vinegar

¼ cup mixed seeds, such as pumpkin, sunflower, sesame

3–4 tablespoons chopped fresh cilantro

1 small ripe avocado

○ Put the rice and water in a heavy-based saucepan that comes with a tight-fitting lid, and bring to a boil. Once it's bubbling, clamp on the lid, turn the heat down very low, and simmer for 25 minutes. Then turn off the heat, leaving the lid on, and let it stand for a further 5 minutes, by which time the rice will be cooked – but still nutty – and the water absorbed.

○ While the rice is cooking, use a vegetable peeler to shave the ginger into very thin strips. Cut the radishes into quarters or eighths lengthways, depending on their size.

○ When the rice is cooked, spoon into a mixing bowl. Add the tamari or soy sauce and the apple cider vinegar to the bowl and toss with a fork to combine, and then do the same with the ginger shavings, radishes, and seeds. Stir all but a little of the chopped cilantro into the rice, still using a fork.

○ Divide between 2 smallish bowls and top with avocado, cut either into gondola-shaped slices or chunks, as wished. Sprinkle each with the remaining cilantro, and eat serenely.

MAKE AHEAD NOTE

If you want to eat this cold, the rice can be cooked 1 day ahead. Spread cooked rice out on a large plate to cool quickly. Cover and refrigerate within 1 hour.

Sweet potato macaroni and cheese

I'm just going to say it: this is the best macaroni and cheese I've ever eaten – better than the macaroni and cheese I ate as a child; better than the macaroni and cheese I brought my own children up on when they were little (they don't agree); better than any fancy restaurant macaroni and cheese with white truffle or lobster; better than any macaroni and cheese I have loved in my life thus far, and there have been many.

I don't feel it's boastful to say as much, as the greatness lies not in any brilliance on my part, but in the simple tastes of the ingredients as they fuse in the heat. That's home cooking for you.

I do rather love the way these little macaroni and cheeses, with their pixie-penne, look like they've been made with artificially colored, cheap squeezy cheese or out of a box, when in fact their exotic glow comes courtesy of the earthy goodness of a sweet potato.

SERVES 4

1 pound sweet potatoes

10 ounces (approx. 2 cups) pennette or other small short pasta

4 tablespoons soft unsalted butter

3 tablespoons all-purpose flour

2 cups whole milk

1 teaspoon English mustard

¼ teaspoon paprika, plus ¼ teaspoon to sprinkle on top

3 ounces feta cheese (approx. ¾ cup crumbled)

1¼ cups grated sharp Cheddar, plus ¼ cup to sprinkle on top

4 fresh sage leaves

salt and pepper to taste

○ Preheat the oven to 400°F. Put on a large-ish saucepan of water to boil, with the lid on to make it come to a boil faster.

○ Peel the sweet potatoes and cut them roughly into 1-inch pieces. When the water's boiling, add salt to taste, and then the sweet potato pieces, and cook them for about 10 minutes or until they are soft. Scoop them out of the water into a bowl using a "spider" or slotted spoon and lightly mash with a fork, without turning them into a purée. Don't get rid of this water, as you will need it to cook your pasta in later.

○ In another saucepan, gently melt the butter and add the flour, whisking to form a roux, then take the pan off the heat, slowly whisk in the milk, and, when it's all combined and smooth, put back on the heat. Exchange your whisk for a wooden spoon, and continue to stir until your gently bubbling sauce has lost any floury taste and has thickened. Add the mustard and the ¼ teaspoon of paprika. Season to taste, but do remember that you will be adding Cheddar and salty feta later, so underdo it for now.

○ Cook the pennette in the sweet-potato water, starting to check 2 minutes earlier than package instructions dictate, as you want to make sure it doesn't lose its bite entirely. Drain (reserving some of the pasta cooking water first) and then add the pennette to the mashed sweet potatoes, and fold in to combine; the heat of the pasta will make the potatoes easier to mix in.

○ Add the feta cheese to the sweet potato and pasta mixture, crumbling it in so that it is easier to disperse evenly, then fold in the bechamel sauce, adding the 1¼ cups grated Cheddar as you go. Add some of the pasta cooking water, should you feel it needs loosening up at all.

○ Check for seasoning again, then, when you're happy, spoon the brightly sauced macaroni and cheese into 4 small ovenproof dishes of approx. 1½–1¾ cup capacity (or 1 large rectangular dish measuring approx. 12 x 8 x 2 inches deep and 6½-cup capacity). Sprinkle the remaining Cheddar over each one, dust with the remaining ¼ teaspoon of paprika, then shred the sage leaves and scatter the skinny green ribbons over the top, too.

○ Put the dishes on a baking sheet, put into the oven, and bake for 20 minutes (or, if you're making this in a larger dish, bake for 30–35 minutes), by which time they will be piping hot and bubbling, and begging you to eat them.

MAKE AHEAD NOTE

The macaroni and cheese can be made 1 day ahead. When the pasta has cooked, reserve 7 tablespoons of the cooking water and add this to the white sauce (it may look a little thin but the pasta absorbs the sauce as it cools). Transfer to the ovenproof dishes (without the sage topping). Once cool, cover and refrigerate within 2 hours of making. Sprinkle with the Cheddar, paprika, and sage just before baking and cook for an extra 5–10 minutes, checking that the macaroni and cheese is piping hot in the center before serving.

Pasta alla Bruno

Since this book contains a recipe for Chicken Cosima (**p.149**), inspired by my daughter, it seems only fair to include a recipe for my son as well. This is his favored pasta – which can also be made with chorizo, should that be at hand – and I have been greeted on many mornings with the tell-tale signs of it in the kitchen from the late night before. A variant also includes fresh mozzarella, added at the end of the cooking time, while the pasta is sitting, calmly absorbing its sauce, but I think it better without. Not that, at home, it's my call. You must do as you wish.

SERVES 2, OR 1 TEENAGE BOY

8 ounces casarecce pasta or pasta of your choice	1 clove garlic, peeled and finely grated or minced
1 teaspoon salt for pasta water, or to taste	8 ounces ripe cherry tomatoes, quartered
1 teaspoon regular olive oil	1 teaspoon crushed red pepper flakes
6 slices thin-cut smoked bacon	Parmesan or mozzarella, to serve

° Put a saucepan of water on to boil for the pasta, and when it's bubbling, add a teaspoon of salt, or to taste, and put the casarecce on to cook. The make I use stipulates 11 minutes' cooking time, but I feel it needs rather less, so keep testing. Get on with the sauce when the pasta goes in, or even before, should you prefer, as it can stand, with the lid on, once it's cooked.

° Heat the oil in a wok or heavy-based frying pan that comes with a lid, then scissor in the bacon, and stir-fry until crisp. (If you want the bacon to stay crisp, remove now to a plate, uncovered, and toss back in just before eating.) Remove the pan from the heat, just while you add the garlic, then stir, and place back on the heat. Tumble in the quartered cherry tomatoes and the red pepper flakes, stir well, and put on the lid. Shake the wok from time to time while cooking, and lift the lid once or twice to give a stir, and a check.

° Once the pasta is cooked, but still with a bit of bite to it, use a "spider" or wire basket ladle to scoop out the pasta into the wok, stirring in a little of the pasta cooking water just to help the sauce amalgamate. Put the lid on and leave to stand on the ring it cooked on, though with the heat turned off, for 5 minutes.

° Stir the bacon back in, check for seasoning, then tip into a bowl, and eat heartily.

Pasta snails with garlic butter

I have rather a weakness for the culinary pun, and find this one particularly pleasing. This is snails in garlic butter, only the snails are pasta. Since, really, the reason people eat snails is for the garlic butter, it seems to me that this is no second best. And while it is obviously rich, the pasta snails make it rather less so than the original escargots. I'm afraid it's all too easy to eat, and copiously.

SERVES 2

6 ounces pasta snails (lumache rigate)

salt for pasta water to taste

3 tablespoons soft unsalted butter

2 fat or 4 smaller cloves garlic, peeled and finely grated or minced

pinch sea salt flakes or kosher salt, plus more to taste

1 cup finely chopped parsley

○ Put on a saucepan of water for the pasta, salt it, and then cook the pasta following the package instructions, though do start to taste 2 minutes before it says it'll be ready.

○ In a saucepan that will take the pasta later, melt the butter over a lowish heat, then add the garlic and a pinch of sea salt flakes and fry for 1 minute, making sure the garlic doesn't color. Add the parsley, and stir over the heat for another minute, until you have a velvety green sauce.

○ When the pasta's cooked, but still has a bit of bite, reserve some of the pasta cooking water and then drain.

○ Add the drained pasta to the pan of sauce, then add a tablespoonful of the pasta cooking water, and stir again – with the pan still over the heat – adding another tablespoonful or so, as much as is needed to make the sauce coat the pasta well. Season to taste and eat immediately.

Merguez meatballs

This is a recipe of fabulous ease and speed, but you'd never guess it to eat it. These meatballs taste as if they had been slowly and lovingly tended, and their deeply spiced sauce tastes as if it had been cooked over days. I make no apology for the shortcuts – the meatballs are made of squeezed-out merguez sausages, and the sauce's rich base is a jar of roasted red peppers – because what you end up with is honest and flavorful and just so good.

1 pound merguez sausages	2 teaspoons cumin seeds
2 tablespoons regular olive oil	1 teaspoon ground allspice
1 x 14-ounce can diced tomatoes	1 teaspoon ground cinnamon
¾ cup drained roughly chopped roasted red peppers in oil (or mixed colors if available)	2 teaspoons sea salt flakes or kosher salt
	1 tablespoon honey

○ Squeeze the sausage meat out of the casings and then form into small meatballs, using about 2 teaspoonfuls per ball. I get 34 out of this mixture, but I have to concentrate on not making the meatballs bigger as I go – they should each be about the size of a cherry tomato.

○ Heat the oil in a wide, heavy-based saucepan or Dutch oven (with a lid), and fry the meatballs for about 3 minutes or so, then spoon out as much excess oil as you can and discard.

○ Add the canned tomatoes, then snip or chop the roasted red peppers into pieces, before adding to the pan as well.

○ Sprinkle the spices over the contents of the pan, add the salt and – oiling the tablespoon first – the honey, then bring up to a boil before partially covering the pan with its lid, and leaving to simmer for 10 minutes. Obviously, you can make rice or couscous to eat with this, or just get some good bread to dunk in.

MAKE AHEAD NOTE	FREEZE NOTE
The meatballs and sauce can be made 1 day ahead. Cool, cover, and refrigerate within 2 hours of making. Reheat gently until piping hot, being careful not to break up the meatballs.	The cooked and cooled meatballs and sauce can be frozen, in an airtight container, for up to 3 months. Thaw overnight in refrigerator before reheating as in Make Ahead Note.

Indian-spiced shepherd's pie

A reader kindly sent me her recipe for "Indian Shepherd's Pie" (at my request, as I'd seen her mention it on Twitter), which certainly inspired this, although the recipe here is totally different. And cooking is like this: we each play out the themes differently in our own kitchens, but carrying with us, gratefully, the ideas and practices of others.

My children love this. Actually, I don't know anyone who's eaten it and doesn't. While it's spicy (though you can reduce the heat to taste) and vibrant, it is also cozy and comforting, and blends the familiar with the less traditional in a way that gives me quiet satisfaction.

The impetus to use mashed sweet potatoes for the topping was simply because it was so much easier than peeling and mashing regular potatoes, and they work so well against the hot, exuberantly spiced meat, especially when tempered with lime and ginger juice. And see overleaf for my ginger-juicing trick, which can be brought into play on any number of occasions – I often squeeze this juice into soups or stews at the end if I feel they need gingering up.

FOR THE TOPPING:

2¼ pounds sweet potatoes

2 teaspoons sea salt flakes or kosher salt

2 tablespoons white peppercorns

6 cardamom pods, cracked

peeled strips from 1 lime, preferably unwaxed, and juice of ½ lime

approx. 1 quart cold water

1½-inch piece fresh ginger, peeled, plus more for filling (see below)

FOR THE FILLING:

3 cloves garlic, peeled

1½-inch piece fresh ginger, peeled

1 onion, peeled

seeds from 6 cardamom pods

2 teaspoons cumin seeds

2 teaspoons coriander seeds

2 tablespoons cold-pressed coconut oil

2 teaspoons garam masala

1 teaspoon crushed red pepper flakes

1 teaspoon ground turmeric

1 pound ground lamb, preferably organic

1 x 14-ounce can diced tomatoes

¾ cup red lentils

1 teaspoon sea salt flakes or kosher salt

2 tablespoons Worcestershire sauce

TO DECORATE:

4 teaspoons nibbed or finely chopped pistachios

○ Preheat your oven to 425°F. Start with the topping, cutting each of the sweet potatoes into approx. 2-inch chunks.

○ Put the unpeeled potato chunks into a large saucepan (with a lid) and add the salt, peppercorns, cracked cardamom pods, and lime strips (you don't need the ginger just yet), then add just enough cold water (about 1 quart) to cover.

○ Bring to a boil, then reduce the heat slightly, put the lid on, and cook for about 30 minutes – or until the sweet potatoes are tender – while you get on with the filling.

○ Slice the garlic and ginger roughly, quarter the onion, and put them all into the bowl of a food processor with the cardamom, cumin, and coriander seeds, and whizz until finely chopped. Alternatively, use a bowl and a stick blender, or just chop everything very finely by hand.

○ Heat the coconut oil in a heavy-based pan (with a lid), and then tip this paste in.

○ Cook for a few minutes or so to soften, stirring frequently, then stir in the garam masala, red pepper flakes, and turmeric, and tip in the ground lamb, turning it in the spiced onion mixture and breaking it up gently.

○ Add the canned tomatoes, then fill the empty can with cold water and, swilling it around, pour this in as well. Stir in the red lentils.

- Season with the salt and Worcestershire sauce, then bring to a boil, clamp on the lid, lower the heat, and simmer for about 25 minutes, stirring once or twice to stop it catching on the bottom of the saucepan.

- When the sweet potatoes are cooked, drain them, reserving the liquid, and leave until cool enough to peel away the skins. Put the flesh into a wide bowl.

- Mash the sweet potatoes, using a potato masher, or any gadget of your choice (even a fork would do) and slowly beat in some of the potato cooking water – adding as much as you need to make the potatoes a less dense, more spreadable consistency – and squeeze in the juice of half the lime.

- Grate the peeled ginger onto a plate – I use a coarse microplane grater – then spoon the grated ginger into the center of a piece of paper towel. Moving quickly, pull up the edges of the paper and twizzle them, so you have a little wrapped swag-bag, then squeeze and wring out over the potatoes (an intense ginger juice will drip out). Beat this juice into the potatoes. Check the seasoning, tasting to see if you want any more lime or ginger, too.

- Once the lamb filling has had its time, ladle equally between 4 small ovenproof bowls or dishes of approx. 1¾-cup capacity (or a larger rectangular dish, measuring approx. 12 x 8 x 2 inches deep and 6½-cup capacity), and then top with the potatoes, also dividing this equally between the bowls, spreading it to cover the rim of the dishes.

- Sit the dishes on a baking sheet and place in the oven for 10–15 minutes (or, if you're cooking this in one larger dish, it will need 30–35 minutes). The potatoes should be piping hot (though they won't get a crust) with the filling bubbling underneath.

- On serving, sprinkle 1 teaspoon of nibbed pistachios over each bowl.

MAKE AHEAD NOTE	FREEZE NOTE
The pies can be assembled up to 2 days ahead. As soon as the pies are cool (and within 2 hours of making), cover each one and refrigerate until needed. Bake for an extra 10–15 minutes, making sure that the pies are piping hot in the center before serving.	Wrap each pie tightly in a double layer of plastic wrap and a layer of aluminum foil, and freeze for up to 3 months. Thaw overnight in refrigerator and bake as in Make Ahead Note.

Warm spiced cauliflower and chickpea salad with pomegranate seeds

This is one of my favorite suppers, although there's nothing that says you can't serve this as a vegetable side as part of a more conventional meal. And you could also bolster it further by crumbling in some feta. But for me, it is perfect just as it is: the tomatoes almost ooze into a dressing in the oven, and the cauliflower softens, but not soggily. For choice, I'd always use home-cooked chickpeas (I cook batches in my slow cooker and freeze them in 1½-cup portions for everyday use; see **p.211**), but otherwise I like the pre-cooked Spanish chickpeas in jars. Yes, they are more expensive than the canned variety, but the cheapest option is always to buy dried. Don't feel bad about using chickpeas out of a can, though – I have been known to, myself. One can't always be so organized to have the freezer stashed with cooked chickpeas, and so I am always well stocked with canned chickpeas. They do work here, it's just that they won't be as soft; but then, you don't necessarily need them to be. The cauliflower and juicy tomatoes can stand some nubbliness.

The parsley is not a garnish – ugh, that word – but used, here, as a salad leaf. And this is also very, very good cold, so if you have some left over, it makes a fabulous box lunch, or provides instant gratification on those days you have to eat fridge-side, with your coat still on, you're so hungry.

1 small head cauliflower

3 tablespoons regular olive oil

½ teaspoon ground cinnamon

2 teaspoons cumin seeds

1½ cups chickpeas, home-cooked or drained from a can or jar

1–2 tablespoons harissa, to taste (and depending on the heat of the harissa)

4 smallish ripe vine tomatoes (approx. 6 ounces total)

1 teaspoon sea salt flakes or kosher salt, or to taste

3–4 tablespoons pomegranate seeds

2½ cups Italian parsley leaves

○ Preheat the oven to 425°F. Trim the cauliflower and divide into small florets. Pour the oil into a large bowl, add the cinnamon and cumin seeds, and stir or whisk to help the spices disperse. Tip in the prepared cauliflower and toss to coat. Pour the contents of the bowl into a small oven pan (I mostly use a disposable foil baking pan measuring 12 x 8 inches) and place in the oven for 15 minutes. Don't wash out the bowl you've been using just yet.

○ Add the chickpeas to this bowl, and add the harissa, tasting it first to see if you want both tablespoonfuls, and, at the risk of being repetitive, toss to coat. Quarter the tomatoes and add them to the bowl, and shake or stir to mix. When the cauliflower has had its 15 minutes, remove the pan, quickly tip the chickpeas and tomatoes over the cauliflower, and toss to combine before returning to the oven for a further 15 minutes until the cauliflower is tender.

○ When it's ready, remove from the oven and sprinkle the salt over the vegetables, then (and this isn't the last time) toss to combine with half of the pomegranate seeds before dividing between 2 bowls. Divide the parsley leaves – without chopping them – between the 2 bowls and toss to mix. Scatter with the remaining pomegranate seeds.

STORE NOTE

Cool leftovers, then cover and refrigerate within 2 hours of making. Will keep in refrigerator for up to 2 days. Serve cold.

Stir-fried rice with double sprouts, red pepper flakes, and pineapple

This is one of my quick-fire, bowlfood specials – instant comfort, instant joy. And here's what I'm not ashamed of doing: I use those pouches of ready-cooked brown basmati rice and supermarket containers of ready-cubed fresh pineapple. There, I've said it. And although I've stated (truthfully enough) that it will feed 2–4, I often make the full quantity for myself and, with a glad heart, stash any leftovers in the refrigerator to be eaten cold later. But if you want to make this as an accompaniment to a plate of cold ham or suchlike, then know that this amount will happily feed 6.

8 ounces Brussels sprouts, trimmed

2 scallions, trimmed

6 ounces (approx. 1 cup) fresh pineapple cubes

1-inch piece (2 teaspoons) fresh ginger, peeled and finely grated

½ teaspoon crushed red pepper flakes

2 tablespoons cold-pressed coconut oil

1½ cups cooked and cooled brown rice

8 ounces bean sprouts

2 tablespoons soy sauce

2 tablespoons lime juice

3 tablespoons chopped fresh cilantro

- With a sharp knife and a patient frame of mind, slice the Brussels sprouts thinly. Also thinly slice the scallions, and mix the two together.

- Cut the pineapple cubes into ½-inch dice and put in a bowl. Add the ginger and red pepper flakes and stir to mix.

- Get out a wok (or similar) and over a vigorous heat, melt the coconut oil. Toss in the sliced Brussels sprouts and scallions and stir-fry (I use a spatula-type implement in each hand) for about 3 minutes (the sprouts will start scorching in parts).

- Add the rice and toss to mix quickly, then add the bean sprouts and the chilified, gingery pineapple (and any juice that has collected) and stir-fry for a minute or so, before adding the soy sauce, lime juice, and 2 tablespoons of chopped cilantro. Stir-fry for another minute, or until everything (most importantly the rice) is hot, and transfer to a warmed bowl or bowls, sprinkling the top with the remaining tablespoon of cilantro.

STORE NOTE

Cool leftovers, then cover and refrigerate within 1 hour. Will keep in refrigerator for up to 1 day. Serve cold.

Middle-Eastern minestrone

This is in no sense an authentically Middle-Eastern recipe, but a fancy of mine. To elucidate: it is a vegetable soup that is imbued with Middle-Eastern flavors and, in place of the pasta that you'd cook for a traditional Italian minestrone, I use bulgur wheat.

Like many such soups, it thickens on standing, in which case you can either add more liquid, or eat it as a stew. Either way, it is fragrant and filling, and is fast becoming one of my favorite recipes.

2 tablespoons regular olive oil

1 red onion, peeled and chopped

sea salt flakes or kosher salt, to taste

1 butternut squash, peeled, seeded, and chopped into 1-inch cubes

1 clove garlic, peeled and finely grated or minced

2 teaspoons cumin seeds

2 teaspoons coriander seeds

2–3 preserved lemons (depending on size), finely chopped

1½ cups chickpeas, home-cooked or drained from a can or jar

1½ quarts mild vegetable broth

⅔ cup bulgur wheat

chopped fresh cilantro, to serve (optional)

- Heat the olive oil in a heavy-based saucepan that comes with a lid, and sauté the chopped onion sprinkled with a little salt for about 3 minutes until softened.

- Add the chopped butternut squash, the garlic, and the cumin and coriander seeds and stir around, letting everything cook for about 10 minutes.

- Tip in the chopped preserved lemons and the drained chickpeas, then pour in the vegetable broth and partially cover with the lid to keep the liquid from evaporating too much. Simmer for about 20 minutes, by which time the butternut should be just cooked.

- Add the bulgur wheat, then re-cover the pan and cook gently for another 10 minutes, by which time the vegetables should be tender and the bulgur wheat soft but still nutty. Sprinkle with chopped cilantro on serving, if so desired.

STORE NOTE	FREEZE NOTE
Cool leftovers, then cover and refrigerate within 2 hours of making. Will keep in refrigerator for up to 3 days. To reheat, pour the soup into a saucepan, adding extra water or broth if needed, then heat gently, stirring occasionally, until piping hot.	Cooled soup can be frozen, in an airtight container, for up to 3 months. Thaw overnight in refrigerator and reheat as in Store Note.

Split pea soup with chiles, ginger, and lime

This is one of those thick, wintry soups made spiky and fresh with chiles, ginger and lime. It has the hit of a hot and sour soup, but the nubbliness of the split peas gives those clear, piercing flavors an unfamiliar edge, while adding coziness at the same time.

SERVES 6–8, MAKES APPROX. 2 QUARTS

2½ cups yellow split peas

6 scallions, trimmed and thinly sliced

3 fresh red chiles, finely chopped (with or without seeds)

2 cloves garlic, peeled and finely grated or minced

2 quarts water

2 teaspoons vegetable bouillon powder, or to taste

2-inch piece fresh ginger, peeled and finely grated (3½ teaspoons)

zest and juice of 2 limes, preferably unwaxed

salt to taste (optional)

TO SERVE:

chopped fresh cilantro, or sliced scallions, or chopped fresh chiles, or all 3

○ Put the split peas, scallions, chiles, and garlic into a large Dutch oven or heavy-based saucepan that comes with a lid, and pour in the water. Bring to a boil, and once it's bubbling, clamp on the lid, lower the heat slightly, and cook for 40–60 minutes, stirring occasionally, until the split peas are cooked and breaking up in the liquid. You may well have to add more water if the soup gets too thick, although there is a school of thought that holds that this soup should be thick, a positively biblical mess of potage.

○ Once the split peas are cooked and soft, you will need to season with the bouillon powder. Go gently, adding just a little, as specified, at first, as you have fierce flavorings to come. Add the ginger to the soup, then grate in the zest of the limes and squeeze in the juice. Taste for seasoning – you may need to add a little more bouillon powder, or salt if you prefer – and immediately pour into bowls, topping with chopped cilantro or some more sliced scallions or red chiles if wished, or all of them.

STORE NOTE	FREEZE NOTE
Cool leftover soup (without toppings), then cover and refrigerate within 2 hours of making. Will keep in refrigerator for up to 3 days. Reheat gently in a saucepan, stirring occasionally and adding extra water if needed, until piping hot.	Cooled soup can be frozen, in an airtight container, for up to 3 months. Thaw overnight in refrigerator and reheat as in Store Note.

Spiced parsnip and spinach soup

Spiced parsnip soups were the staple of my childhood and teens – those of my vintage and over will most definitely remember the popularity of the curried parsnip soup – but this, while inspired by that memory, is very different. It's rich (though without the butter that was the hallmark of the time), sweet, and a glorious billiards-baize green. The spinach improves the texture and taste, adding a robust earthiness, which, once added, seems the obvious partner to the more mutedly earthy parsnips.

I keep frozen organic leaf spinach (which comes in cubes, and unfurls into leaves as it thaws and cooks in the soup) in the freezer at all times. Someone once told me that spinach draws its nutrients from deep in the soil, and it's one of those vegetables where it makes a real difference if it's organic. I don't know if it's true, but somehow this message has gone deep into my consciousness and now I have to obey.

1 pound parsnips

1 fat clove garlic, peeled

1 quart chicken or vegetable broth

1 teaspoon garam masala

6 ounces frozen organic leaf spinach

lots of freshly ground nutmeg

salt and pepper to taste

○ Peel the parsnips and cut them into equal-sized pieces that will cook in about the same time: that's to say, leave the skinny twigs as they are, and cut the wider bits into smaller pieces. Cut the garlic into 3, then drop these and the prepared parsnips into a large saucepan (with a lid). Cover with broth, bring to a boil, then reduce the heat slightly, put the lid on, and leave to simmer with a certain amount of brio for 15 minutes, or until the parsnips are soft.

○ Stir in the garam masala, add the frozen spinach, then put the lid back on and cook for 5 minutes, by which time the spinach should be thawed and hot.

○ Take the pan off the heat to cool slightly and, using a stick blender, carefully blend the soup until smooth. Add a generous amount of freshly ground nutmeg and season to taste. You may need to add water as this soup does tend to thicken as it stands.

STORE NOTE	FREEZE NOTE
Cool leftovers, then cover and refrigerate within 2 hours of making. Will keep in refrigerator for up to 3 days. Reheat gently in a saucepan, stirring occasionally and adding extra water if needed, until piping hot.	Cooled soup can be frozen, in an airtight container, for up to 3 months. Thaw overnight in refrigerator and reheat as in Store Note.

Sweet potato, ginger, and orange soup

I have this regularly for supper, and I tend to make life easier for myself by always having a stash of baked sweet potatoes in the refrigerator. If you don't, I advise baking the potatoes the night before, so that when you come to make this soup the next or another night, you are about 3 minutes away from a soothing, comforting, gutsily flavored big bowlful. But even if you do roast the sweet potatoes to order, as it were, you need do nothing while they're in the oven, and not much after.

SERVES 2–4, MAKES APPROX. 1 QUART

2 medium-sized sweet potatoes (approx. 1 pound total)	zest of ½ orange, preferably unwaxed, and 2 teaspoons juice
3 cups vegetable broth	1 teaspoon lime juice
2 teaspoons finely grated fresh ginger	¼ teaspoon cayenne pepper
	salt to taste

○ Preheat the oven to 425°F. Put the sweet potatoes in a small roasting pan, lined with aluminum foil, or a disposable foil one (the scorched syrup that oozes out of the sweet potatoes as they cook is hell to wash up), and prick them a few times with the tip of a sharp knife or the tines of a fork. Then bake for 1 hour, or until the potatoes are soft within their skins. Remove from the oven and leave to cool. I like to do this the day before, or any time I've got the oven on, and space to spare in it.

○ Get out a saucepan (one with a lid) and, holding one of the sweet potatoes over it, rip open the skin and let the cooked sweet orange flesh drop into the pan. Repeat with the second potato. Pour in the broth, add the grated ginger, the zest of ½ an orange, and 2 tablespoons of orange juice, along with the lime juice and the cayenne pepper. Then stir to mix, before clamping on the lid, turning on the heat, and bringing the soup to a boil.

○ Taste for seasoning, leave to cool slightly, and then use a stick blender to whizz it smooth, although you could just beat it with a fork if you want a rougher-textured soup.

MAKE AHEAD NOTE	STORE NOTE	FREEZE NOTE
The potatoes can be baked up to 2 days ahead. Transfer to a suitable container, leave to cool, then cover and refrigerate until needed.	Cool leftovers, then cover and refrigerate within 2 hours of making. Will keep in refrigerator for up to 3 days. Reheat gently in a saucepan, stirring occasionally and adding extra water if needed, until piping hot.	Cooled soup can be frozen, in an airtight container, for up to 3 months. Thaw overnight in refrigerator and reheat as in Store Note.

Pea and broccoli soup

You can never have too many pea soups for my family and, indeed, previous books have been rich in pea soups, all of which I still cook. Not for nothing does the great Nigel Slater call me "the queen of the frozen pea" (an accolade I am most proud of) and this is my latest version, which I've been cooking for the past couple of years, and am more than happy to unveil now.

Along with the frozen peas, you could easily use frozen broccoli and, what with these 2 ingredients in the freezer, and the mint teabag, this makes for a great store cupboard supper. This is not the soup's chief virtue: the sweetness of the peas and the brassic boldness of the broccoli hold each other in check; and the merest touch of mint in its hinterland gives this a certain delicate grace.

I don't quite remember what induced me to use a mint teabag as broth for the soup, but very pleased I am too with my innovation. Please do, though, use pure mint tea and not some fancy mixture. Or rather, by all means try whatever fancy mixture you have in the house, only bear in mind it was your addition should you be less than pleased with it.

It occurs to me only now that this soup is most virtuous in its ingredients, but, believe me, it tastes nothing of restraint. It was devised to give pleasure, not to deprive — and I'm glad to say it delivers — and with speedy ease.

SERVES 4–6, MAKES APPROX. 1 ½ QUARTS, OR 6 CUPFULS

5 cups hot water, from a recently boiled kettle	2 fat or 4 small cloves garlic, peeled
1 pure mint teabag	2½ cups frozen peas
2 teaspoons sea salt flakes or kosher salt	3 cups fresh or frozen broccoli florets

○ Pour the water into a saucepan, one that comes with a lid and that is also large enough to take all the ingredients later, then drop in the teabag, stir in the salt, and leave to infuse for 5 minutes.

○ Take out the mint teabag, squeezing out all its minty juices as you do so, then put the lid on the saucepan and bring the mint water to a boil.

○ Once the mint water is boiling, add the garlic and frozen peas, and then let the pan come back to a boil with the lid on.

- Now add the broccoli and cook, this time with the pan only partially covered, for about 10 minutes, or until the broccoli is soft. You do not have to alter this procedure should you be using frozen broccoli rather than fresh.

- Let the soup cool just a little before blitzing with a stick blender until smooth, then season to taste and serve.

STORE NOTE	FREEZE NOTE
Cool leftovers, then cover and refrigerate within 2 hours of making. Will keep in refrigerator for up to 3 days. Reheat gently in a saucepan, stirring occasionally and adding extra water if needed, until piping hot.	Cooled soup can be frozen, in an airtight container, for up to 3 months. Thaw overnight in refrigerator and reheat as in Store Note.

DINE

DINE

This chapter may sound a bit Silver Service, but relax – I don't throw dinner parties, and don't suggest that you do. So, this is not some encomium to any Stepford Wife life, but an attempt to Redefine Dine. I have learned something about myself, and it's this: I can't invite people over to eat if I wouldn't be comfortable were I in my pajamas and no makeup. This is not to say I *have* to be in pajamas and no makeup but, as friends can testify, that is often the case.

But then, I've always been relaxed about the way I feed people: the perfectionist drive makes life hell for host and guest alike. An informal atmosphere is not only the most welcoming one, but – for me – the only way to ensure that I don't regret inviting people over in the first place. I don't do plated appetizers; I don't lay the table properly, but leave canisters of flatware about for people to help themselves; and my food never, ever emulates restaurant service. I don't do smart, I do cozy. You know all those magazine "entertaining" articles, studded with their cook-to-impress checklists? This chapter is the antithesis of all that.

Not all the food I make when cooking for friends is collected here: the Breathe chapter is another trusted resource, and, perhaps self-evidently, the Sweet chapter provides dessert. But here you will find the picky bits I serve, sofa-side, to have with drinks, and those recipes that I rely on for lunch, dinner, or a low-key party, when I want to feed people but, most importantly, want to make my friends feel welcome, and all of us to feel happy.

As for drink, while I generally just offer Prosecco, beer, and red or white wine, along with a lot of water, there are times when it makes life easier to have something you can pour out of a pitcher. In which case, I suggest 3 cocktails: the first, a zingy grapefruit number, is nothing harder to mix up than combining a 750ml bottle of (preferably) pink, sweet, fizzy Muscat (or other sweet, fizzy wine) and 1 cup of freshly squeezed, sharp white grapefruit juice, which is about 2 grapefruits' worth. The second, a heady Cosmopolitan Cup, is made by adding, to each 750ml bottle of Prosecco or other dry, fizzy wine, 2 cups of cranberry juice from a carton, ¼ cup of vodka, and 1–2 tablespoons of freshly squeezed lime juice to taste, so ½–1 lime. The third is my Saketini, which is made much as a vodka martini, but using sake in place of vermouth, in the ratio 2 parts vodka to 1 part sake, shaken over a lot of ice and poured from a cocktail shaker. I agree this last suggestion is not the pitcher-cocktail I promised, but is too good to leave out, and if you can get someone else to shake up the saketinis, then so much the better. I generally like to put someone else on bar duty, anyway.

The recipes that follow, bolstered, too, by those in Breathe, in which the focus is on slow-cooked, make-ahead dishes – and, indeed all the recipes in this book – are really just a record of the food I've made for friends as I've settled into my new life and new home. And now I'm happy to share them with you.

Caramelized garlic hummus

While I am quite happy to have a tub of good-quality hummus in the refrigerator for family fridge-foraging, I don't tend to bring it out for eating out loud, as it were, without some zhuzhing up. Making your own from scratch, I have concluded, is scarcely any harder, and much more satisfying. I am aided in this enterprise by the fact that I cook chickpeas, unsoaked, in my slow cooker (see **p.211**) and sometimes even freeze them (see Freeze Note, overleaf), plus I always have a couple of jars of fabulous pre-cooked Spanish chickpeas in the cupboard; and I am a compulsive garlic-caramelizer. I cannot stop wrapping heads of garlic in aluminum foil and baking them in the oven, until the cloves are sweet and soft. I always store some in the refrigerator (where they keep, in an airtight container or wrapped in foil, for up to 1 week), ready to have this rich, heady purée squeezed into baked potatoes, soups, stews, yogurt – you name it – without any notice. I have given instructions on the overleaf, should you choose not to follow suit, but what you should know is that I wouldn't fire up the oven specially for them: I just cook them at whatever heat the oven's on at the time; thus, you will see for the Spiced Lamb Stew on **p.197**, I cook the heads of garlic, prepared as on overleaf, for 2 hours at 325°F, because that's what the oven's on for the lamb.

As for the chickpeas, I have specified home-cooked ones or those out of a jar, as they are so much better than the canned ones, which can make the hummus too bitty. True, the canned chickpeas are much cheaper, but I go for the least expensive option (dried, which I then cook myself) or the most expensive (Spanish ones from a jar) and miss out the middle path, which has none of the virtues of either of the others. However, 2 x 15-ounce – drained – cans of chickpeas can be used in place of those specified. The seed-sprinkled shards of crisp bread you see alongside the hummus here are simple to make: I split open some whole wheat flatbreads, bought from a nearby Middle-Eastern shop, pour some olive oil on them, sprinkle them with sesame seeds, and bake them, on a rack, in a 425°F oven for 5 minutes, then break them up when they are handle-able. True, they are too delicate to dip, so you have to spoon the hummus on, but they are very good. Otherwise, grissini, toasted pitas torn into bits, or crudités make the perfect accompaniment for greedy dippage.

1 large head of garlic, whole and unpeeled

3 cups chickpeas, home-cooked or drained from cans or jars

zest and juice of 1 unwaxed lemon

¼ cup tahini

¼ cup extra-virgin olive oil, plus more to drizzle on top

¼ cup cold water

1 teaspoon sea salt flakes or kosher salt, or to taste

good grinding of white pepper

- ◦ Preheat the oven to 425°F. Cut the top off the head of garlic, so that you can just see the tops of the cloves peeking through, discard the top, then sit the garlic on a piece of aluminum foil and seal the ends tightly, while leaving the parcel slightly baggy. Sit it on a small foil pan (or similar) and bake in the oven for 45 minutes. Let it cool in the foil wrapping.

- ◦ Drain and rinse the chickpeas (if using canned or jarred), then tip into a food processor.

- ◦ Add the lemon zest and juice, and squeeze in the soft flesh from the caramelized garlic.

- ◦ Spoon in the tahini and the ¼ cup of olive oil and then blitz to a smooth purée.

- ◦ Tip in enough, or all, of the cold water to get the right consistency, adding and blitzing as you go, then add the salt and pepper and check the seasoning. Decant into a bowl and drizzle, if wished, with some more olive oil.

MAKE AHEAD NOTE	STORE NOTE	FREEZE NOTE
Can be made up to 2 days ahead and kept, covered, in refrigerator. If using frozen and thawed chickpeas, best eaten within 24 hours of making.	Cooked chickpeas should be cooled and refrigerated as quickly as possible and used within 2 days.	The cooked and cooled chickpeas can be frozen, in airtight containers or resealable bags, for up to 3 months. Thaw overnight in refrigerator.

Miso mayonnaise

I am forever indebted to Yotam Ottolenghi for his mother's mayonnaise recipe, in which she uses a whole egg rather than just the yolk – for all that my late mother would definitely not approve. When I was in New York recently, I ate a miso mayonnaise alongside a black-and-blue steak on a wooden board (we were in hipster territory), but I felt that had the egg been a bit less dominant, I'd have seen the point of the miso more. And I do love miso. So this is my version, and even though fresh cilantro certainly adds pungency, it works, matching the miso tonally as well as adding a leafy freshness at the same time.

Should you want to roast some sweet potato wedges to eat with this, I wouldn't try to dissuade you, but I love it just with some herbal, crunchy fennel and sweet, crisp sugar snaps to dip in.

1 egg

1½ cups vegetable oil

2 tablespoons apple cider vinegar or white wine vinegar

3 tablespoons sweet white miso

leaves from large bunch cilantro

- Crack the egg into the small bowl of a food processor – these days, most processors come with a smaller bowl that can be clipped on top of the big bowl. (If you don't have a processor, you could use a bowl and a stick blender, or make this – as I was taught by my mother when I was so young I had to stand on a chair to reach the table – by hand with a bowl and whisk.)

- With the motor running, slowly and patiently pour in the oil and then – still with the motor running – slowly pour in the vinegar. You should have a thick, pale mayonnaise in front of you.

- Take off the lid, scrape down, add the miso and the cilantro, put the lid back on, and process again until the cilantro leaves are chopped into small pieces in the mayonnaise. Take off the lid, scrape down to catch any straggling whole cilantro leaves, then put the lid back on and give it a final pulse or two before decanting into a bowl and serving with the accompaniment of your choice.

STORE NOTE

The mayonnaise will keep in refrigerator for up to 4 days from day of making. Transfer to a container, cover, and refrigerate as soon as possible. (Do not leave out of refrigerator for more than 2 hours.)

Note: since this recipe contains raw egg, you should not serve it to anyone with a weak or compromised immune system, such as pregnant women, young children, or the elderly.

Sweet potato and chickpea dip

I cooked my first Thanksgiving dinner last year, which felt both significant and pleasurable, and this was the dish I presented with drinks before the great feast. I adore its harvest-festival colors and sweet earthiness and, bejeweled with pomegranate seeds at the end, it is simple but resplendent.

The making of it also happens to rely on two of my favorite cooking tricks, the pre-roasting of whole sweet potatoes and garlic. Baking a batch of sweet potatoes for plundering later will make your cooking life much easier, and never is this more useful than on big occasions. But I should add that, just because this made its first public appearance at Thanksgiving, it certainly doesn't need to be limited to that. It inspires immense gratitude in me throughout the year, and isn't the attitude of gratitude meant to be one of the great happiness indicators?

1 ¾ pounds sweet potatoes

1 head of garlic, whole and unpeeled

2 limes, preferably unwaxed

2 teaspoons smoked sea salt flakes (though regular sea salt flakes or kosher salt will do), or to taste

½ teaspoon pimentón dulce or paprika

1 ¼ cups chickpeas, home-cooked or drained from a can or jar

1 ½-inch piece (2 ½ teaspoons) fresh ginger, peeled and finely grated

2 tablespoons pomegranate seeds

- Preheat the oven to 425°F, and prick the sweet potatoes before placing them on a baking sheet and cooking them whole for about 1 hour, depending on their size. You want the flesh inside to be very soft, and no doubt the skin will be burnt in parts by the hot-roast syrup that can dribble out as they cook. This is good.

- The minute the sweet potatoes are in the oven, cut the stalk end off the garlic, leaving the tips of the cloves exposed, and then wrap loosely in aluminum foil, sealing the ends tightly to form a baggy parcel, and roast with the sweet potatoes. This should probably be ready in 45 minutes, but I leave it for the hour with the sweet potatoes.

- Let the soft and tender sweet potato and garlic cool; you can do this ahead of time (see Make Ahead Note, below).

- When you are ready to prepare the dip, peel the skin gently away from the sweet potatoes and scoop out the orange pulpy flesh, leaving behind any of the scorched bits. Tip it all into a bowl and then squeeze in the soft, caramelized garlic purée from the exposed cloves.

- Add the finely grated zest from both limes, and the juice from one, the smoked salt, pimentón dulce (or paprika), chickpeas, and finely grated ginger, and then blitz with a stick blender (or use a food processor) to make your dip.

- Check the seasoning as well as acidity – you may want more lime juice – and serve, for beauty's sake, sprinkled with pomegranate seeds. I couldn't resist the autumnally hued vegetable chips alongside, but I actually serve golden corn chips and crudités, as these last two are, indeed, rather more robust as a dipping vehicle.

MAKE AHEAD NOTE	STORE NOTE
The sweet potato and garlic can be made up to 3 days ahead and kept, wrapped in aluminum foil or in a covered container, in refrigerator.	Leftover dip can be stored, in a covered container, in refrigerator for up to 2 days from making.

A simple salsa

As far as I'm concerned, you can never go wrong with a simple, spiky salsa and a bowlful of tortilla chips. True, this is on the fiery side – those who want a little less heat should seed the chiles – but that, for me, is the whole point. I also make it, as a matter of course, to go with the Oven-Baked Egg Hash on **p.390**, but I am sure you won't have any difficulties finding a wide application for this in your daily life.

I think it's important to treat the salsa with respect and serve only proper corn tortilla chips alongside. If you can get blue corn chips, I'd go for those; otherwise plain, unsalted, yellow corn chips, and no funny flavors, please.

MAKES ENOUGH FOR 6–8 PEOPLE, TO DIP INTO OVER DRINKS

1–2 tablespoons regular olive oil

1 small red onion, peeled and finely chopped

2 fat cloves garlic, peeled and finely grated or minced

1 teaspoon cumin seeds

1 teaspoon sea salt flakes or kosher salt

3 fresh jalapeño peppers, finely chopped with seeds intact

2 x 14-ounce cans good-quality diced tomatoes

○ Heat 1 tablespoonful of oil in a medium, heavy-based saucepan over a medium heat, and cook the finely chopped red onion, stirring every now and again, until it's soft but not colored (beyond its natural hue) in any way, about 5 minutes, adding more oil if necessary – it rather depends on the diameter of your saucepan. Add the garlic to the pan, and give it a good stir before adding the cumin, salt, and jalapeños.

○ Cook, stirring, for another minute, with the heat a little higher, making sure nothing catches, then tip in the canned tomatoes, stir well, and when it comes to a boil, lower the heat slightly and simmer for about 15 minutes. You want the sauce to thicken and gain in richness.

○ Check for seasoning, and pour into a bowl to cool before serving with the tortilla chips of your choice.

STORE NOTE	FREEZE NOTE
Cool leftovers, then cover and refrigerate within 2 hours of making. Will keep, covered, in refrigerator for up to 3 days.	The cooled salsa can be frozen, in an airtight container, for up to 3 months. Thaw overnight in refrigerator and use within 2 days.

Brazilian cheese bread

I have a wonderful Brazilian friend, Helio, mentioned elsewhere in this book and, indeed, others of my books, who has been plying me with *pão de quiejo* for years, but it wasn't until I went to Brazil that I realized what a statement of national identity it is. That's to say, I don't think I ever went into any Brazilian's house without a warm bowl of these cheese breads being forced upon me (in the loveliest way) the minute I stepped through the door. I've tried a number of recipes, but this amalgam of a few of them is the best I've come up with for those outside Brazil, and Helio has given me the nod of approval (it was he who suggested the store-bought shredded Parmesan, by the way). And now I have found myself pressing these upon anyone who comes to my house. I recommend you do what they do in Brazil, which is to make the dough, form it into balls, and then freeze it so that you can always be ready to serve up a warm batch. Alas, I am not always so organized myself.

But before we proceed, I feel I do need to explain what these are like, because cheese bread doesn't quite convey their unfamiliar gooey chewiness. At first you may find them underwhelming: shortly, you will find them addictive; this, a friend tells me, is the working definition of "more-ish." They are rather like cheese-scented choux buns, but with a more papery outside and a softer inside. And they look rather like golf balls, lit up from within. None of this sounds great, I know, but I can't get enough of them, and nor can anyone I give them to.

They are made from manioc flour but you can use tapioca flour (also sometimes called starch), which I found online and is, so far as I can tell, the same thing. You can otherwise find manioc or tapioca flour wherever Brazilians shop or, indeed, in Asian and Middle-Eastern stores, too.

And it is worth mentioning, I feel, that tapioca flour is gluten-free.

2 cups tapioca flour (see Intro)	½ cup vegetable oil
1 teaspoon fine sea salt	2 large eggs, beaten
1 cup whole milk	1 cup shredded Parmesan

- Preheat your oven to 425°F and line 2 large baking sheets with parchment paper, or use 1 sheet and bake in batches.

- In a freestanding mixer, using the flat beater, or with a hand-held electric whisk and bowl, combine the tapioca flour and salt.

- In a saucepan, heat the milk and oil, bringing gently to a boil, and once it's bubbling, take the pan off the heat before it becomes a full rolling boil. Pour immediately into the flour mixture and turn on the motor, though not too fast at first, beating until it forms a sticky batter.

- Carry on beating the dough for at least 5 minutes (as you want it to cool down before you add the eggs) then scrape down and check with your fingers to see if it is still hot to the touch. You need it to cool to about body temperature, which could take up to 10 minutes of beating.

- Once you have reached this point, duly whisk in the beaten eggs, spooning them in very gradually, about a tablespoon or so at a time, and make sure that the egg is fully amalgamated before you add the next spoonful.

- Finally, add – still beating – the Parmesan cheese in 2 batches, and continue to beat until all ingredients are, again, well combined.

- Scoop teaspoon-sized balls onto the lined baking sheets, or use 1 sheet and bake in batches. If you are baking in batches then refrigerate the unused batter as it waits. I use a rounded measuring spoon and, if needed, dip the spoon in water every couple of scoops, as the dough then drops out of the spoon more easily.

- Put in the oven, then immediately turn the heat down to 375°F, and bake for 12–15 minutes, until puffed and with a golden tinge. Let the cheese breads cool a little before serving.

MAKE AHEAD NOTE	FREEZE NOTE
The dough can be made 1 day ahead and kept, covered, in refrigerator until needed.	The dough can be scooped in balls onto baking sheets lined with parchment paper and frozen. Once solid, transfer to resealable bags or airtight containers and freeze for up to 3 months. Bake directly from frozen, following the directions in recipe, above.

Chicken crackling

The great Simon Hopkinson, author of *Roast Chicken and Other Stories*, gave me — appropriately enough — a bag of chicken crackling as a present, and I pressed him for the recipe. Although I have impatiently cooked my version at a higher heat and for a shorter time than he ordained, I hope he will not be too disapproving.

Since butchers spend a lot of their time skinning chicken for their customers, you shouldn't find it difficult to buy the skin, nor should it cost much; if you're buying other things, they'll probably throw it in for free. And although there is something a bit Hannibal Lecter about the way the raw skin looks, stretched out on the wire rack before it goes into the oven, the finished article is unspookily inviting.

SERVES 4–6, TO PICK AT OVER DRINKS

8 ounces chicken skin	¼ teaspoon cayenne pepper
¼ teaspoon fine sea salt	oil for greasing

- Preheat the oven to 350°F.

- Oil a large wire rack that can sit over an oven pan or baking sheet, and then stretch the pieces of skin over the rack so that each piece lies flat with none of them overlapping.

- Sprinkle the salt and cayenne over the chicken skin and then place in the oven for 30 minutes. The chicken skin should be golden and crisp, but watch that it doesn't catch too much.

- Take out of the oven and pull the pieces of chicken crackling gently off the rack — you will need a metal spatula to help lift them off — and leave to cool.

- Once cooled, break into nibble-sized pieces and serve with drinks.

MAKE AHEAD NOTE

The crackling can be made up to an hour ahead and left at room temperature. Consume within 2 hours of making.

Sake-sticky drumsticks

I'm always in favor of food that can be eaten by hand: whether over drinks, at the table, or straight from the refrigerator. But however you eat these, many napkins are called for.

Do consider making the Miso Mayonnaise on **p.115** to go with them, though I'm happy enough with just some limes to spritz over, too. And I know some people are nervous of making party food too spicy (I'm not one of them) so I want to reassure the fire-afeared that none of the gorgeous umami stickiness and savoriness is ruined by leaving out the red pepper flakes.

MAKES 20 DRUMSTICKS

½ cup sake	1 teaspoon Asian sesame oil
¼ cup fish sauce	1 teaspoon crushed red pepper flakes
¼ cup soy sauce	20 chicken drumsticks, skin on
¼ cup vegetable oil	2 tablespoons honey

○ Mix the sake, fish sauce, soy sauce, vegetable oil, sesame oil, and red pepper flakes together in a measuring cup. Put the chicken drumsticks into a large resealable bag, pour over the contents of the cup, seal the bag, place it in something like a lasagna dish (just in case the bag leaks), and leave in a cool place for 40 minutes or in the refrigerator for up to 1 day.

○ When you are ready to cook, preheat the oven to 400°F and line a large, shallow oven pan (I use a half sheet pan with a small lip of ½ inch) with aluminum foil and, being careful not to let the bag spill out its precious juices, place the drumsticks, curved-side up, on it. If they've been in the refrigerator, let them come up to room temperature. Pour off ½ a cupful of the marinade, reserving it, pouring the scant remaining marinade onto the drumsticks. Cook in the oven for 45 minutes.

○ While the chicken's in the oven, pour the reserved ½ cup of marinade into a small saucepan, add the honey, and boil until it's reduced to a sticky glaze. This will take 5–7 minutes.

○ When the drumsticks have had their 45 minutes, test to see if they're more or less cooked through, then carefully pour the juices that have collected in the pan into the glaze. Stir and pour over the chicken drumsticks, then place back in the oven for 10 minutes. After which, spoon the sticky juices over the drumsticks and roast for another 10 minutes.

○ Remove from the oven, then spoon any glaze from the bottom of the pan over the drumsticks, and let them stand until cool enough to be eaten by hand.

MAKE AHEAD NOTE	STORE NOTE	FREEZE NOTE
The drumsticks can be marinated 1 day ahead. It is also possible to freeze the drumsticks in the marinade for up to 3 months (as long as the meat has not been previously frozen); thaw overnight in refrigerator before cooking.	Cool leftovers, then cover and refrigerate within 2 hours of making. Will keep in refrigerator for up to 3 days.	Cooled leftovers can be frozen, in an airtight container, for up to 1 month. Thaw overnight in refrigerator before using.

Lamb ribs with nigella and cumin seeds

Stop what you're doing: I bring you important news. Lamb ribs, almost unknown in the UK, are one of the most delicious ways of eating lamb, and certainly the least expensive. I'd love to see them more widely available (without the hike in price that so often follows), but until then you will need to find a compliant butcher and ask for them.

Incidentally, in the US they're known as "Denver ribs," since Denver is the largest producer of lamb in America, although one could argue that even there these are not exactly widely known. I feel now's the time for them to garner a little more universal appreciation. I'm certainly evangelical about spreading the word.

Actually, I used to buy breast of lamb (which is where the ribs come from) when I was an undergraduate in the UK for 25 cents per breast (I was cooking on a student budget, after all). I'd braise it, slowly, with spices, in one piece, and it was considered a pretty odd thing to do back then, too. The breast and, consequently, the ribs do cost a bit more now, I concede, but they're still a gratifying good buy. Not that they taste bargain-basement: everyone who's eaten these has said they're the best spareribs they've ever had.

I like to keep the flavor of the meat to the fore, so don't coat them in a glaze, but give them the scantest covering before they go into the oven. And while it might seem unnecessary to use oil, it does help the spices to stick and the ribs to crisp; anyway, so much of the fat drips off into the pan under the rack. Even so, they are, without question, a fatty cut, but for those of us who love the flavor and the lip-smacking stickiness that this gives, it's a bonus, not a warning. If you're a lean-cut kind of a person, these are not for you. Commiserations.

4 teaspoons nigella seeds

4 teaspoons cumin seeds

4 teaspoons regular olive oil

¼ cup soy sauce

4 cloves garlic, peeled and finely grated
or minced

24 lamb ribs, cut from 3 lamb breasts, bones in

○ Preheat the oven to 325°F. Line a large roasting pan with aluminum foil and sit a
rack on top. If you haven't got a large enough pan (the one that came with my oven
is half sheet size), then use 2 pans, and just swap them over in the oven halfway
through cooking, and be prepared to add a further 10–15 minutes on to the
roasting time.

○ Get out a dish and add the nigella and cumin seeds, pour in the oil and soy, and
add the garlic. Stir to combine.

○ Dip and schmoosh the ribs, one by one, in this mixture, so that they are lightly
coated on both sides; you may think this scant amount won't be enough for all the
ribs, but it is – just – and you don't want them wet, merely colored by the liquid and
with some seeds adhering to them.

○ Arrange them on the rack above the lined baking pan and cook in the oven for
1½–2 hours (they can differ in size), or until the fat on the ribs is crisp and the
meat tender.

○ Arrange on a warmed platter and make sure you have a good supply of napkins
to hand.

STORE NOTE	FREEZE NOTE
Cool leftovers, then cover and refrigerate within 2 hours of making. Will keep in refrigerator for up to 3 days.	Cooled leftovers can be frozen, in an airtight container, for up to 1 month. Thaw overnight in refrigerator before using.

Butternut and halloumi burgers

While these are not actually burgers, there is something meaty about a slice of roasted butternut squash that lends itself to this way of eating, and the salty halloumi, welded on by the heat of the oven, is the perfect foil to the squash's densely fleshed sweetness. It's always difficult with squash, just as it is with pumpkin, to tell before cooking whether you have a good, juicy one, or if the flesh is going to be stringy and tasteless. But I have found that sweet butternut squash seems to be very reliable, plus its long shape, before it bulges into the round seedy bit, is well suited to this recipe. Choose a butternut that has a long neck, as it is this part that you cut to make the "burgers." The remaining part of the squash can be usefully employed in the Tray of Roasted Veggies (**p.237**) for another meal.

These, for me, are perfect for Saturday lunch all year round, or for a sunny summer supper – icy cold beers and rosé wine close at hand. But they're quick and simple enough to rustle up whenever you need to feed people without much notice.

1 butternut squash

1 tablespoon regular olive oil

1 teaspoon dried oregano

1 x 8-ounce block halloumi cheese

4 pita breads

TO SERVE:

salad leaves of your choice

2 large tomatoes, thickly sliced

○ Preheat the oven to 400°F. Slice the long part of the butternut into approximately ½-inch rounds; if it is a uniform size you can get about 6–8 slices before you hit the bulbous, seeded end. Pour the oil onto a large, shallow baking sheet and then put the slices of butternut on top. Sprinkle with half of the oregano, then flip the rounds over and sprinkle on the rest.

○ Put in the oven to roast for 20–30 minutes, or until tender and browning at the edges. Then cut the block of halloumi cheese in half, to give 2 square-ish pieces, and stand each half upright, to make it easier to cut each into 3 or 4 slices, depending on how many slices of butternut you have. Place a slice on each round of butternut.

○ Roast in the oven for another 10 minutes, by which time the cheese should be soft and melting – bearing in mind that halloumi never gets very melty – on top of the butternut.

○ While the butternut and halloumi are getting toward the end of their time in the oven, cut the pitas in half crossways and briefly warm them, too, in the oven.

○ Open the mouths of the pita halves slightly in order to load them with some salad leaves and slip a cheese-loaded butternut round into each pita pocket, top the butternut burger with a thick slice of tomato, and eat straightaway.

Fish tacos

I am a broad church: when I'm not craving a bowl of food that delivers the same soothing taste from mouthful to mouthful, I like the sort of meal that involves a table full of bits and pieces, much DIY assembly, and a lot of condiments. I certainly think this latter way of eating is one of the most relaxing ways of sitting around a table with friends.

These fish tacos are a case in point (see also the Oven-Cooked Chicken Shawarma on **p.157**), and rest assured that the actual preparation is much more low-effort than you might think. For one, I roast the fish that goes in the tacos rather than, as is more traditional, fry it; the quick-pickled onions involve no more than cutting a small red onion into half-moons and steeping them in lime juice; the corn relish is mainly made out of a can (for which, no apologies), and the spicy sauce comes simply by adding some Korean gochujang into some store-bought mayo. Yes, I know there is a little cultural melding going on here, but if you have the gochujang for the Slow-Cooker Korean Beef and Rice Pot on **p.218** (much advised) then you will long to find other uses for it. Otherwise, any store-bought hot sauce of your choice will do or, if you're feeling like getting a little more stuck in, then please, *please* try the Chile, Ginger, and Garlic Sauce on **p.254**, which I eat with practically everything.

SERVES 4–6, AS A MAIN COURSE

FOR THE QUICK-PICKLED ONION:

1 small red onion

juice of 2 limes

FOR THE HOT SAUCE:

½ cup mayonnaise

2 teaspoons gochujang paste, or other hot sauce, to taste

FOR THE CORN RELISH:

1 cup drained canned corn

1 fresh red chile

3 tablespoons chopped fresh cilantro

salt to taste

FOR THE FISH TACOS:

4 skinless fillets of firm white fish, such as hake or haddock (1¾–2 pounds total), from the thicker loin end

1 teaspoon ground cumin

½ teaspoon paprika

1 teaspoon sea salt flakes or kosher salt

1 clove garlic, peeled and finely grated or minced

2 tablespoons regular olive oil

8 soft corn tortillas

FOR THE AVOCADO:

2 ripe avocados

juice of 1 lime

TO SERVE:

salad leaves of your choice

1–2 tablespoons chopped fresh cilantro

2 limes, cut into wedges

- Preheat the oven to 425°F for the fish, and begin by preparing the sides for your tacos. Peel and halve the red onion, then thinly slice into half-moons. Put the red onion slices into a bowl and cover with the lime juice. Stir with a fork to mix the onion well in the juice. Actually, if you can get this done ahead of time (up to 1 day), so much the better, but even 20 minutes is fine.

- Make the hot sauce by mixing together the mayonnaise and the gochujang paste (or other hot sauce) in a small bowl. Set aside.

- For the corn relish, put the canned corn into a bowl. Finely dice the chile (seed if you don't like too much heat) and add to the corn, along with the chopped cilantro and some salt to taste. Give it all a good stir, and set aside.

- Cut the fish fillets in half lengthways, so you have long sticks, and arrange in a shallow roasting pan. Mix together the cumin, paprika, and salt, and sprinkle over the fish fillets.

- Mix the garlic and the oil in a small bowl. Drizzle the fish with the garlicky oil, and roast in the oven for 8–10 minutes, depending on the thickness of your fillets. Check to see if the fish is cooked through (though only just) before taking out of the oven.

- Once you've taken the fish out (though don't let it get cold) turn off the oven and warm the tortillas in the fading heat. Meanwhile, peel, pit, and slice the avocados, then spritz with the juice of the lime, ready to serve with the other accompaniments.

- Arrange the fish on a plate (lined with salad leaves, if so desired), sprinkle with some chopped fresh cilantro, and take to the table along with the warmed tortillas. If you don't want to add any salad to the fish directly, you may want to put a bowl of shredded iceberg or some other crisp leaves nearby.

- Put the bowls of soused, but drained, red onions, the corn relish, hot sauce, and a plate of sliced avocados on the table so that everyone can load their tortillas. A plate of lime wedges and a pile of napkins are both good ideas, too.

MAKE AHEAD NOTE

The pickled onions, hot sauce, and relish (minus the cilantro) can be made 1 day ahead. Cover and refrigerate until needed. Stir the chopped cilantro into the corn relish just before serving.

Greek squid and orzo

The aniseed flavor that underscores this fabulously easy baked squid and orzo pasta dish is gentle enough not to frighten away any but hardcore fennelphobes and, even then, I have surprised those who profess aniseed-antagonism with just how well it goes down. And it's joyously simple to make, too: all it takes is a little desultory chopping and stirring, and then it cooks itself in the oven, until the squid is so tender that the lightest touch of a spoon cuts through it.

Thank you to Alex Andreou for showing me how to cook this, along with the Strapatsada on **p.49** and Old Rag Pie on **p.318.** I feel the Greek kitchen has been given a fine showing in these pages, and I'm grateful to have been able to do so, not least because learning new recipes that you know will become part of your own trusted repertoire is one of the great joys of cooking.

SERVES 4–6, AS A MAIN COURSE

4 shallots or 1 small red onion

½ bulb fennel

2 cloves garlic

¼ cup extra-virgin olive oil, plus a little more for later

1½ pounds squid (cleaned weight)

1¾ cups orzo pasta

1 x 14-ounce can diced tomatoes

1 tablespoon tomato paste

2 tablespoons ouzo

large bunch (approx. 4 ounces) fresh dill

1 cup hot water, from a recently boiled kettle

salt and pepper to taste

- Preheat the oven to 325°F. Get out a large Dutch oven or pan (one with a tight-fitting lid) that's big enough to take everything, and that can go on the stove and into the oven later. The shallow braiser you can see in the picture is 12 inches in diameter, and the one I always use.

- Peel and halve the shallots (or small red onion), then cut into chunky half-moons. Cut the core out of the fennel, and discard it, then slice the fennel, including the tubey parts, into rough chunks. Don't discard the fronds. Press down on the garlic cloves with the side of a heavy knife to bruise them, then peel off the skins.

- Pour the olive oil into the pan, put it over a low heat, and add the sliced shallots (or onion), chopped fennel, and bruised garlic, along with the squid, left just as it is, and cook it all, stirring every now and again, for 10 minutes. The squid (and the fennel) will give out quite a bit of liquid, so you won't be frying so much as braising.

- Stir in the orzo pasta and the diced tomatoes. Add the tomato paste to the empty tomato can, then fill it up with cold water and give it a good stir, before pouring this into the pan. Now pour in the ouzo and give the pan another stir. Do not season at this stage. Turn up the heat, and once it comes to a boil, clamp on the lid, then transfer the pan to the oven and cook for 1 hour and 20 minutes. When you're near the end of the cooking time, finely chop the dill and put the kettle on to boil.

- When time's up, take the pan out of the oven and remove the lid. The orzo will have absorbed all the liquid and the squid should be tender enough to be cut into with a wooden spoon. Add the hot water and stir well to scrape up any bits stuck to the bottom (these are the bits full of flavor). Add salt and pepper to taste and most of the chopped dill, then stir before putting the pan back in the oven, with the lid off, for 10 minutes.

- Remove from the oven, sprinkle with the remaining dill, and eat with no more than a crisp green salad alongside. And if you wish to grate Parmesan over it as you eat, despite the Italian no-cheese-with-fish-pasta rule, I will not try to put you off. The Greeks do eat this with grated cheese after all.

STORE NOTE

Cool leftovers, then cover and refrigerate within 2 hours of making. Will keep in refrigerator for up to 2 days. Leftovers are best served cold, with a spritz of lemon juice.

Chicken traybake with bitter orange and fennel

I don't think I could say how often I've made this since settling into my new kitchen. Not that I'm ashamed of being repetitive – I find that comforting – but I've simply cooked it too often to count. It will always, no matter wherever and whenever I cook it, be the taste of my new home, evoking the strength and robust sense of coziness that emanates from that.

I never quite feel that a house is a home until a chicken has been roasted in it (with apologies to all vegetarians and, indeed, chickens) and this, as it cooks, fills your kitchen with its gentle anise and citrus scent, working as well in midwinter with in-season Seville oranges as it does in summer with eating oranges, their sweetness soured by lemon. Apropos of this, although I normally consider not using the zest of a lemon a culinary hanging offense, here I don't use it, as it would flagrantly, if fragrantly, overpower the essential orange.

I always get the chicken in its marinade a day ahead, but if you don't have time, an hour would be fine (out of the refrigerator, but in a cool place) so long as you start off with good chicken. If you can afford good organic chicken, buy it. It is this chicken that provides a strong natural "gravy," and the other reasons to do so are even more compelling.

The fennel I've been finding lately has been large but no less full of herbal flavor for all that; if you find only smaller bulbs of fennel, maybe use 3, and just quarter them.

As for what to serve alongside, depending on the time of year, I'd say a pile of mashed potatoes or steamed baby white potatoes and perhaps some just-blanched sugar snaps, glossed with butter or oil, for crunch.

SERVES 6

2 large bulbs fennel (approx. 2¼ pounds total, though less wouldn't matter)

7 tablespoons extra-virgin olive oil, plus 1 tablespoon or so for drizzling on the chicken when cooking

zest and juice of 2 Seville oranges (scant ½ cup juice), or zest and juice of 1 eating orange and juice of 1 lemon

2 teaspoons sea salt flakes or kosher salt

4 teaspoons fennel seeds

4 teaspoons Dijon mustard

12 chicken thighs, skin on and bone in, preferably organic

- Remove the fronds from the fennel and put them in a resealable bag in the refrigerator for serving. I discard (that's to say, eat) the tubey bits of the fennel, but if you have a roasting pan big enough, use everything. Cut the bulbs of fennel into quarters and then cut each quarter, lengthways, into 3. Leave on the cutting board while you get on with the marinade.

- Placing a large resealable bag in position inside a wide-necked measuring cup or similar, pour in the oil, add the orange zest and juice (and lemon juice, if using), and spoon in the salt, fennel seeds, and mustard. Stir briefly to mix.

- Remove the bag from the cup and, holding it up, add a quarter of the chicken pieces, followed by a quarter of the fennel pieces, and so on until everything's been used up.

- Seal the bag tightly at the top, lay the bag in something like a lasagna dish, and squelch it about so that you make the small amount of marinade cover as much of the chicken as possible. It will look as if it isn't enough, but it is, I promise. Leave in the refrigerator overnight or up to 1 day.

- When you want to cook, remove the marinating chicken and fennel from the refrigerator and tip the contents of the bag — marinade and all — into a large shallow roasting pan (I use a half sheet pan with a lip of ½ inch). Using tongs, or whatever implement(s) you prefer, arrange the chicken pieces so that they are sitting, skin-side up, on top of the fennel. Leave it for 30 minutes or so, to come up to room temperature while you preheat the oven to 400°F.

- Drizzle some more golden oil onto the chicken, and cook in the oven for 1 hour, by which time the fennel will be soft and the chicken cooked through and bronzed on top.

- Put the chicken and fennel onto a warmed serving plate and put the pan over a medium heat (use a saucepan if your pan isn't stove-friendly) and boil the juices, stirring as you watch it turn syrupy; this should take about 1½–2 minutes in the pan, and about 5 in a saucepan.

- Pour the reduced sauce over the chicken and fennel, and then tear over the reserved fennel fronds.

MAKE AHEAD NOTE	STORE NOTE
The chicken can be marinated 1 day ahead. Store in refrigerator until needed.	Cool leftovers, then cover and refrigerate within 2 hours of making. Will keep in refrigerator for up to 3 days.

Roast chicken with lemon, rosemary, garlic, and potatoes

I am back to familiar territory with this: the smell of chicken roasting with lemon, rosemary, and garlic has always seemed to me the essence of all that is comforting. But this version is so sprightly and robust that I feel it uplifts as it soothes: it is good-mood food, and good-mood cooking, too. You just throw everything in the pan with brio and let it roast away merrily.

¼ cup regular olive oil

2 teaspoons finely chopped rosemary needles, plus more to serve

1 head of garlic, separated into (unpeeled) cloves

2 leeks

2¼ pounds waxy potatoes, such as Yukon Gold, washed if necessary, but unpeeled

2 unwaxed lemons

1 medium chicken (approx. 3 pounds), preferably organic

sea salt flakes or kosher salt, to taste

- Preheat the oven to 425°F. Get out the biggest roasting pan you have, and pour all but a teaspoon or so of the oil into it. Throw in the chopped rosemary needles and the garlic cloves.

- Trim the leeks and cut each in half lengthways, then slice into half-moons and drop these leek curls into the pan, too.

- Cut the potatoes into ½-inch slices, then cut each slice into 4, or just halve them if the potatoes are small, and add these to the pan.

- Quarter the lemons, then cut each quarter in half, take out as many pips as you can without exerting yourself unduly, and toss the lemon quarters into the pan. Now schmoosh everything to mix, and then make a space in the middle of the pan for the chicken to sit in.

- Untruss the chicken, place it in the reserved parking space, pour the tiny bit of remaining oil on top of it, and sprinkle sea salt flakes on top of the chicken only. Place in the oven for 1 hour and 10 minutes, and if the juices of the chicken run clear when you push the tip of a knife into the joint where the thigh meets the body, remove the chicken to a board to sit, letting the juices from its cavity spill back into the pan as you do so, then put the potato mixture back in the oven for 10 minutes until soft and golden. If the chicken needs longer, keep everything in the oven until the chicken's cooked.

- When it's ready, and the chicken has rested, either carve it or cut into joints as wished – I find the chicken goes further if carved. If you don't want to serve the lemony, garlicky potatoes from their pan (I never mind), transfer them to a serving plate or dish and sprinkle with ½ a teaspoon or so of finely chopped rosemary needles and sea salt flakes to taste.

STORE NOTE	FREEZE NOTE
Transfer leftover cooked chicken to a container, then cover and refrigerate within 2 hours. Will keep in refrigerator for up to 3 days.	Cooked and cooled chicken can be frozen, in airtight containers or resealable bags, for up to 2 months. Thaw overnight in refrigerator before using.

Chicken Cosima

I am smiling as I'm writing this, as it is what I cooked for my daughter to celebrate her 21st birthday, not long after we'd moved into our new home. Actually, I cooked huge vats of it, in a pan so big that both the children could fit into it together when they were little – and have the lid put on, too. Not that I was in the habit of squeezing them into saucepans.

I made this for the momentous event, as I wanted to create something that had all my daughter's favorite ingredients in it, that would be easy to make, and amenable once made. It sits comfortably on a low heat or in a low oven if you need to wait before serving, and it doesn't require anything more than to be ladled out into shallow bowls. The Leek Pasta Bake on **p.208** was also presented, for non-meat-eaters, and both are great for a party and can be scaled up or down easily.

2½–3 tablespoons all-purpose flour

1 teaspoon ground coriander

1 teaspoon ground cumin

½ teaspoon ground turmeric

½ teaspoon paprika

½ teaspoon sea salt flakes or kosher salt

6 large skinless and boneless chicken thighs, cut into bite-sized chunks

1 tablespoon cold-pressed coconut oil or regular olive oil

1 onion, peeled and chopped

1 pound sweet potatoes, peeled and cut into 1-inch chunks

2 cups hot chicken broth

3 cups chickpeas, home-cooked or drained from cans or jars

chopped fresh cilantro, to serve

- Preheat the oven to 400°F.

- Measure the flour, spices, and salt into a resealable bag and then tip in the chicken. Shake the bag around to coat the chicken with the floury spice.

- Heat the oil in a wide Dutch oven or pan (with a lid), and then fry the onion until softened but not really colored.

- Add the chicken and all the contents of the bag to the pan, and stir around for a minute or so, then add the peeled and chopped sweet potatoes and stir again.

- Pour in the hot broth, then bring the pan up to a boil and tip in the drained chickpeas. Give it another good stir, then clamp on the lid and put in the oven for 25 minutes.

- Check that the chicken is cooked through and the sweet potatoes are tender, then take out of the oven and leave with the lid on to stand for about 10 minutes.

- Ladle into bowls, sprinkling each with chopped cilantro.

STORE NOTE

Transfer leftover chicken to a container, then cool, cover, and refrigerate within 2 hours of making. Will keep in refrigerator for up to 3 days. Reheat leftovers gently in a saucepan until piping hot. Stir occasionally, adding a splash of water or chicken broth if needed.

Tequila and lime chicken

Someone once said to me on Twitter that Mother Hens must use me as a warning to frighten their chicks when they were misbehaving. There's no denying it, I do cook an awful lot of chicken. But you cannot have too many chicken recipes in my book and this is, after all, my book.

This is relatively new to my repertoire but firmly established for all that. True, the tequila doesn't exactly convey flavor, or not so that you could name it, but it sure brings fire – augmented by the red pepper flakes – and tenderizes the chicken beautifully.

If you want to bulk it out, then look no further than the Cuban Black Beans on **p.214** or simply chop up some sweet potatoes and roast them in cold-pressed coconut oil and cumin in the oven at the same time. But when I want something lighter, a simple green salad does me. At all times, some avocado mashed with salt then sprinkled with fresh cilantro and a few more red pepper flakes, to be dolloped on the plate, is highly desirable.

It was while cooking this, during an extended (work) stay at the Chateau Marmont in LA, that I set off the fire alarm. Somehow that feels entirely appropriate.

1 medium chicken (approx. 3 pounds), preferably organic, cut into 8 pieces

5 tablespoons tequila blanco

zest and juice of 2 limes, preferably unwaxed

½ teaspoon crushed red pepper flakes, plus more to sprinkle on at the end

2 teaspoons sea salt flakes or kosher salt

2 tablespoons regular olive oil

TO SERVE:

chopped fresh cilantro

lime wedges

° First, put the jointed chicken pieces into a resealable bag.

° Mix together the tequila, zest and juice of the limes, the red pepper flakes, salt, and olive oil, and then tip this into the resealable bag with the chicken. Seal or tie tightly (letting out the air first) and place it (in a dish) in the refrigerator to marinate for 6 hours or overnight, or up to 2 days, or leave outside the refrigerator, but in a cool place, for 40 minutes if you're short of time.

° Preheat the oven to 425°F. If the chicken is in the refrigerator, take it out and remove the chicken pieces from the bag, reserving the marinade. Sit the chicken pieces on a smallish, shallow roasting pan for about 30 minutes to allow them to come to room temperature. It's important that the chicken pieces sit on the pan without a lot of room to spare, or else the marinade will immediately evaporate in the hot oven. When you are ready to put it into the oven, pour half of the marinade over the chicken pieces and transfer to the hot oven for 25 minutes.

° Take the chicken out of the oven, pour the other half of the reserved marinade over it, then put the chicken back in for another 25–30 minutes. Check it is cooked through before removing from the oven.

° Put the chicken pieces on a serving plate. Then add a little boiling water to the pan to help get every last bit of flavor-sticky juice out, and pour it over the chicken on its plate. Scatter with chopped cilantro and – if you like it hot – some more crushed red pepper flakes, and serve with some lime wedges alongside.

MAKE AHEAD NOTE	STORE NOTE	FREEZE NOTE
The chicken can be marinated up to 2 days ahead. Store in refrigerator until needed.	Transfer leftover cooked chicken to a container, then cool, cover, and refrigerate within 2 hours. Will keep in refrigerator for up to 3 days.	The chicken can be frozen in its marinade – as long as the meat has not been previously frozen – for up to 3 months. Thaw overnight in refrigerator before using. Leftover cooked and cooled chicken can also be frozen, in airtight containers or resealable bags, for up to 2 months. Thaw overnight in refrigerator before using.

Chicken and wild rice

I've been cooking this, or a version of it, for years, but it wasn't until I returned to it recently for this book – having found a scribbled recipe in an old notepad – that I realized that it was really a version of my newly learned squid and orzo dish; the cooking method is virtually identical. Everything is linked: Only Connect.

Of course, the flavors are very different, and so, therefore, is the finished dish. And I love the mellow depth of the spices against the sour-sweet cranberries and glistening spikiness of the wild rice. The strange thing is, when I first cooked this, I hadn't planned it out at all, but simply raided my refrigerator and cupboards and set to, scribbling down what I'd cobbled together only afterward. But then, I am a person guided so much more by instinct than strategy. And it's a reminder that in cooking, as in life, without risk there is no reward.

2 tablespoons regular olive oil	8 skinless and boneless chicken thighs, each chopped into 4 pieces
1 onion, peeled and chopped	
1 clove garlic, peeled and finely grated or minced	1¼ cups wild rice
	½ cup dried cranberries
1 teaspoon ground turmeric	1 quart chicken broth
2 teaspoons coriander seeds	salt and pepper to taste
2 teaspoons cumin seeds	handful finely chopped fresh cilantro

- Preheat the oven to 350°F. Put a wide, flameproof Dutch oven, that will take all the ingredients snugly, and that comes with a lid, on the stove. Add the oil, and cook the onion for 5–10 minutes, stirring once or twice, on a low to medium heat, until just softened. Since we have turmeric a-coming, I'd advise against using a wooden spoon or spatula.

- Add the garlic to the oniony pan and then stir in the spices.

- Turn the heat to high and add the chicken pieces, stirring for 3 minutes until sealed, although they will not color much.

- Add the rice and stir for 1 minute, followed by the cranberries and the chicken broth, and bring to a boil. Clamp on the lid and transfer to the oven, and cook for 1 hour.

- Remove from the oven, check the rice is cooked – the grains will be swollen and starting to split open but still have bite to them – and season with salt and pepper, then put back in the oven for another 15 minutes without the lid on this time. Because the wild rice (actually a grass, not a rice) doesn't absorb all of the liquid, this isn't dry like a regular pilaf, but makes a scant, rich, yet runny sauce. And it's wonderfully dramatic looking: the chicken and cranberries now golden against the blackly gleaming spikes of wild rice.

- Stir in half the cilantro and then sprinkle the rest over the top. That's if you're serving straight from the pan you've cooked it in, as I have here; otherwise, stir in half the cilantro, transfer to a serving dish, and scatter the remaining cilantro over the top.

STORE NOTE

Cool leftovers, then cover and refrigerate within 2 hours of making. Will keep in refrigerator for up to 2 days. Reheat in a saucepan, with a little extra liquid, stirring occasionally until piping hot all the way through.

Oven-cooked chicken shawarma

Chicken shawarma is usually cooked on a spit, but I saw a recipe by the excellent Sam Sifton (a home cook, therefore eminently trustworthy) in the *New York Times* (where he is the food editor) for roasting it in the oven, and felt it was therefore safe to give it a go. Though I should say that, while my recipe is inspired by him, it is not his recipe. And though I was delighted with it, for me the crucial test was my son's approval. For a while, we lived on what I could loosely call London's Shawarma Strip, and my son went out nightly – after dinner, if you please – for at least one shawarma. I proffered my version tentatively, and he pronounced in its favor.

Here, I've served it modestly, on a pile of shredded iceberg, with some warmed (proper) pitas, lemon wedges, and a tahini sauce, as made below. Although here my son dissented, and said that only lamb shawarma should be served with tahini sauce. When I make this for friends, or for a family lunch or supper, I certainly also include my Caramelized Garlic Yogurt Sauce (**p.256**) and slice up some fresh tomatoes sprinkled with mint, and bring out my Quick-Pickled Carrots (**p.262**) and Quick Dill Pickles (**p.258**), or I just cut some cucumbers into wedged slices, and macerate some red onions, cut into half-moons, with red wine vinegar or lime.

SERVES 6–10, DEPENDING ON HOW YOU CHOOSE TO SERVE IT

12 skinless and boneless chicken thighs

2 unwaxed lemons

7 tablespoons regular olive oil

4 fat or 6 smaller cloves garlic, peeled and finely grated or minced

2 dried or fresh bay leaves

2 teaspoons paprika

2 teaspoons ground cumin

1 teaspoon ground coriander

1 teaspoon crushed red pepper flakes

¼ teaspoon ground cinnamon

¼ teaspoon freshly grated nutmeg

2 teaspoons sea salt flakes or kosher salt

lettuce leaves, to serve

FOR THE SHAWARMA SAUCE:

1 cup plain yogurt

¼ cup tahini

1 fat or 2 smaller cloves garlic, peeled and finely grated or minced

fat pinch salt, or to taste

1 tablepoon pomegranate seeds

- Take a large resealable bag and put the chicken thighs in it.

- Using a fine microplane grater (for choice), grate in the lemon zest, then squeeze the lemons and add the juice. Pour in the olive oil and add the garlic, then add all the remaining ingredients, except for those for the sauce.

- Squish everything together, then seal the bag, place it on a plate or in a dish, and refrigerate for at least 6 hours, or up to 1 day.

- When you're ready to cook, preheat the oven to 425°F, remove the chicken from the refrigerator, and allow it to reach room temperature.

- Tip the contents of the resealable bag onto a sheet pan – mine is a half sheet with a small lip of ½ inch – and make sure all the chicken thighs are lying flat and not on top of one another (if possible) before roasting in the hot oven for 30 minutes, by which time they should be cooked through (though obviously you must check) and golden on top.

- When the chicken's more or less cooked, make the sauce simply by combining the yogurt with the tahini and garlic, stir and salt to taste, and sprinkle with a few pomegranate seeds.

- Line a platter or a couple of plates with crisp lettuce, shredded or torn into pieces, and then top with the piping hot chicken, pouring the oily juices over them, unless you are, for some inexplicable reason, anti-oily-juices. If you wanted to make the chicken go further, you could cut the thighs into chunky slices rather than leaving them whole. And please do add any of the suggested accompaniments, itemized in my Introduction.

MAKE AHEAD NOTE	STORE NOTE	FREEZE NOTE
The chicken can be marinated 1 day ahead. Store in refrigerator until needed.	Transfer leftover cooked chicken to a container, then cool, cover, and refrigerate within 2 hours. Will keep in refrigerator for up to 3 days.	The chicken can be frozen in its marinade – as long as the meat has not been previously frozen – for up to 3 months. Leftover chicken can also be frozen, in airtight containers or resealable bags, for up to 2 months. Thaw overnight in refrigerator before using.

Tamarind-marinated flank steak

Flank steak is eaten a lot in America, and in France, but hardly at all in the UK. This is madness, as it is so much cheaper than any other sort of steak and so rich in flavor. I think what has put people off in the past is that, in Britain, it has been cooked in low and slow braises, which turns it into shoe leather. Flank is the external part of the abdomen (hanger being the internal connecting tissue) and all you need to do to cook it is, as my butcher puts it, "sear the hell out of it and serve it rare." I find 2 minutes a side on a very hot, ridged grill pan optimum, but this does mean it's only for those who like their steak blue. The other key point is how you carve it: it must be sliced against the grain. That holds true with all steak, but with a cut like flank, it will be inedibly chewy if you disobey. Luckily, the grain is very distinct (as you can see on the left of the picture) so it's very easy to identify and then cut across it.

You don't have to get the whole piece. I don't like cooking individually cut steaks, as it's all in the thin slicing as far as I'm concerned, but a 1 pound piece will be plenty to feed 4, and is the size I often go for, cooking it for exactly the same amount of time as in the overleaf. Skirt steak could also be used instead of flank, and should be cooked in exactly the same way.

The tamarind and soy marinade tenderizes the meat, but also gives such a glorious tanginess (I have a sour tooth). I keep Thai tamarind paste, which is condensed almost into a brick, in my refrigerator, and that's why I proceed as below. But if you are using tamarind paste out of a jar (which tends to be runny), then use 5 tablespoons and simply add it to the rest of the marinade ingredients, without cooking it or adding water. Either is fine, but it just so happens that the genuine article is better, and less expensive.

I serve this thinly sliced, as if it were a large cut of beef, but it would also make for fantastic beef tacos, and is wonderful cold, stuffed into a baguette or tossed into a salad, so leftovers are a real boon.

3 tablespoons tamarind paste	2 tablespoons vegetable oil
¼ cup soy sauce	1 tablespoon honey
¼ cup hot water, from a recently boiled kettle	1 whole piece flank steak (approx. 1 ¾ pounds)

○ Put the tamarind paste, soy sauce, and hot water into the smallest saucepan you have, and stir over a low heat to dissolve the tamarind. When it's as smooth as you think you can get it – the tamarind paste I use says it's without pits, but I do find the odd one, and I don't bother to get rid of them – remove to a bowl or pitcher, whisk in the oil and honey, and leave to cool. Do not use until it is cold.

○ Put the flank steak into a resealable bag, pour in the cold marinade, and squelch it about so that the thin steak is covered on both sides, then seal, lay on a plate, and put in the refrigerator overnight or for 1 day.

○ Bring it back to room temperature, prepare a large piece of aluminum foil, then heat a ridged grill pan till very, very hot. Lift the steak out of its marinade, letting any excess (and there will be a lot) drip back into the bag, and then slap the meat on the pan and cook for 2 minutes a side.

○ Immediately (I use tongs for all this) transfer the steak to the piece of foil and make a tightly sealed but baggy parcel, and let the meat rest, on a cutting board, or any surface that is not too cold, for 5 minutes. Then unwrap the foil, transfer the steak to a board, and carve in thin slices against the grain.

MAKE AHEAD NOTE	STORE NOTE	FREEZE NOTE
The steak can be marinated 1 day ahead. Store in refrigerator until needed.	Transfer leftover cooked steak to a container, then cool, cover, and refrigerate within 2 hours. Will keep in refrigerator for up to 3 days.	Leftover cooked and cooled steak can be frozen, in airtight containers or resealable bags, for up to 2 months. Thaw overnight in refrigerator before using.

Butterflied leg of lamb

So long as you don't have to butterfly it yourself, this is the quickest way to cook a cut of lamb, and the easiest way of carving it. And although lamb has become the most expensive of meats now, serving it this way at least means it goes further.

In this recipe, I've brought together a favorite cut and a long-beloved flavor combination: anchovies bring out the sweet richness of lamb quite extraordinarily. There is nothing original about the pairing, just as it is hardly novel to cook lamb with thyme and garlic, but the gloriousness of home cooking is that it relies on the comforting rituals of familiar flavors rather than losing itself in a mad pursuit of novelty.

I have specified an approximate weight for the lamb, but the reality is, a leg of lamb will weigh as much as it does, according to season. Whatever the weight, I give the lamb its half-an-hour blast in the oven – any less and the skin won't brown. It is the amount of time you let it rest *out* of the oven that will determine how pink it is.

SERVES 8

3-pound (approx.) boned and butterflied leg of lamb

1 tablespoon fresh thyme leaves, plus more to sprinkle on at the end

6 anchovy fillets (the sort packed in oil)

4 fat cloves garlic, peeled

2 tablespoons extra-virgin olive oil

1 teaspoon sea salt flakes or kosher salt

- Preheat the oven to 425°F. Get out a large, shallow sheet pan and put the butterflied leg of lamb in, skin-side down. If there is any thick part still not very "butterflied" or flattened, then put another slit in with a knife.

- Put the tablespoonful of thyme leaves on a cutting board and place the anchovy fillets on top. Cut the garlic cloves in half lengthways, then add to the thyme and anchovy fillets on the board.

- Roughly chop all these ingredients together to make a paste to spread on the lamb.

- Rub this paste into the slashes in the butterflied lamb, and then spread the remainder on top of the meat, smearing all you can onto it.

- Drizzle the extra-virgin olive oil over and then leave the lamb to come to room temperature (this could take up to 30 minutes).

- When you are ready, carefully turn the lamb over, still in its pan, and rub some of the oil in the pan onto the skin, then sprinkle with the salt.

- Put in the oven for 30 minutes, then take it out and tent with aluminum foil, leaving it to rest for 10–15 minutes if you want the meat pink. If you prefer your lamb less pink, leave it to stand for 30 minutes.

- Transfer the meat to a board and cut it into very thin slices across. Pour the cooking juices into a small saucepan and heat on the stove. Pour some over the sliced meat. Sprinkle with some chopped thyme leaves and serve with the remaining juices.

STORE NOTE	FREEZE NOTE
Transfer leftover cooked lamb to a container, then cool, cover – or wrap tightly in aluminum foil – and refrigerate within 2 hours of making. Will keep in refrigerator for up to 2 days.	Cooked and cooled lamb can be frozen, in airtight containers or resealable bags, for up to 2 months. Thaw overnight in refrigerator before using.

BREATHE

BREATHE

Most of our lives are spent rushing about, scrabbling for time and having to cook in snatched moments, with scarcely a minute to catch our breath. This chapter sets a different, slower, pace and yet the recipes in it couldn't suit our modern, frenzied life better.

It is essential to realize that slow cooking isn't about a dream of olden-days farm-house living: it makes your life easier in the here and now. These are the recipes I rely on when I have friends over midweek and no time to get anything together on the evening itself, and this is the food we eat together as a family. I try to keep a stash of everyday supper portions in the freezer – money in the bank. These recipes really cook themselves, needing no more than to be left in a low oven, with no interference from me. All I have to do is reheat them later. Strictly speaking, you have to be there only to throw everything into a pot and bung said pot in the oven, though I know there are those who are anxious about leaving the house with the oven left on. Since I work from home, that isn't a factor for me, but anyway, that is where the slow cooker comes in.

I have grown to love my slow cooker, not least because I've found one that suits my way of cooking. The bowl itself is made of cast iron and is removable, so if I want to brown anything on the stove first, I don't need to add to the dishwashing by using a frying pan. And I can serve straight from the pot itself when the food's ready. I have professed my deep and elemental love for cooking with cast iron earlier (see my encomium on p.xiii), and even when I am not actually doing the cooking, but leaving the food to cook itself, I feel it makes a difference, bringing that old-fashioned, cooked-at-the-fireside depth of flavor that synthetic materials, however efficient, cannot replicate.

Similarly, I use enameled cast iron Dutch ovens for slow cooking stews in the oven. The heat is much more evenly generated, so you don't get hot spots, and the flavor really does seem better. They are expensive, I know, but as I said in *Kitchen*, they last forever (one of mine was a wedding present to my parents in 1956), which also means you don't have to buy them new – and I always like an excuse to go eBaying. But much as cooking is about practicality, we also form emotional attachments to old, loved and trusted pots and pans, and those heavy-duty Dutch ovens that have been with me so much of my adult life make cooking part of an important continuum. The slow cooked stews that are ushered out of them form a thread of cooking and eating that runs through my life, and my children's. Though that's not to say I don't enjoy adding to my collection, but I do so knowing that one day my son and daughter, and maybe even their children, will be cooking out of them.

This sense of continuum is at the heart, too, of why I so love this way of cooking. It buys me breathing space, and this is space I can relax into, in the secure and happy knowledge that food will be on the table later. And, for me, it's a boon that the recipes that follow are better if left for a couple of days before being reheated. In fact, I insist upon it. The happy knowledge that the food is there and, furthermore, that I don't have to worry or fuss about it, makes me breathe easier.

Malaysian red-cooked chicken

Yasmin Othman is my patient teacher in the arts of Malaysian cooking, and I am grateful to her. This, properly called *ayam masak merah*, gets its red color as much from the fiery chili paste at its base as from the tomatoes. In fact, when I posted a picture of my first attempt online, I was strictly enjoined by a chorus of Malaysians to add more chiles. They could tell my error just by the color. Yes, it is hot, but not frighteningly so, yet what is more unfamiliar is the desirably dry texture of the curry. Dry, in the context of curries, and more particularly here, simply means that the chicken mustn't swim in a sauce, but be thickly coated by it. I require nothing more alongside it than plain rice.

SERVES 4–6

6 long dried red chiles (not the small dried bird's eye chiles)

1 large red onion, peeled and roughly chopped

3 cloves garlic, peeled and roughly chopped

2-inch piece fresh ginger, peeled and sliced

3 fresh red chiles, roughly chopped with seeds intact

2 tablespoons vegetable oil

2 stalks lemongrass, trimmed and bruised

3 tablespoons tomato paste

12 chicken thighs, bone in and skin removed

1 x 14-ounce can diced tomatoes

scant 1 cup coconut milk

½ teaspoon sea salt flakes or kosher salt

TO SERVE:

2 shallots, peeled and thinly sliced

3–4 tablespoons vegetable oil

○ Soak the dried chiles in hot water for 5 minutes to soften; many will float rather than be submerged by the water. Remove them from the water, tearing into pieces – best to use disposable vinyl CSI gloves for this – and shake out as many seeds as possible.

○ Blitz the onion, garlic, and ginger into a paste with the fresh red chiles and soaked dried chiles in a bowl with a stick blender.

○ In a large wok (that comes with a lid), heat the oil, then add the just-blitzed-up chili paste and bruised lemongrass to the wok and fry for 5 minutes over a medium heat, stirring every now and again.

○ Add the tomato paste and fry for 1 minute, then add the chicken thighs to the pan, stirring to coat them well in the mixture.

◦ Add the canned tomatoes, then add water from the cold tap to the empty can so that it is quarter-filled, then swill the can and pour the water into the wok, followed by the coconut milk, stir well, and add the salt.

◦ Bring to a boil, then cover with the lid, turn down the heat, and leave to simmer for 30 minutes, lifting the lid every so often to stir the chicken in the sauce.

◦ Remove the lid, turn the heat up a little, and cook, uncovered, at a bold simmer for 30 minutes; the sauce will start to thicken and become a deeper red. Transfer to a dish to cool, and refrigerate, covered, for at least 1 day and up to 3 days (see Make Ahead Note, below).

◦ To reheat, put the chicken in its sauce back in the wok, put on the lid, and cook over a medium to low heat until the chicken is hot all the way through, about 20 minutes, lifting the lid to stir every so often to make sure the heat is evenly distributed. Remove the lid, turn up the heat, and let the sauce bubble away for about 15 minutes, so it becomes more like a thick paste that sticks to the chicken thighs. Once the sauce is the right consistency, taste and add more salt if you wish.

◦ You don't have to sprinkle crisp shallot rings over the top, but you will be glad if you do. Heat the oil in a cast iron skillet or heavy-based frying pan and fry the sliced shallots until they are golden and crisp. As soon as they are cooked, carefully transfer to some paper towels and leave to cool. Indeed, you can cook these at any time while the chicken's cooking, or even before. Sprinkle over the red-cooked chicken on serving.

MAKE AHEAD NOTE	FREEZE NOTE
The shallots can be fried up to 4 hours ahead. Leave at cool room temperature until needed. The chili paste can be made 2 days ahead then covered and stored in refrigerator until needed. The chicken (without shallots) can be made up to 3 days ahead. Cool, cover, and refrigerate within 2 hours of making. Will keep in refrigerator for up to 3 days. Reheat as per recipe, above.	Freeze in an airtight container for up to 2 months. Thaw overnight in refrigerator and reheat as in Make Ahead Note.

Note: the chicken should be reheated once only.

Massaman beef curry

This is another recipe inspired by my Thai travels and I have cooked it many, many times since. It is essentially a beef and potato stew, with all the comfort that this implies, but the rich mellow flavors bring a vibrancy not immediately conveyed by that description. A massaman curry is a relatively mild curry, so don't feel that the amount of paste I use will blow you away. I do feel strongly, though, that unless you use authentic Thai pastes, you will not get a curry that truly delivers on flavor. Anyway, I buy my coconut milk, tamarind paste, and all my curry pastes from a Thai provisioner online and not only is the quality much better, but the prices are much lower than the supermarket varieties.

As for the coconut, you will see that I add the cream from the top first, but I can't tell you how often I open the can upside down, and so can't then follow my own instructions. In other words, relax: with good pastes and coconut milk, this cannot go wrong.

I like to blanch some green beans, chopped into short lengths, which I then refresh in cold water and mix with some thinly sliced shallots to sprinkle on top, or – for the family supper version – I just serve a bowl of plain-cooked green beans alongside.

2½ teaspoons tamarind paste

2 tablespoons palm sugar or light brown sugar

2 cups hot water, from a recently boiled kettle

1 x 14-ounce can coconut milk

½ cup massaman curry paste, or to taste

1 teaspoon sea salt flakes or kosher salt

2 pounds beef shank off the bone, cut into 2-inch cubes

1¾ pounds waxy potatoes, peeled

small bunch Thai basil or cilantro, to serve

○ Preheat the oven to 325°F. Put the tamarind paste and the sugar in a large measuring cup and add boiling water to the 1 cup mark. Stir with a fork to help dissolve the paste and sugar.

○ In a large, heavy-based pan or Dutch oven that has a tight-fitting lid – I use one of 10 inches in diameter – spoon in the cream from the top of the coconut can. Add the curry paste and then heat, stirring every now and again, until boiling (some of the oil may separate out at this stage, but that's fine). Add the contents of the measuring cup – with its water, tamarind, and sugar – and the rest of the coconut milk, along with the salt, and stir to combine, before adding the beef. Stir well, and let it come to a boil. As soon as it does, clamp on the lid, turn off the heat, and transfer to the oven to cook for 2 hours.

○ Once it's out of the oven, leave to cool, then refrigerate for at least 1 day, or up to 3 days, to allow the beef to get tender and the flavors in the sauce to develop.

○ About half an hour before you want to eat, preheat the oven to 400°F, and cut the potatoes into similar-sized chunks as the beef, then add them to the pot of curry. Place on the stove, add 1 cup of boiling water, and bring to a boil, then clamp on the lid and transfer to the oven for 30 minutes, or until the stew is piping hot and the potatoes are tender. Sprinkle with some shredded Thai basil leaves, should you be able to get hold of them, or scatter with chopped cilantro, and bring to the table immediately.

MAKE AHEAD NOTE	FREEZE NOTE
Cook curry for 2 hours as per recipe, above, then cool, cover, and refrigerate within 2 hours of making. Will keep in refrigerator for up to 3 days.	Freeze cooled curry in an airtight container for up to 3 months. Thaw overnight in refrigerator before reheating as per recipe, above.

Note: the curry should be reheated once only.

Oxtail on toast

Sometimes I get obsessed with a recipe, and this is such a one. I first ate the most divine oxtail on toast at a restaurant called Hubbard & Bell, and could talk of nothing else for days. Some months later, I came across a recipe for Oxtail Marmalade in Jody Williams' *Buvette* cookbook and knew I had to have a go myself. My recipe is much simpler than either version, but I am grateful for the inspiration from both.

It is quite extraordinary how much mileage you get from this: it makes enough to spread on 6–8 pieces of toast, and you'll still be able to conjure up a sauce with what's left to eat with wide egg noodles, or over polenta. Just make sure to reheat only as much as you need for each outing. I freeze mine in portions – enough to spread on 4 pieces of toast – for much comfort and joy at later dates.

MAKES 8 CUPS, ENOUGH FOR 6–8 PIECES OF TOAST, PLUS A STEW FOR 4
OR A SAUCE TO POUR OVER 1 POUND PASTA (DRIED WEIGHT) FOR 4–6

1 onion, peeled and roughly chopped

1 clove garlic, peeled and roughly chopped

1 carrot, peeled and roughly chopped

1 stalk celery

small handful fresh parsley

1 tablespoon duck, goose, or bacon fat

zest and juice of 1 clementine or ½ orange, preferably unwaxed

2 teaspoons dried thyme, or 1 tablespoon fresh thyme leaves

2 teaspoons ground allspice

2 teaspoons unsweetened cocoa powder

¼ cup red vermouth or ruby port

2 cups beef broth (a good quality store-bought one is fine)

2 tablespoons Worcestershire sauce

2 teaspoons sea salt flakes or kosher salt

2¾ pounds oxtail, cut into 2-inch slices

2 bay leaves

fresh thyme, to serve (optional)

○ Preheat the oven to 325°F.

○ Put the chopped onion, garlic, and carrot into the bowl of a food processor fitted with the steel blade. Tear the celery stalk into 2 or 3 pieces and drop that in too, along with the parsley, and blitz till finely chopped. Or you can simply do this by hand.

○ Melt the duck (or other) fat over a medium heat in a Dutch oven (with a tight-fitting lid), and when hot, grate in the zest of the clementine (or orange), stirring it in the warm fat and letting the scent waft up, before adding the mixture from the processor. Cook, stirring every now and again, for 5 minutes.

○ Add the dried thyme (or fresh thyme leaves), ground allspice, and cocoa and stir together before pouring in the vermouth (or port). Let it bubble up, then pour in the beef broth and Worcestershire sauce, squeeze in the juice of the clementine or orange (don't worry if you get a bit of pulp), and sprinkle in the salt. Give it a stir, then add the oxtail to the liquid in the pan, bring to a boil, add the bay leaves, clamp on the lid, and transfer to the oven to cook for 3½ hours.

○ You'll know the oxtail is ready when it's falling off the bone. Using 2 forks, start pulling the meat off and shredding it. If you want to wait until it's a little cooler, by all means do. Cool the stew, remove the bones, then keep in the refrigerator in a covered container for at least 1 day, or up to 3 days.

○ When you're ready to reheat the oxtail, remove the fat, which will have risen to the surface in a solid disc, and add as much oxtail as you need to a saucepan that's big enough for the portion size you've settled on. It will seem dry, but this is just because the juices have jelled – you do not need to add water, however much you itch to. But you must make sure the heat under the pan is low, and the lid is tightly clamped on, to preserve the liquid you do have, and make sure it is piping hot before serving.

○ Spread on toast made with good bread – I find a cupful of stew, in its cold jelled state, is enough for 3 pieces of toast, maybe 4 – and strew with some fresh thyme leaves, should you have some.

MAKE AHEAD NOTE	CONVERSION NOTE TO SLOW COOKER	FREEZE NOTE
The oxtail can be made up to 3 days ahead. Cool, cover, and refrigerate within 2 hours of making.	Halve the broth and cook on low for 8 hours, until the oxtail is tender enough to shred, before adding the dried or fresh thyme, ground allspice, and cocoa and continuing as per recipe, above.	Freeze cooled oxtail in an airtight container for up to 3 months. Thaw overnight in refrigerator before reheating.

Note: the oxtail should be reheated once only.

Asian-flavored short ribs

Since America is such a big beef country, short ribs are found easily and every-where. The meat is luscious and sweet, and if that weren't inducement enough, they are poetically known in the British butchery business as Jacob's Ladder.

I make this stew – which is almost embarrassingly easy – when I want full-on gorgeousness but nothing much to do when people actually turn up. You might need to order the ribs in advance, as you will also need to ask for them to be cut into 2-inch cubes. You'll need a large pan (with a lid) to cook them in – I use one of 14 inches in diameter – as, unless you can more or less fit the ribs into one layer, the liquid they cook in won't cover them sufficiently. If you don't have a pot big enough, then use a large roasting pan and cover tightly with aluminum foil.

I like to eat this with some short grain brown rice cooked with a few cardamom pods, and the Roasted Radishes on **p.227** or some crunchy green beans.

5½ pounds beef short ribs, cut into 2-inch squares

1 cup hoisin sauce, from a jar

2 cups water

¼ cup soy sauce

½ cup Chinese (Shaoxing) rice wine

2 tablespoons Chinese 5-spice powder

1 tablespoon crushed red pepper flakes

1 tablespoon Asian sesame oil

4 fat cloves garlic, peeled and finely grated or minced

TO SERVE:

1 fresh red chile, finely chopped

2–3 tablespoons chopped fresh cilantro

3–4 limes, cut into wedges

○ Preheat the oven to 300°F. Clatter the chunks of short ribs into a large pan, and read the Introduction for pointers here, if you haven't done so already.

○ Mix together all the remaining ingredients and pour over the ribs.

○ Cover with a layer of parchment paper, tucking it in tightly to seal as best you can, before putting on a lid, or cover the top of the pan with aluminum foil and seal the edges securely. Cook in the oven for 4–4½ hours: the meat should be tender and starting to come away from the bones.

○ Transfer the ribs to a vessel that will fit in the refrigerator later to cool, and then tenderly remove as many of the bones as possible, before covering and refrigerating for at least 1 day, or up to 3 days.

○ Before you reheat them, remove the hard layer of fat that will have formed on the top (I do this with my hands, encased in a pair of disposable vinyl gloves, CSI-style), transfer to a large ovenproof dish that you can also serve the ribs in – I use a ceramic dish measuring 11 x 10 x 3 inches just because I like the way its shape mirrors the cubes of meat – and reheat, covered with foil or a lid, depending on what you're cooking in, at 400°F for 1 hour, or until piping hot.

○ Scatter some finely chopped chile and chopped fresh cilantro over the ribs on serving, and put some lime wedges on the table so that everyone can squeeze this sour juice into their rich, sweet stew, to taste, on eating.

MAKE AHEAD NOTE	FREEZE NOTE
The ribs can be made up to 3 days ahead. Cool, cover, and refrigerate within 2 hours of making.	Freeze in an airtight container for up to 3 months. Thaw overnight in refrigerator before reheating as per recipe, above.

Note: the ribs should be reheated once only.

Beef chili with bourbon, beer, and black beans

I refer to this at home as The Texas Chili Massacre, as my recipe is far from being authentic in the eyes of Americans serious about their chili. My offenses are double: the inclusion of beans is not considered proper Stateside, and my addition of maple syrup is a further heresy in the South. But while I apologize to anyone I may offend, I do not, *cannot*, apologize for this. It is everything I dream of in a chili: deeply flavored and resonantly fiery but not burning. But you have seen my casual disregard for rules, so feel free to reduce the chile quotient if you wish.

As for the chiles, I find ancho chiles in the spice aisle at my supermarket, but if you can't get them easily, then just add another 2 teaspoons of red pepper flakes. You won't have the smokiness, but you will have the intense heat. Also, you could blister the fresh chiles over a flame to compensate. One last note: if you are a contact lens wearer, as I am, you must wear disposable vinyl gloves for the chile wrangling.

I haven't made a mistake with the beans, by the way: they don't need pre-soaking; indeed they – and the eventual chili – are much better for not being soaked.

There's nothing wrong in eating this with no more than some hunks of good bread, but my accompaniment of choice would be baked potatoes and coconut milk yogurt that's had some chopped fresh cilantro stirred into it. Sour cream is also an option. And some salving slices of avocado atop your bowlful of chili is always a good way to go.

2 dried ancho chiles (approx. 1 ounce total)

1 cup hot water, from a recently boiled kettle

2 tablespoons vegetable oil

1 large onion, peeled and chopped

4 fresh jalapeño peppers or other chiles, chopped but not seeded

3 fat cloves garlic, peeled and finely grated or minced

2½ teaspoons ground cumin

2½ teaspoons ground coriander

1 teaspoon crushed red pepper flakes

4 pounds boneless beef shank, cut into cubes

2/3 cup bourbon whiskey

1 x 12-ounce bottle Mexican beer, or other lager

2½ cups dried black beans

1 quart cold water

2 teaspoons sea salt flakes or kosher salt

2 tablespoons maple syrup

○ Preheat the oven to 300°F.

○ Put the ancho chiles in a measuring cup and add boiling water to the 1 cup mark.

○ Heat the oil in a large, heavy-based pan – bearing in mind, you have many good things to go in it – then add the onion and cook, stirring every now and again to make sure it isn't burning, for about 5 minutes, or until beginning to soften. Add the chopped jalapeños and cook, stirring, for another 3 or so minutes, before adding the garlic, followed by the cumin, coriander, and red pepper flakes. Stir well.

○ Add the cubes of beef, followed by the bourbon, and let it bubble up in the hot pan before pouring in the beer.

○ Add the black beans, and – wearing disposable vinyl gloves – tear the soaked ancho chiles into pieces (discarding the tough stalks) and drop them into the pan, then pour in the soaking liquid, followed by the quart of cold water, and the salt and maple syrup. Bring to a boil, then clamp on a lid and transfer to the oven to cook for 4 hours, by which time the meat will be meltingly tender. My children won't let me wait when I make this and want to eat it immediately, but this dark, rich, heat-packed stew is even better if left to cool, then reheated in a day or two.

MAKE AHEAD NOTE	CONVERSION TO SLOW COOKER	FREEZE NOTE
The chili can be made up to 3 days ahead. Cool, cover, and refrigerate within 2 hours of making.	Reduce the quart of cold water in recipe to ¾ cup. Cook on low for 8–10 hours, until the beans have softened and the meat is tender. After 6 hours, check on the chili and, if the beans have absorbed most of the liquid, add a little water from a freshly boiled kettle.	Freeze cooled chili in an airtight container for up to 3 months. Thaw overnight in refrigerator before reheating. Reheat gently, stirring occasionally, until piping hot.

Note: the chili should be reheated once only.

Italian veal shank stew

Perhaps this is a bad thing for someone who writes cookbooks to admit, but I do find myself, when I come across a recipe I love, cooking it over and over again whenever people come for supper. This is a case in point, and I actually have to find a reason *not* to cook it. I first ate it years ago, made by the most generous and talented cook I know, Helio Fenerich of Helio's Kitchen, and this is my version of the recipe he was kind enough to give me.

I need at this point to repeat a small lecture I gave in *Nigellissima*: I know there is widespread revulsion at the idea of eating veal, but it is crucial to know that Compassion in World Farming are urging us to eat veal, so long as it is pasture raised (labeled as "certified humane" or maybe called "rose veal"), otherwise countless animals are needlessly destroyed. It is time to rethink our prejudices. Lecture over.

SERVES 8–10

2 carrots, peeled and roughly chopped

1 large onion, peeled and roughly chopped

4 cloves garlic, peeled and roughly chopped

4 stalks celery, torn into pieces

small bunch fresh thyme

3 tablespoons vegetable oil

2 whole veal shanks (ask butcher to cut the ends off to reveal the marrow)

½ x 14-ounce can diced tomatoes

1 cup dry white vermouth or white wine

1 teaspoon sea salt flakes or kosher salt

good grinding of pepper

- Preheat the oven to 350°F. Put all the vegetables, along with 2 tablespoons of thyme leaves – reserving the rest for later – into the bowl of a food processor, and blitz until finely chopped. You can also do this by hand.

- In a large roasting pan that will go on the stove, heat the oil over a medium to high heat, and brown the veal shanks. They are quite big, and this does involve a bit of comedy wrangling to get them brown on all sides, but you do not have to be fanatical about it. Remove the meat once it's browned.

- Add the finely chopped vegetables – your soffrito – and cook over a medium heat, stirring, for 10–15 minutes, or until the mixture has softened.

- Add the canned tomatoes (if you can't bear having half a can of tomatoes roaming free in the refrigerator afterward, then nothing too terrible will happen if you chuck the whole can in, but I am restrained, and don't), the vermouth (or wine), and sprinkle with the salt and a good grinding of pepper. Stir well, then return the veal shanks to the pan, and turn them in the vegetably juices, spooning a little on top of the shanks. There won't be much liquid, but that's how it's meant to be.

- Turn off the heat, and cover with parchment paper, tucking it around the meat in the pan, then cover the whole pan with 2 layers of aluminum foil, sealing the edges tightly. Transfer to the oven and cook for 3 hours, or until the meat is beginning to fall off the bone.

- Remove the foil and the parchment paper, and when the meat has cooled down enough to handle, pull the meat off the bones, shredding it with your hands, and discard any gluey bits of rind. Actually, I eat them then and there, as my treat, but not everyone has a taste for the glutinous. Now for the fun part: rap the bones against the inside rim of the pan so that the marrow shoots out into the stew; this is not for the squeamish.

- Transfer the rich stew to a dish that will fit in the refrigerator to cool, then cover it and refrigerate for at least 1 day, and up to 3 days. When you want to eat it, preheat the oven to 400°F, transfer the stew to a Dutch oven or ovenproof dish with a lid, stirring in the layer of marrow fat, and let it come to room temperature, then put the lid on and reheat in the oven for 30 minutes, or until piping hot. Taste to see if you wish to add more seasoning, and serve immediately, strewn with the reserved thyme.

MAKE AHEAD NOTE	FREEZE NOTE
The stew can be made up to 3 days ahead. Cool, cover, and refrigerate within 2 hours of making.	Freeze cooled stew in an airtight container for up to 3 months. Thaw overnight in refrigerator before reheating as per recipe, above.

Note: the stew should be reheated once only.

Barbecuey pork butt

It's embarrassingly childish of me to find this name funny, but I do, and that's why I'm keeping it. Pork butt is from the shoulder, although my butcher says that it is more properly the upper blade bone part, which is why I have specified so in the ingredients. What I've made below, though, is essentially pulled pork, and I'm sure any part of the shoulder would do just fine.

The real treat about this – apart from the ease of preparation and the joy of eating – is that you cook it for such a long time in a low oven, that not only does your house smell magnificent (I put this in late at night, and come down at breakfast to be heralded by it), but you don't need to do anything when the hungry hordes arrive, except shred it. But I have also given an option for a shorter cooking time, should that make life easier.

If you have a double oven, ask the butcher to give you the scored rind too, snip it into pieces with kitchen scissors, and roast in an oven preheated to 425°F for 25 minutes, then turn them over for a final 5 minutes. Serve alongside the pork.

This is very, very good squidged into burger rolls, or eaten alongside the Cuban Black Beans (**p.214**) or the Sweet and Sour Slaw (**p.240**), or both.

4½-pound boneless pork shoulder (pork butt), with a good layer of fat remaining, rolled and tied

2 tablespoons light brown sugar

2 tablespoons Dijon mustard

2 tablespoons sherry vinegar

2 teaspoons sea salt flakes or kosher salt

2 teaspoons Chinese 5-spice powder

2 teaspoons hot chili powder

4 cloves garlic, peeled and finely grated or minced

- Line the base and sides of a small roasting pan, just large enough to take the pork, with a double layer of aluminum foil, sit the pork in it, fat-side up, and let it come to room temperature, which takes about 40–60 minutes, depending on your refrigerator and the weather. When it's almost there, heat the oven to 450°F.

- Mix the sugar, mustard, and vinegar in a bowl, stir in the salt, 5-spice and hot chili powders, then add the garlic.

- When the pork is ready to go into the oven, mix the rub ingredients together again (I use a rubber spatula for this, and for smearing the pork) and cover the pork with as much as you can. The barbecuey rub may not look very appealing at this stage, but that need be of no concern. Put the smeared pork into the very hot oven and leave for 10 minutes – by which time the top will be beginning to burn in parts – and turn down the oven to 200°F and cook for at least 12 hours, or up to 18, tenting with foil after 14–15 hours.

- Alternatively, after the 10 minute blast at 450°F, turn the heat down to 300°F and cook for 5½–6 hours, tenting with aluminum foil after 3 hours.

- Remove from the oven, untie, discard any bits that are too blackened to eat (though the burnt bits are my favorite), and pull to pieces with a couple of forks. Pour over some of the juice (though you might want to spoon off a little of the fat first) and serve immediately.

STORE NOTE	FREEZE NOTE
Cool leftovers, then cover and refrigerate within 2 hours of making. Will keep in refrigerator for up to 3 days. Reheat in an ovenproof dish, covered with aluminum foil – or wrap pork in foil, if small portions – in an oven preheated to 300°F for about 30 minutes (timing will depend on quantity) until piping hot. Add a splash of water, if needed, to prevent it from becoming too dry.	Freeze in an airtight container for up to 2 months. Thaw overnight in refrigerator before reheating as in Store Note.

Note: the pork should be reheated once only.

Pork buns

Where do I start? I know: in New York, in Momofuku Noodle Bar in the East Village, to be precise. The name of the restaurant is Japanese; David Chang, the owner and head chef, is Korean-American; the slow-braised pork belly, squished into their steamed buns, definitely has Chinese heritage, though it is not to be confused with those other – *char sui* – pork buns. These are more like sandwiches, or belly-pork burgers, and within the steamed bun that holds the slices can be placed all manner of deliciousness. For me, that means the Chile, Ginger, and Garlic Sauce on **p.254**, the Thai Pickled Peppers on **p.261**, or just freshly chopped chiles, some cilantro leaves simply torn from their stalks, plus some shredded scallions and slender cucumber sticks, and, if in the mood, some crisp, fried shallot rings, but the game-changer here is the pork belly.

In the West we eat pork belly roasted, so that the skin goes crisp, making for soft meat with a roof of crackling. But there is another way, though it's not for fatphobes. When the meat is softly braised, the fat remains and is, indeed, essential to the dish. It is all succulence: every bit of it.

While it's a time-consuming recipe, it is a very simple one. And if it makes your life even easier, you can cook the pork ahead of time, and reheat it quickly when you want to eat it. Here's the thing: the pork looks much more beautiful to serve if you slice to order, but it is actually much easier to slice the meat if you do it once it's cold. And the buns do taste rather more Momofuku-like that way too.

You will need to go to a Chinese supermarket to get the steamed buns although I suppose you could use regular soft bread rolls, but bear in mind that these juicy slices of meat can be eaten with rice or noodles, or however you please.

MAKES ENOUGH TO FILL 14–28 PORK BUNS

½ cup sea salt flakes or ⅓ cup kosher salt

½ cup sugar

2¾-pound boneless and rindless pork belly (though still with some fat covering), cut in half lengthways to make 2 pieces

¼ cup hoisin sauce, plus more to serve

14–28 Chinese soft "bao" buns (see Intro), or soft bread rolls, to serve

TO ACCOMPANY:

2–4 shallots, thinly sliced

3–4 tablespoons vegetable oil for frying

½ English cucumber

4 scallions, trimmed

large bunch cilantro

Chile, Ginger, and Garlic Sauce (see p.254) or any hot sauce

○ Fill a large measuring cup with 4 cups of cold water from the tap. Add the salt and sugar, and stir to dissolve. Put the 2 pieces of pork belly into a large resealable bag and pour in the brining liquid. Seal the bag, sit it in a dish, and leave in the refrigerator for at least 8 hours, and up to 24.

○ When you are ready to cook, remove the pork from the refrigerator to let it come to room temperature, and preheat the oven to 450°F. Pour 1 cup of cold tap water into a measuring cup, add the hoisin, and stir to mix well. Take the pork out of its brine (over the sink), pat it dry, and put the 2 slabs, fat-side up, into a roasting pan in which they will sit snugly; I used one measuring 11 x 10 x 2½ inches. Moisten the top of each slab with 1 tablespoonful of the hoisin mixture and cook in the oven for 30 minutes, by which time the fat will have colored and scorched in parts.

○ Take it out of the oven, turn the heat down to 300°F, and pour the remainder of the hoisin cup into the roasting pan, avoiding the top of the meat. Cover the pan tightly (and carefully – it will be hot) with a layer of thick aluminum foil (or 2 layers of regular foil) and put back in the oven for 2 hours, by which time the meat will be cooked through and tender. While the pork's cooking, you could always fry your sliced shallots in hot oil till crisp, and leave them to cool on a double layer of paper towels, to be sprinkled on later.

○ Remove the cooked pork from the oven and onto a cutting board. If you are serving straightaway, leave it to stand for a few minutes while you microwave or steam the buns, then carve each slab of pork into ½-inch slices – I get 14 slices out of each piece. If the pork falls to pieces slightly as you carve, do not worry, as it tastes as good shredded and, indeed, is often served in the buns this way.

○ Cut the cucumber and scallions into thirds, crosswise, then slice both into fine strips, lengthways, tear some cilantro leaves from the stalks, and transfer these to small dishes to go alongside the pork, along with the chili sauce and some hoisin.

○ If I've made this ahead and reheated the slices, I make up the buns and hand them round myself, filling each bun with 2 slices (though if you want this to go further, just 1) of pork belly, along with the strips of scallion and cucumber, cilantro, hoisin, and fried shallot if wanted, and the chile sauce. If I'm slicing the pork there and then, I let everyone make up their buns themselves.

MAKE AHEAD NOTE	FREEZE NOTE
Leave the pork to cool out of its cooking liquid (and pour the liquid into a bowl or pitcher, to be refrigerated), then wrap each slab tightly in foil and refrigerate for up to 3 days. To reheat, remove the solid disc of fat from the pork's cooking liquid, then add ¼ cup of the jelled broth to a shallow baking pan, smoosh it around to cover the base, then slice the pork. Sit these slices in a single layer in the pan, cover with foil, and cook for 15 minutes in an oven preheated to 400°F until piping hot. Turn the slices in the liquid before serving.	Cooled, cooked pork can be tightly wrapped in a double layer of aluminum foil and frozen for up to 3 months. Thaw overnight in refrigerator, and slice and reheat as in Make Ahead Note.

Note: the pork should be reheated once only.

Lamb shank and black garlic stew

This is a very lazy take – with some additions of my own – on a wonderful lamb tagine in Sabrina Ghayour's gloriously inspiring *Persiana* cookbook. The first time I made it, I followed standard procedure and provided a shank per person, but it occurred to me that actually, no one needs a whole shank, so I now shred the sweet meat (making sure I extract every little bit of marrow from the shank bones) which makes it go much further. Couscous might seem the obvious accompaniment, and it's a good one, but I prefer to produce a pile of proper pita or good bread and the Chickpeas with Cumin and Spinach (**p.211**). If you haven't come across black garlic, you must try to find it: it has a flavor that tastes somehow caramelized and fermented at the same time, and adds a fabulous musky richness. It's much easier to get now, but if this eludes you, or doesn't appeal, then use 2 heads of home-caramelized garlic in its place (see Caramelized Garlic Hummus, **p.113**, for instructions). If you're using this rather than black garlic, then just chop the onions by hand and squeeze the garlic pulp into the pan once the tomatoes have gone in.

SERVES 10–12

2 large onions (1 pound total), peeled and quartered

2 heads black garlic (see Intro), broken into cloves and peeled

3 tablespoons goose or duck fat or olive oil

2 teaspoons cumin seeds

2 teaspoons ground allspice

2 teaspoons ground cinnamon

1 cup red vermouth or full-bodied red wine

2 x 14-ounce cans diced tomatoes

2 teaspoons sea salt flakes or kosher salt

6 lamb shanks

○ Preheat the oven to 300°F. Put the onions and black garlic cloves into the bowl of a food processor and chop finely. You could also do this by hand, but the black garlic is very sticky. It also disperses better in the stew if it is blitzed to a near-pulp.

○ In a large pan, big enough to take everything later (I used one of 12 inches in diameter and 6 inches deep) and that comes with a lid, melt the goose or duck fat, then add the contents of the food processor, scraping with a spatula to get every last bit. Cook, stirring frequently, for 3 minutes over a medium heat, or until the onion starts to soften, and then stir in the cumin seeds, ground allspice, and cinnamon.

○ Turn the heat up to high, and then pour in the red vermouth or wine. Let this bubble up before adding the contents of the 2 cans of tomatoes, then fill each can with cold water from the tap, and pour that in, too.

○ Stir in the salt and add the lamb shanks, bring again to a boil, then clamp on the lid and transfer to the oven to cook for 4 hours, by which time the sauce will be rich and the meat will begin to fall off the bone.

○ Leave in a cool place with the lid off and when the shanks are not too hot to handle (you might need to leave this for 1 hour, depending on the sensitivity of your hands; I plough in after 30 minutes), strip the meat from the shanks, and knock each shank bone against the inside rim of the pan to make sure the marrow and any juices in the bone go into the stew. This can be messy. Discard the bones, and shred the lamb a little more, using 2 forks. I then pour this into the pan I'm going to reheat and serve this in later – a pan of 11 inches in diameter and 4 inches deep, or one with a 6-quart capacity, should be fine – as being in the cold pan will help the lamb cool faster. Once cooled, cover and stash in the refrigerator for at least 1 day, or up to 3 days. Or, if this is easier for your refrigerator, decant when cool into airtight containers or a dish of fridge-friendly size.

○ Before reheating the stew, take it out of the refrigerator, remove any fat from the surface, and leave for 1 hour (less if in airtight containers) to come to room temperature, and preheat the oven to 400°F. Cook for 1–1¼ hours, until piping hot, and if everyone's not ready to eat, just switch off the oven, and let the pan sit there for up to 30 minutes.

MAKE AHEAD NOTE	FREEZE NOTE
The shanks can be made up to 3 days ahead. Shred and cool as quickly as possible, then cover and refrigerate within 2 hours of making.	Freeze in an airtight container for up to 3 months. Thaw overnight in refrigerator before reheating as per recipe, above.

Note: the shanks should be reheated once only.

Spiced lamb stew with a goat cheese and thyme cobbler topping

A mellow, aromatic stew, this has established itself as a Sunday stalwart in my house, and although there is nothing wrong in serving the stew just as it is, for me it achieves everything it ought when topped with scone-like, tender biscuits, tangy with goat cheese and fragrant with thyme. It also saves you making any potatoes or other starch to serve alongside. And if you whizz over to the instructions for the cobbler topping, you will see how dreamily easy it is to make. As, indeed, is this.

Caramelized garlic has become a leitmotif in my cooking life, and here is where it all started.

SERVES 8

2 heads garlic, whole and unpeeled

2 tablespoons regular olive oil

2 onions, peeled and roughly chopped

1½ teaspoons dried thyme

2½ teaspoons ground cinnamon

2¾ pounds lamb stew meat, cut into 1-inch cubes

1 cup red vermouth or full-bodied red wine

4 carrots (12 ounces), peeled, quartered lengthways (halved if they're skinny carrots), and sliced into 1-inch chunks

2 eggplants (1 pound), chopped into roughly 2-inch chunks

1½ cups hot water, from a recently boiled kettle

2 teaspoons sea salt flakes

3 star anise

- Cut the tops off the garlic heads, so that you can see the tops of the cloves peeking through. Discard the tops, and sit each head on a separate piece of aluminum foil, then seal the ends tightly to form a slightly baggy parcel. Sit these on a small foil pan or dish that will go in the oven. Preheat the oven to 325°F.

- In a large – wide rather than tall – Dutch oven or pan (one that has a tight-fitting lid and will go in the oven), heat the olive oil and add the chopped onions. Cook over a medium to low heat for about 10 minutes, stirring frequently to make sure that they soften without burning. If they go golden, that's fine, you just don't want them to go any further than that. Stir in the dried thyme and cinnamon.

- Turn the heat up under the pan, then add the chunks of lamb, and stir well, though don't expect the lamb to sear.

- Pour in the vermouth or wine, stirring to try and pick up some of the bits sticking to the bottom of the pan, then add the carrots, eggplants, hot water, salt, and star anise, stir again, and let the panful of stew come to a boil.

- Clamp on the lid, then transfer to the oven, putting the prepared garlic in at the same time, and cook for 2 hours. Once out of the oven, let the stew cool, with the lid off, and as soon as you can handle the garlic, squish the caramelized cloves into the stew, stir and let it cool. Then transfer to a suitable container, cover, and keep in the refrigerator for at least 1 day, or up to 3 days, before reheating.

- To reheat, remove any fat from the surface, then transfer the stew to a dish that will fit both it and the cobbler topping – I use a wide, shallow braiser of 12 inches in diameter and 3 inches deep – and bring to a boil on the stove. Let it simmer for 30 minutes.

- If you're making the cobbler topping, preheat the oven to 425°F while the stew is simmering, and see next recipe. Or, if you want to serve the stew unadorned, then make sure the meat is piping hot on the stove before taking to the table.

MAKE AHEAD NOTE	FREEZE NOTE
The stew can be made up to 3 days ahead. Cool, cover, and refrigerate within 2 hours of making.	Freeze in an airtight container for up to 3 months. Thaw overnight in refrigerator before reheating as per recipe, above.

Note: the stew should be reheated once only.

Goat cheese and thyme cobbler topping

I first made this to go on top of the Spiced Lamb Stew in the previous recipe, but please don't feel you have to restrict its usage to this. I certainly don't. Regard it, rather, as a helpful blueprint. You can change the goat cheese to Cheddar, use all butter, add other spices, or vary the herbs. Any stews, adorned with this gorgeously golden topping, are most highly recommended contenders for a cozy Sunday dinner, and I also often top a regular meat sauce with a cobbler, made with half Colby or orange Cheddar, half butter (both grated), and in place of the turmeric I add a pinch of mace and whisk ½ teaspoon of English mustard into the soured milk, and do without the herbs altogether. As the cobbler topping cooks in the oven, with a hot stew beneath it, the little biscuits both bake and steam, becoming light and tender as they rise in the oven with their tops crisp and golden, while the underside fuses with the sauce below.

These are really a doddle to make. I love the feel of the soft dough under my hands, and the quiet mood that descends on me as I pat and roll them into being. Indeed, the very act of making them reduces rather than adds to any stress.

½ cup whole milk, plus 2 teaspoons	½ teaspoon ground turmeric
1 teaspoon lemon juice	1 tablespoon fresh thyme leaves, plus a few sprigs for later
1 cup plus 2 tablespoons all-purpose flour, plus more for rolling and cutting	2 ounces crumbled goat cheese (approx. ⅓ cup)
2 teaspoons baking powder	3 tablespoons fridge-cold unsalted butter
¼ teaspoon baking soda	1 egg
½ teaspoon fine sea salt, plus a pinch	

○ Pour the ½ cup milk into a cup or small pitcher, stir in the lemon juice, and let it stand while you get on with the rest.

○ Mix the flour, baking powder, baking soda, ½ teaspoon of salt, turmeric, and thyme leaves in a mixing bowl. Crumble in the goat cheese, and grate in the butter. I use a microplane ribbon grater, the sort you might use for shaving chocolate. Stir together lightly with a fork.

○ Now, as if you were making a crumb topping, rub the butter and goat cheese into the spiced flour with your fingers. In other words, work the fats into the dry ingredients – by using a flutteringly light movement, like a butterfly's wings – rubbing the pads of your thumbs against the middle 3 fingers of each hand, catching the mixture as you go. When you have a flaky, oat-like texture, pour in 7 tablespoons of the lemon-soured milk and mix together with a wooden spoon until you have a slightly damp, squidgy dough. If you find you don't need the remaining tablespoon of lemon-soured milk, then don't use it.

○ Lightly flour a surface you can roll out on, then tear off a large piece of parchment paper and place it nearby. Form the soft dough into a ball, press it down into a fat disc, and sit this on the floured surface, then immediately turn the dough the other way up. Roll or pat it into a thickness of just under ½ inch, dip a 2½-inch round cutter – or the rim of a glass will do – into a little extra flour and start cutting out discs, sitting them on the sheet of parchment paper. Gather up the remaining dough, and start again by making a ball, flattening it into a fat disc, and continue rolling and re-rolling like this until you have used up all the dough. You should have approximately 20 biscuits.

○ When the stew you want to cover is warmed through, and the oven is preheated to 425°F, you can top it with these little scone-like biscuits. First, though, make an egg wash by whisking together the egg, 2 teaspoons of milk, and a pinch of salt. With the hot stew in front of you, arrange the soft shallow biscuits on top and, moving quickly but calmly, brush the egg wash onto the biscuits and place back in the oven for a further 15 minutes until the biscuits are risen and golden and the stew is bubbling.

Slow-cooked molasses ham

Nothing will ever take the place of my Ham in Coca-Cola from *Nigella Bites* – in my heart or on my table – but this slow-baked ham is a revelation of a different sort. Instead of being boiled and then transferred to a hot oven to be glazed, I cook it so, so slowly, in the oven, draped with molasses, then wrapped in aluminum foil, so that it steams sweetly in the low heat. I then remove the ham from the oven and its foil, take off the rind, stud the layer of fat on top with cloves and cover with a mustardy molasses glaze, and put the ham briefly back in a very hot oven. Cooked like this, the meat is astonishingly tender and carves into thin slices with ease; there is also very little shrinkage, and no wrangling with large cuts of meat in boiling liquid.

I always like a ham on Christmas Eve, which means that there is cold ham as well as cold turkey for the following days (and general sandwich duty), and this is the way to cook it to make your life easier. And if the 12–15 hours' cooking doesn't suit you, you can cook it for 5 hours in a 350°F oven instead, before proceeding with the glaze.

The juices that collect from the first step of cooking are gorgeously flavored, but very intense. I pour a little of them over the cut slices of meat, but go sparingly.

If you are able to buy a cured, uncooked ham then you may well prefer to soak it in several changes of cold water before cooking, to reduce the saltiness, and you should check the information from the producer for more details. Fully cooked hams are more common in the US and if you use one of these, then try to choose one with the rind still on and not spiral cut. Smear the rind of the ham with 2 tablespoons of molasses then wrap it in a baggy aluminum foil package with tightly sealed edges. Sit it in a roasting pan and reheat following the producer's instructions for oven temperature and time. When the ham has heated through uncover it and reserve juices and use sparingly to moisten ham once sliced. Carefully remove the rind, leaving a good layer of fat, then follow the instructions for glazing the ham.

By the way, when you measure out your molasses, it'll make life a lot easier if you oil your receptacle first.

SERVES 10–12, WITH LEFTOVERS

7½-pound boneless cured uncooked ham, rind on

½ cup molasses

FOR THE GLAZE:

approx. 1 tablespoon whole cloves

¼ cup molasses

¼ cup turbinado sugar

1 tablespoon Dijon mustard

- Preheat the oven to 450°F, and let your ham come to room temperature.

- Line a large roasting pan with a layer of aluminum foil, and then sit a wire rack on top of this foil. Tear off a large piece of foil (big enough to wrap around the ham) and place this over the rack on the roasting pan. Tear off a second large piece of foil and place on top, but in the opposite way to the first, so you have 4 corners of foil ready to wrap your ham in.

- Sit the ham on the foil and then pour the molasses over it, straight onto the rind, letting it run down both sides. Don't worry too much about spreading it over the ham, as once it's in the heat of the oven, it will coat the ham well enough.

- Now lift up the sides and ends of the first layer of foil and make a seal at the top, leaving some room around the ham, then seal the ends. Then take up the other piece of foil and do the same: you are trying to create a good seal around the ham, so pinch together any open gaps that remain. Finally, tear off another piece of foil and put over the top of the whole parcel, making sure it's well sealed.

- Put carefully into the oven and let it cook for 30 minutes, then turn the oven down to 200°F and leave for a further 15–24 hours.

- The following day, take the ham out of the oven and open up the foil seal. It will have made some liquid, which you can reserve to moisten the carved meat later. Carefully lift the ham out onto a board, snip and remove the string, and peel off the rind to leave a good layer of fat.

- Increase the oven temperature to 400°F. Using a sharp knife, cut a diamond pattern in the fat layer, drawing lines one way and then the opposite way, about ¾ inch apart.

- Stud the center of each diamond with a clove, then mix together the molasses, turbinado sugar, and Dijon mustard in a bowl and spread over the fat on the ham. It will dribble off a bit, so just spoon it back over the ham before putting back in the oven for 20 minutes, by which time the glaze will be burnished and blistered in the heat. Remove from the oven, and transfer to a board. Let it rest for 10–20 minutes before carving into thin slices.

STORE NOTE	FREEZE NOTE
Cool leftovers as quickly as possible, then cover (or wrap tightly in aluminum foil) and refrigerate within 2 hours of making. Will keep in refrigerator for up to 3 days.	Freeze in an airtight container (or wrapped in foil, and then put in a resealable bag) for up to 2 months. Thaw overnight in refrigerator before using.

Make-ahead mashed potatoes

No one is doubting the glory of mashed potatoes, and while they are not difficult to make, they can be quite a faff in large quantities at the last minute. This is the answer: a tangy, subtly cheesy dish, with a crunchy topping, that has revolutionized my cooking life. I made them for the first time last year for Thanksgiving, and they have happily appeared on my table several times since. They come heartily recommended with the ham on the previous page, and any time you want to spread the load when you have people coming over.

SERVES 12

5½ pounds potatoes for mashing, such as Yukon Gold

salt for potato water to taste

1¼ sticks (12 tablespoons) soft unsalted butter

1 cup sour cream

good grinding of nutmeg

good grinding of pepper

⅓ cup shredded Parmesan

sea salt flakes to taste or kosher salt

FOR THE TOPPING:

¾ cup dried bread crumbs

5 tablespoons soft unsalted butter

½ cup shredded Parmesan

○ Peel the potatoes, then cut each one roughly into quarters, put into a large saucepan of salted water, and bring to a boil. Lower the heat slightly and cook until the potatoes are tender and soft but not disintegrating. The timing will depend on the size of your pan, but allow about 30 minutes once the water has come to a boil.

○ Before you drain the potatoes, reserve 2 cupfuls of the cooking water, then drain the potatoes and put them back in the hot, and now dry, pan with the lid on, but off the heat.

○ Melt the butter and sour cream in a saucepan, then pour this over the cooked and drained potatoes in their warm pot, and mash them while slowly adding some of the reserved potato cooking water to get the right softness and consistency. I keep this a fairly loose mixture, since it will thicken on standing and reheating. Add the nutmeg, pepper, Parmesan, and sea salt to taste.

○ Once you are happy with your mashed potatoes, spoon them into a wide, shallow ovenproof dish and smooth the top. You can let this cool and then refrigerate it, covered with plastic wrap, for up to 3 days, although if you want, you can, of course, proceed to the next stage immediately.

○ When you're ready to reheat, preheat the oven to 400°F and take the dish of potatoes out of the refrigerator to come to room temperature.

○ Tip the bread crumbs into a bowl, then add the butter, a teaspoonful at a time, and mix together to form a lumpy crumb topping. Dot over the top of the potatoes, and then sprinkle with the Parmesan. Bake for 30 minutes, or until piping hot all the way through.

MAKE AHEAD NOTE

The potatoes, without the topping, can be made up to 3 days ahead. Cool, cover, and refrigerate within 2 hours of making. Allow to come to room temperature (about 30 minutes) before adding the topping ingredients and baking.

Note: the potatoes should be reheated once only.

Leek pasta bake

This had its first outing, together with the Chicken Cosima on **p.149**, for my daughter's 21st birthday, as a dish made for non-meat-eaters, and to provide ballast later on in the night. I have since found out that Parmesan is not vegetarian; it is fine to do without it, and use 3½ cups of a vegetarian-friendly Cheddar. Indeed, feel free to use whatever cheese you have at hand.

SERVES 8, AS A MAIN DISH

1 pound leeks (trimmed and cleaned weight)	2 teaspoons Dijon mustard
1 cup dry white vermouth or white wine	½ cup shredded Parmesan
2 cups cold water	3 cups grated sharp Cheddar
2 teaspoons sea salt flakes or kosher salt	grinding of pepper
2 cups whole milk	1 pound tortiglioni or rigatoni pasta
5 tablespoons soft unsalted butter	salt for pasta water to taste
½ cup all-purpose flour	

○ Cut the leeks into ½-inch slices before putting them into a wide, heavy-based saucepan, one that has a tight-fitting lid. Add the vermouth (or wine) and water and salt – the leeks should be just covered – then put on the lid and bring to a boil. Once they are bubbling, keep them covered – you will need the cooking liquid later, so you don't want it to evaporate – and cook until soft and no longer squeaky, about 10 minutes. About 5 minutes in, it's a good idea to take the lid off briefly and give a robust stir or two to help the rounds of leek unfurl a bit.

○ Drain the leeks and set aside, reserving their cooking water. I do this by sitting a large strainer over a wide-necked measuring cup; you should have about 2 cups' worth. Add the milk to this leek-cooking-liquor, and if it doesn't make the liquid come up to the 4 cup mark, just top it up with a little more milk. This might be a good moment to put the pasta water on to boil.

○ Make sure there isn't any stray leek left in the pan, and then melt the butter in it over a medium heat. Add the flour and mustard, and whisk to form a roux, then cook, whisking, for 1–2 minutes or so until the bubbling mixture thickens a bit.

○ Take the pan off the heat, and then gradually pour in the milky-leek liquor, making sure you keep whisking to incorporate the liquid and to get rid of any lumps.

- Once all the liquid is added, put the pan back on a medium heat, and – swapping your whisk for a wooden spoon or spatula – cook it, stirring all the while with the spoon or spatula, until the sauce is thick, smooth, and has lost its floury taste. This will take about 10 minutes.

- Once the sauce is thickened, turn the flame off under the pan (or, if you're cooking on electric, remove the pan from the stove) and, using your wooden spoon or spatula, beat in the Parmesan and 2¼ cups of the Cheddar, seasoning with pepper to taste, making sure the cheeses are fully incorporated, before stirring in the leeks. Take off the heat and cover.

- When your pan of pasta water has come to a boil, salt to taste, then add the pasta and cook until rather more al dente than you'd normally want it. Reserve a couple of cups of the pasta water before you drain it.

- Beat ½ cup of pasta cooking water into the sauce and then pour half of the sauce into a lasagna dish of about 11 x 5 inches or a roasting pan, or receptacle of your choice. Tip in the drained pasta, then pour the remaining sauce over this and stir gently to make sure all is mixed together. Add more pasta water if needed; you'll want this quite runny as it will thicken both on standing and baking. Let this stand for 10 minutes (or leave to cool and then refrigerate for up to 3 days, making sure it comes back to room temperature before baking).

- When you're ready to bake, preheat the oven to 425°F. Sprinkle the remaining ¾ cup grated Cheddar over the top of the pasta and bake in the hot oven for about 20–25 minutes, or until bubbly and golden on top. Check it is hot all the way through by inserting the tip of a knife into the center. It should come out feeling hot. If you want the top crusty and burnished, place under a hot broiler for a couple of minutes, keeping a careful eye on it. Or just leave it for longer in the hot oven. Let it stand out of the oven for 10–20 minutes before serving.

MAKE AHEAD NOTE

The pasta bake can be made up to 3 days ahead. Cool, cover, and refrigerate within 2 hours of making. Allow to come to room temperature (about 30 minutes) before baking.

Note: the pasta bake should be reheated once only.

Slow-cooker Moroccan chicken stew

My chook-from-the-souk is a lightly fragranced golden stew that gains more succulence from having the bones of the chicken thighs in as well. If you make this in advance (and all stews are better this way), you can easily remove the fat that the skin produces once the stew has sat in the refrigerator. The skin gives flavor, too, and both skin and bones are removed on serving and the tender meat shredded.

SERVES 6

8 chicken thighs, skin on and bone in

1 onion, peeled and finely chopped

2–3 preserved lemons (depending on size), roughly chopped

3 cups chickpeas, home-cooked or drained from cans or jars

2 teaspoons cumin seeds

1 teaspoon ground ginger

1 long or 2 short sticks cinnamon

pinch (¼ teaspoon) saffron threads

2 cups chicken broth

⅓ cup golden raisins

1 cup (approx. 3 ounces) pitted green olives

chopped fresh cilantro, to serve

○ Put everything into the slow cooker and cook on low for 4 hours.

○ Once the stew's ready, remove the slow cooker from its base and let the stew stand for 10–15 minutes with the lid off, before shredding the chicken. Discard the skin and bones. Place in a warm bowl to serve and scatter with cilantro.

STORE NOTE	CONVERSION TO OVEN	FREEZE NOTE
Cool leftovers, then cover and refrigerate within 2 hours of making. Will keep in refrigerator for up to 3 days.	Heat 1 tablespoon olive oil in a cast iron Dutch oven or heavy-based pot (big enough to take the chicken in one layer) and cook the onion for 5 minutes, until softened. Add the remaining ingredients and bring to a boil, then cover with a piece of parchment paper and the lid, and cook in an oven preheated to 350°F for 1 hour, or until the chicken is tender and falling off the bone.	Freeze in an airtight container for up to 3 months. Thaw overnight in refrigerator before using. Reheat in a covered saucepan over a low heat, stirring occasionally, until piping hot.

Note: the stew should be reheated once only.

SIDES

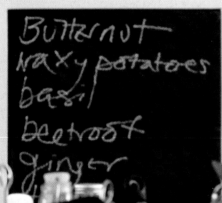

Butternut
waxy potatoes
basil
beetroot
ginger

SIDES

A doctor once told me that I was the only person she had advised to eat fewer vegetables. I am a carnivore who can regularly make 2 pounds of broccoli, hot with chiles and ginger, for my supper, without fleshy accompaniment and with breezy disregard for my digestive system.

But then, my mother thought nothing of eating an entire cabbage, dressed just with butter and white pepper, in one undistracted sitting. I have inherited that desire to wallow in the splendor of just one bowl of food, and in the singularity of its deliciousness. But I have recently found myself searching, as I cook, for simple side dishes that have the grace to accompany a flesh, fish, or fowl recipe without upstaging it and yet, at the same time, having the confidence to hold their own. There is something so aesthetically gratifying about cooking vegetables: their colors make my kitchen sing, and, if only I could, me along with it. I am embarrassed about the number of times I simply roast a chicken for supper, but these are the recipes that combine the comforting rituals of the familiar with the exuberance of the new – something that we all need, both in and out of the kitchen.

They are not the only vegetable recipes in the book, however: many in the preceding chapters provide ideas for side dishes by stealth, in the introductions. Here, though, the admiring focus is on them alone. And, being something of a condiment queen, I have relished the opportunity to throw in a sauce or two. A meal, however pared back it is, feels complete to me only when I have within my reach a jar or bowl of something I can spike my food with as I eat.

This brings me to the new love in my cooking life: I cannot stop pickling things; I have become a toursomaniac. But toursomania – the compulsive need to pickle; the coinage is my own – is not something I see myself being cured of any time soon. As someone who once compiled her Kitchen Gadget Hall of Shame, I should be embarrassed to admit this, but I have recently purchased a Japanese pickle-press.

Don't be alarmed, though, all the pickles here are simple affairs. Along with most of the kitchen contraptions I buy (late at night and online, usually), the pickle-press may well not see the light of day but rather, in the time-honored fashion, languish in the dusty depths of the cupboard under the stairs. These pickles are unruffling to make, requiring no special skills, equipment, or patience, and you can allow yourself a moment of quiet satisfaction, and greedy anticipation, both while you conjure them into existence and as you bring them to the table, too.

Roasted radishes

I came across a recipe for roasted radishes on thekitchn.com and was immediately prompted to make my own version. The only work lies in halving the radishes in question, and they need hardly any time in the oven. Their peppery crunch is transformed in the heat to a piquant juiciness – and, oh, their pink-cheeked prettiness! I make them nearly every time people come for supper, and they have never failed to charm.

You can also turn them into a salad: for the amount of radishes below (though you may want to halve them) toast 1 cup hazelnuts while the radishes are in the oven, then chop them, and toss radishes and nuts in a tangle of watercress and a dressing made with orange juice, olive oil, and sea salt flakes.

SERVES 8–10

1½ pounds radishes

2 tablespoons olive oil

1–2 tablespoons finely chopped fresh chives or scallions

1 teaspoon sea salt flakes or kosher salt, or to taste

° Preheat the oven to 425°F.

° Slice the radishes in half from top to tail: they look beautiful with the green parts left on, though you may want to trim them if they have long tails.

° Put into a bowl and pour in the olive oil, then toss the radishes so they are coated evenly.

° Tip out onto a baking sheet, or shallow roasting pan, and turn all the radishes cut-side down, so that you have a sea of pink humps.

° Roast in the hot oven for 10 minutes, then take them out and toss with the chopped chives (or scallions) and salt, checking the seasoning and adding more of either if you wish. Serve hot, though a stash of these, cold, should you have leftovers, is a rich resource, to be called upon later in the week, added to salads or noodle soups, or simply, pinkly, spooned onto the side of your plate as you eat.

STORE NOTE
Cool leftovers, then cover and refrigerate. Will keep in refrigerator for up to 5 days. Eat cold.

Broccolini with clementine and red pepper flakes

This recipe came about as so many recipes do: I was in a kitchen (my publisher's, in fact) and just seized upon the most immediately available ingredients. It worked so gloriously, and I have stayed true to it, cooking it faithfully and frequently in my own kitchen.

SERVES 4–6

1 pound broccolini

salt for broccolini water

zest and juice of 1 clementine or ½ orange, preferably unwaxed

¼ teaspoon coarse celery salt or ½ teaspoon sea salt flakes or kosher salt, or to taste

1 heaping teaspoon Dijon mustard

2 tablespoons extra-virgin olive oil

½ teaspoon crushed red pepper flakes

- Put a saucepan of water on to boil for the broccolini, adding salt to taste once it comes to a boil. Trim any woody ends from the broccolini.

- Put half of the clementine (or orange) zest into a jar or bowl, and reserve the other half for the time being. Add the clementine (or orange) juice, celery salt (or sea salt flakes), Dijon mustard, oil, and a ¼ teaspoon of the red pepper flakes to the jar, and give everything a good shake. Or, if making this in a bowl, just whisk together.

- Cook the broccolini for about 2 minutes, until just tender, but still with some crunch to it. It's impossible to give a precise timing guide as it really depends where in the season it is. Drain the broccolini and return to the hot but dry pan, add the dressing ingredients, and toss gently but thoroughly before transferring to a plate or bowl. Sprinkle with the remaining zest and red pepper flakes, and serve.

STORE NOTE

Cool leftovers, then cover and refrigerate as quickly as possible. Will keep in refrigerator for up to 5 days. Eat cold.

Broccoli two ways, with ginger, chile, lime, and pumpkin seeds

I may be extravagant, but I am never wasteful (something I am called upon to say often) and I can never bear to see the stalk from a head of broccoli go into the trash. Even if I'm cooking a head of broccoli and want just the florets, I now keep the stalk in a resealable bag in the refrigerator, to be peeled and stir-fried a day or so later.

SERVES 6

1-inch piece fresh ginger, peeled

¼ cup pumpkin seeds

1 head broccoli (approx. 1 pound)

salt for broccoli water

2 teaspoons lime juice

pinch salt

½ teaspoon Asian sesame oil

1 tablespoon vegetable oil

FOR THE STALK:

1 teaspoon vegetable oil

1 fresh red chile, seeded and chopped

1-inch piece fresh ginger, peeled and cut into matchsticks

1 tablespoon water

2 teaspoons lime juice

○ Put a saucepan of water on to boil for the broccoli. Coarsely grate the peeled ginger onto a lipped plate (this should yield about 2 teaspoons of grated ginger). Get out a piece of paper towel and spoon the ginger into the center, then – moving swiftly – bring up the sides of the paper, and twirl the ends to form a mini swag bag and squeeze out the juice (you can squeeze this back onto the plate). This should give you about 1 teaspoon of pungent ginger juice. Now that you have performed my new favorite trick, you can move on. You'll need the ginger juice in a minute, though.

○ Toast the pumpkin seeds by shaking them about, in a cast iron skillet or heavy-based frying pan, without oil, over a medium to high heat, until they have colored and are fragrant. Transfer to a plate, but don't wash the pan as you'll need it shortly.

○ Cut the stalk off the head of broccoli, and set it aside. Break the head into florets. Peel the stalk with a vegetable peeler and then slice into thin strips, rather like bamboo shoots.

○ When the broccoli water comes to a boil, add salt to taste, then cook the florets in the boiling water for 2–3 minutes, making sure they still have their bite, drain, and put back into the dry pan, now off the heat.

- Make the dressing for the florets by whisking together the lime juice, ginger juice, salt, and sesame and vegetable oils in a small bowl until combined. Then pour this dressing, along with half of the toasted pumpkin seeds, over the cooked broccoli florets in the pan, and toss together. Let this stand while you get on with the stalks.

- In the pan you toasted the pumpkin seeds in, heat the vegetable oil, then add the sliced broccoli stalks and stir-fry for 1 minute before adding half the chopped chile and the ginger matchsticks and frying for another 30–60 seconds. Add the water and lime juice and stir-fry for another scant minute, until the stems are starting to soften slightly but still have some bite.

- Tip the florets into the center of a platter, scatter most of the stir-fried stalks around, then drop some onto the florets, and sprinkle with the remaining pumpkin seeds and chopped chile.

STORE NOTE

Cool leftovers, then cover and refrigerate as quickly as possible. Will keep in refrigerator for up to 5 days. Eat cold.

Braised peas with mustard and vermouth

I am never without a supply of petits pois in the deep freeze: cooked slowly, with a scant amount of flavorful liquid, they are both comforting and elegant. True, they lose their bright green color, but do not fear the khaki, as what they lack in vividness of hue is more than compensated by the vibrancy of their flavor. And because they can sit for a long time, only improving, they make life very much easier when you have people over for supper, when the less last-minute faffing, the better.

SERVES 8

2 tablespoons extra-virgin olive oil	2 teaspoons sea salt flakes or kosher salt
2 pounds frozen petits pois (approx. 7 cups)	2 teaspoons Dijon mustard
½ cup dry white vermouth or dry white wine	2 bay leaves

○ Heat the oil in a heavy-based pan (with a lid) and tumble in the peas, stirring in the heat, then add the vermouth (or wine) and let it come to a boil.

○ Add the salt, mustard, and bay leaves. Bring to a boil, put the lid on, and simmer for 20–30 minutes, then remove from the heat and leave to stand in a warm place for up to 1 hour with the lid still on. I like these best, however, when they have been left to continue their sweet braising in a 250°F oven for 1–2 hours once they've been cooked on the stove.

STORE NOTE	FREEZE NOTE
Cool leftovers, then cover and refrigerate as quickly as possible. Will keep in refrigerator for up to 5 days. Reheat in a small saucepan over a low heat, stirring occasionally, until piping hot.	Freeze leftovers in an airtight container for up to 3 months. Thaw overnight in refrigerator before reheating as in Store Note.

Quick coconutty dal

This is rather like a spiced pease pudding, though the spicing is delicate rather than shoutily invasive. I wanted coconuttiness, but not the rich heaviness of coconut milk, and the recently (but now less so) modish coconut water proved the perfect solution; but it is the mace that seems to bring everything together.

Although this makes more than you need for 2 people, I make this amount even when there are only 2 eating (and see the Indian-Spiced Cod on **p.27**), and I do this on purpose, for the fabulousness of leftovers. I like recipes that do double-duty, and this makes a wonderful soup on its second outing. I take one cupful, and make soup with it by heating it with a cupful of vegetable broth and a teaspoonful of garam masala. I'll admit the outcome is not a beautiful-looking soup, but it is certainly a beautiful-tasting one.

SERVES 2–4

1½ cups red lentils	scant 1 cup water
1¼ cups coconut water	¼ teaspoon ground mace
1 stick cinnamon	salt to taste
2 cardamom pods, bruised	

- Put the lentils into a saucepan that has a lid, and add the coconut water, cinnamon stick, cardamom pods, and water.

- Bring to a boil, then put on the lid and simmer for 20 minutes. After this time, check to see if the lentils are soft; they should have absorbed the water and be close to a purée. If the lentils are not tender enough, then add a little more water and simmer for another 5 minutes or so.

- Once they are soft and the water is absorbed, beat in the ground mace and salt with a fork, until you have a mushy-pea-like consistency. It thickens on standing, so if you are making this a little ahead of time – it can be left in the pot with the lid on, retaining its warmth for up to 1 hour – you will need to add more liquid on serving, and do check for spicing again, too.

STORE NOTE	FREEZE NOTE
Cool leftovers, then cover and refrigerate within 2 hours of making. Will keep in refrigerator for up to 2 days. Reheat in a small saucepan over a low heat, stirring occasionally and adding extra liquid as needed, until piping hot, or use for soup.	Freeze in an airtight container for up to 3 months. Thaw overnight in refrigerator before reheating as in Store Note.

Note: the lentils should be reheated once only.

Cucumber, chile, and avocado salad

Like poor Becky Sharp biting into a green chile thinking it looked so cool and refreshing, it is easy to be lulled by the soothing greenness of this – the salving avocado, the juicy cucumber – but do not overlook the fierce flecks, made even more zingy by the lime's acid rasp.

SERVES 4–6

1 English cucumber, peeled

1 ripe avocado, peeled

1 green chile, seeded (if desired) and finely chopped

¼ cup chopped fresh cilantro

zest and juice of 1 lime, preferably unwaxed

2 tablespoons extra-virgin olive oil

sea salt flakes to taste

° Cut the cucumber in half lengthways and scrape out the seeds with a small spoon. Slice the half-boats into ¾-inch pieces and tip into a bowl.

° Dice the avocado into similar-sized pieces and add to the bowl, along with the chile, chopped cilantro, the lime zest and juice, the oil, and the sea salt.

° Mix gently but thoroughly, and then tip out onto a serving plate.

Potato and pepper bake

I never feel the need to apologize for using jars of roasted red peppers, for while I don't eat them just as they are, I find them the most useful ingredient, as has already been demonstrated in these pages, and in previous books. Just make sure that you are using peppers that are preserved in oil rather than brine. The potatoes don't roast in this oil, so much as braise: they will crisp up in parts, but mostly just become softened and rich in the sweet peppery juices.

SERVES 8–10

4½ pounds waxy potatoes, such as Yukon Gold

2¼ cups roughly chopped roasted red peppers in their oil (or mixed colors, if available)

2 tablespoons coriander seeds

- ○ Preheat the oven to 425°F.

- ○ Peel the potatoes, cut them into 1-inch slices, then quarter each slice (halving the smaller end slices) and toss them into a large shallow roasting pan.

- ○ Tip the roasted red peppers and their oil all over the potatoes. Add the coriander seeds and toss to combine before baking in the oven for 1 hour, by which time the potatoes will be soft on the inside and their outside golden, but not crisp, except at the corners.

- ○ Using a slotted spatula or slotted spoon (let the excess oil drip back into the pan), transfer the potatoes to a large warmed bowl and either serve immediately, or let them stand for 15 minutes, or up to 45 minutes, as they are also excellent warm rather than hot.

MAKE AHEAD NOTE	STORE NOTE
Peel and slice potatoes, submerge in a bowl of cold water, then cover and refrigerate for up to 1 day. Drain and pat dry before using.	Cool leftovers, then cover and refrigerate as quickly as possible. Will keep in refrigerator for up to 5 days. Reheat on a baking sheet in a 400°F oven for about 20 minutes (timing will depend on quantity).

Quick dill pickles

Now this is where my pickling obsession started. For all that, it isn't really a pickle, more of a sprightly salad, but I eat these spikily soused cucumbers just as I do dill pickles. Indeed, I like them so much better: they taste much fresher (as, indeed, they would), are less mushy, and don't have that coruscating acid sting. If you can get Persian or Lebanese cucumbers, do, as they have much more crunch and flavor, but I have made these as well with regular English cucumbers. And I know it might seem unnecessary to use 2 different vinegars, and I am sure white balsamic vinegar is entirely disreputable (I have it in the house, as my son likes it; that's my excuse) but this combination works, and I'm sticking to it. I dare say if you wanted to, you could use just rice vinegar, in which case up the quantity and add a little sugar.

SERVES 6–8

12–14 ounces Persian cucumbers

1 teaspoon coriander seeds

1 teaspoon sea salt flakes or kosher salt

good grinding of coarse white pepper

2 tablespoons rice vinegar

2 teaspoons white balsamic vinegar

2 tablespoons fresh dill leaves, plus more to serve

° Using a vegetable peeler, peel lengths of skin off the cucumbers so you end up with striped cucumbers, then cut them into long sticks and put into a shallow, non-metallic bowl in which you can fit most of them in one layer. Add the remaining ingredients.

° Cover with plastic wrap and swill everything around, so the cucumbers get a good coating. It may not look like there's enough liquid, but the cucumber sticks will give out more liquid as they sit, and their cucumberiness melds with the spiced vinegar beautifully. Leave for at least 20 minutes before serving.

STORE NOTE

The dill pickles will keep in a sealed jar in refrigerator for up to 1 week.

Thai pickled peppers

When I was in Thailand, a jar of these was offered at every meal. I now do the same, and by that I mean I do not limit their usage to Thai food. As you can see, it is not a difficult recipe: it is simply a matter of slicing chiles and leaving them in vinegar. The rule seems to be 1 part chopped chiles to 2 parts vinegar, so that those who want the chilified vinegar have enough of that, and those who (like me) prefer to drain the liquid away while spooning out the chiles are also kept happy. There is no need to make as much as below: simply chop the chiles you have, measure them in a cup, and then double that volume to get to the requisite amount of vinegar.

MAKES APPROX. 2 CUPS

¾ cup fresh red chile peppers (not bird's eye chiles)

1½ cups rice vinegar

1 x 2-cup preserving jar or similar-sized resealable jar with vinegar-proof lid

- Thinly slice the chiles and put into your preserving jar (though, in fact, I first made this in an empty, cleaned 13-ounce Nutella jar) and pour the vinegar over them. Seal the jar with its lid, and leave in the refrigerator for 48 hours before using.

STORE NOTE

The pickled peppers will keep in a sealed jar in refrigerator for up to 1 month.

Quick-pickled carrots

I look at it like this: if I can summon the patience to cut carrots into julienne strips, then anyone can. I think the trick of making pickling manageable — and the same goes for making preserves — is to deal in small batches only. From experience, when you make masses of jars, you end up pressing them on people in an effort to unload them. If you make one jar, as I do, you will gratefully bring it out for a month, to add crunch and piquancy as you eat, and there is very little that a delicate pickle like this can't enhance.

MAKES APPROX. 2 CUPS

2 large carrots (approx. 8 ounces total), peeled	2 bay leaves
¾ cup apple cider vinegar or white wine vinegar	1 teaspoon mustard seeds
	1 teaspoon fennel seeds
¾ cup cold water	4 cardamom pods
2 tablespoons honey	1 x 2-cup preserving jar or any resealable jar with vinegar-proof lid
2 teaspoons sea salt flakes or kosher salt	

○ Peel the carrots and cut them into matchsticks, and put them into a non-metallic bowl or large measuring cup while you get on with the pickling liquid.

○ Put the vinegar, water, honey, salt, bay leaves, mustard, and fennel seeds into a saucepan. Crush or crack the cardamom pods and put them in, too. Bring to a boil, then take the pan off the heat, and stir to make sure that the salt is dissolved. Pour this liquid over the carrots and leave for about 1 hour to reach room temperature, then stash in the refrigerator for about 1 hour before eating.

STORE NOTE

The pickled carrots will keep in a sealed jar in refrigerator for up to 1 month.

Quick-pickled beets with nigella seeds

I thought until now that the only way I could eat beets was raw, but this gentle, ginger-infused pickle is another step in beet-rehabilitation for anyone with a school-induced loathing for the stuff. It's sweet and tangy, and the perfect accompaniment to sausages (most excellent in a sausage sandwich) and deep and dark stews. I can also recommend removing the ruby strands from their liquid and tossing them into a generous amount of fresh dill for a sprauncy little salad.

MAKES APPROX. 2 CUPS

4 small raw beets (approx. 8 ounces total), peeled

¾ cup cider vinegar or white wine vinegar

¾ cup cold water

3 tablespoons ginger syrup

2 teaspoons sea salt flakes or kosher salt

2 bay leaves

2 teaspoons nigella seeds

1 x 2-cup preserving jar or any resealable jar with vinegar-proof lid

° Wearing a pair of disposable vinyl gloves – or this your hand will *fo sho* the multitudinous seas incarnadine – cut the beets into thin slices, and then cut each slice into matchsticks. This may be boring, but it's not difficult, and there aren't enough beets to deal with to make heavy weather of it. Put them into a non-metallic bowl or pitcher while you get on with the pickling liquid.

° Put the remaining ingredients into a small saucepan, and bring to a boil. Take off the heat, and stir to make sure the salt is dissolved, then pour over the prepared beets and leave until it reaches room temperature. Cover and place in the refrigerator for about 1 hour – or until cold – before eating, or storing in your jar for up to 1 month.

STORE NOTE

The pickled beets will keep in a sealed jar in refrigerator for up to 1 month.

Sushi pickled ginger

Who knew I'd ever turn into the sort of person who makes her own sushi ginger? Given that you could put anything in front of me right now and I'd pickle it, it actually makes sense. After all, I am sure the flavor of these pages indicates how far gone I am on ginger. No matter that I don't make my own sushi – *yet* (anything could change, and often does) – as this fiery stuff is wonderful alongside a piece of grilled fish or chicken, or gorgeously fatty pork.

The beet is there just to bring its beautiful tint; it is not evident in the taste. You could leave it out entirely. I, on the other hand, couldn't.

MAKES APPROX. 1 CUP

5 ounces fresh ginger, peeled

1 teaspoon fine sea salt

½ cup rice vinegar

¼ cup water

¼ cup sugar

small piece raw beet

1 x 1-cup preserving jar or any resealable jar with vinegar-proof lid

° Use a vegetable peeler to slice the ginger into thin strips. Transfer to a bowl, sprinkle with the salt, and mix well. Set aside for 30 minutes to allow the salt to extract excess liquid.

° After 30 minutes, squeeze out and discard any excess liquid from the ginger, and put the strips into your preserving jar.

° To a saucepan, add a ¼ cup of rice vinegar and the water, along with the sugar and beet (if using), and warm over a medium heat until the sugar dissolves. Increase the heat to high and allow to boil for 1 minute.

° Pour the vinegar mixture over the ginger strips in the jar and leave to cool.

° Remove the little piece of beet and add the remaining ¼ cup of vinegar, stir well, and seal the jar. Store in the refrigerator for at least 24 hours, to allow the flavors to develop before eating.

STORE NOTE

The pickled ginger will keep in a sealed jar in the refrigerator for up to 1 month.

Pink-pickled eggs

In my younger days, I ate a whole jar of industrially acid-pickled eggs for a (lucrative) bet; and that still hasn't put me off. But these are in another league altogether. They do rather look like they are a 1960s fabric pattern come to life, but they are as gorgeous to eat as they are pretty to look at. I am not, however, looking to convert those who don't like pickled eggs in the first place.

This method of pickling eggs is not new but a traditional German recipe, lazily but gratifyingly simplified here.

If doing fewer than 18 eggs, I'd still use the same amount of pickling liquid, but a smaller preserving jar; the important thing is that the liquid comes to the top of the jar.

3 ounces raw beets, peeled (approx. ¾ cup diced)

1 red onion

3 tablespoons sea salt flakes or kosher salt

3 tablespoons sugar

2 cups cold water

2 cups red wine vinegar, plus more for topping up later

18 eggs

handful of ice cubes, for cooling the eggs

1 x 6-cup preserving jar or any resealable jar with vinegar-proof lid

- Cut the beet into dice and drop into a saucepan.

- Halve the unpeeled onion and cut it into slices, and drop these – skin and all – into the pan.

- Add the salt, sugar, water, and vinegar and bring to a boil, then let it boil for 1 minute, before taking off the heat. Leave to steep for 1 day in a cool place.

- Put the eggs into a saucepan, cover with cold water, and bring to a brisk simmer, and then let it bubble away – not too rambunctiously – for 7 minutes. Take the pan to the sink, drain, and run cold water over the eggs until they are cool enough to handle. Transfer them to a large bowl, cover with cold water and, if you can, a handful of ice cubes so that the eggs cool swiftly. If you let hard-boiled eggs cool slowly, they get those gray rings around the yolk.

- After the eggs have had no more than 8 minutes in the iced water, peel them (if they sit for too long, it becomes very difficult to peel the eggs) and put them into your jar. Strain the beet and onion liquid into a pitcher and pour over the eggs in the jar. Now add enough red wine vinegar to come up to the top of the jar (I use a scant 1 cup), then seal the jar with its lid and leave in the refrigerator for 4 days before eating, turning the jar upside down and then back again at regular intervals.

STORE NOTE

The pickled eggs will keep in a sealed jar in refrigerator for up to 1 month.

my response is simply "then don't eat dessert." But I am not going to apologize for keeping it sweet: it is a part of life, and, further, a part that is central to the way human society celebrates, and I am more than happy to honor that. Those who disapprove should turn away now.

Many of the cakes below are either gluten-free or dairy-free, or both. Any time I have friends for supper there are always some in these camps, and since I have invited them because I want them to feel welcome, why would I cook them something they can't eat? I'm not making any health claims here, and am not in a position to – and I'm always mindful of the late Marina Keegan's irritation, as a celiac, at what she felt was the craziness of the Hollywood gluten-free diet – but I can certainly attest to their deliciousness. And if more people can enjoy that, the happier I am.

You will see, though, that I haven't constrained myself in any way with the recipes that follow. The joy I feel in baking translates to the joy to be had in eating. Whatever ingredients I use, the aim is always simple: to give pleasure, both to the cook and the eater, without which, life and the sum of human happiness, in this small but essential way, would be much diminished.

ACKNOWLEDGMENTS

In order to keep this page from sounding like the breathy gush of an Oscar acceptance speech, I will keep my thanks brief, and hope that any terseness is not construed as lack of gratitude on my part. Indeed, I am profoundly grateful and in ways that could not adequately be expressed here, first and foremost to Gail Rebuck, who inspired me to write this, and buoyed me up while I was doing so. The same thanks must likewise be conveyed to Mark Hutchinson and Ed Victor, and also to Caz Hildebrand and Keiko Oikawa, whose art direction and photography, respectively, brought the book you hold in your hands to life. Nor could it have come into being without the ministrations of Clara Farmer, Parisa Ebrahimi, Will Schwalbe, Kara Rota, Bryn Clark, Sandi Mendelson, Robert McCullough, Anne Newgarden, Hettie Potter, Yasmin Othman, Caroline Stearns, Camille Blais, Linda Berlin, Violette Kirton, Megan Hummerstone, Zuzana Kratka, and Zoe Wales.

I am also grateful for the good will and generosity of Mud Australia (and in particular, the London outpost), Le Creuset, Netherton Foundry, Grain & Knot, David Mellor, Mason Cash, Fermob, Workshop Living, La Fromagerie, and more particularly my fishmonger, Rex Goldsmith, of The Chelsea Fishmonger, Adam and Daniel of HG Walter, my butchers, and my greengrocer, Andreas, of Andreas Veg.

Finally, I thank my family, my friends, my readers: your support, encouragement, and enthusiasm along the way was what turned this project into a book.

Apricot almond cake with rosewater and cardamom

This is my idea of a perfect cake: simple, beautiful, fragrant, and beguiling. I've been making this sort of cake, in one form or another, since my clementine cake in *How To Eat*, and I can't help but feel, with a certain calm excitement, that it has reached its apogee here. This is invitingly easy to make, and while I love the poetry of its ingredients, the cake doesn't overwhelm with its *Thousand-and-One-Nights* scent. Rosewater can be a tricky ingredient: a little, and it's all exotic promise; a fraction too much and we're in bubblebath territory.

One of the things that makes this so easy is that you can throw all the ingredients into a food processor. But if you don't have one, simply chop the prepared dried apricots and cardamom seeds very finely and then beat together with the remaining cake ingredients.

CUTS INTO 8–10 SLICES

1¼ cups (approx. 6 ounces) "ready-to-eat" dried apricots

1 cup cold water

2 cardamom pods, cracked

2 cups almond meal

⅓ cup fine polenta (not instant), or fine cornmeal

1 teaspoon baking powder (gluten-free if required)

¾ cup sugar

6 extra large eggs

2 teaspoons lemon juice

1 teaspoon rosewater

non-stick cooking spray or vegetable oil for greasing

TO DECORATE:

2 teaspoons rose petal or apricot preserves

1 teaspoon lemon juice

2½ teaspoons very finely chopped pistachios

1 x 8-inch round springform cake pan

○ Put the dried apricots into a small saucepan, cover them with the cold water, and drop in the cracked cardamom pods with their fragrant seeds. Put on the heat, then bring to a boil and let it bubble for 10 minutes – don't stray too far away from the pan, as by the end of the 10 minutes the pan will be just about out of water and you want to make sure it doesn't actually run dry, as the apricots will absorb more water as they cool.

○ Take the pan off the heat, place on a cold, heatproof surface, and let the apricots cool.

○ Preheat the oven to 350°F. Grease the sides of your springform cake pan and line the bottom with parchment paper.

- Remove 5 of the dried apricots and tear each in half, then set aside for the time being. Discard the cardamom husks, leaving the seeds in the pan.

- Pour and scrape out the sticky contents of the pan into the bowl of a food processor. Add the almond meal, polenta, baking powder, sugar, and eggs, and give a good long blitz to combine.

- Open the top of the processor, scrape down the batter, add 2 teaspoons of lemon juice and the rosewater, and blitz again, then scrape into the prepared pan and smooth with a spatula. Arrange the apricot halves around the circumference of the pan.

- Bake for 40 minutes, though if the cake is browning up a lot before it's actually ready, you may want to cover loosely with aluminum foil at the 30-minute mark. When it's ready, the cake will be coming away from the edges of the pan, the top will feel firm, and a cake tester will come out with just one or two damp crumbs on it.

- Remove the cake to a wire rack. If you're using apricot preserves to decorate, you may want to warm it a little first so that it's easier to spread; rose petal preserves are so lusciously soft-set, they shouldn't need any help. Stir a teaspoon of lemon juice into the preserves and brush over the top of the cake, then sprinkle with the chopped pistachios and leave the cake to cool in its pan before unspringing and removing to a plate.

STORE NOTE	FREEZE NOTE
Store in an airtight container in a cool place for 5–7 days. In hot weather (or if the central heating's on) keep in refrigerator.	The cake can be made ahead and frozen for up to 3 months (though the nuts may soften slightly on thawing). Wrap the fully cooled cake (still on the springform pan base) tightly in a double layer of plastic wrap and a layer of aluminum foil. To thaw, unwrap and leave it (still on the pan base) on a plate at room temperature for about 4 hours.

Warm raspberry and lemon cake

Although this started off life as more of a traditional British bake, rather along the lines of the Marmalade Pudding Cake in *Kitchen*, I prefer it in this incarnation: sweet with almonds and the soft crunch of polenta. This also gives it universal appeal in that it is both dairy- and gluten-free. But if you want a more old-fashioned cake taste, then make it with 13 tablespoons soft unsalted butter (plus a little more for greasing the pan), which you cream with the sugar and zest, and use 1½ cups all-purpose flour in place of the almonds and polenta. You will also need 4 eggs rather than 3, and – the flour being less sweet than both the almonds and the polenta – I'd advise you to warm the lemon juice that goes on top with 2 teaspoons of honey first.

In both cases, this is as good cold as it is warm, though I love the way the scent mingles with the taste when it still has the breath of the oven on it. When cold, however, you can make the cake go further, by slicing it into thin rectangles and eating it daintily with a cup of tea.

I've specified frozen raspberries rather than fresh as they don't go so mushy when baked. However, in either case, the fruit has a tendency to sink a bit, but don't let that bother you.

MAKES 9 SLABS OR 18 FINGERS

⅔ cup light olive oil, plus more for greasing	½ teaspoon baking soda
zest and juice of 1 unwaxed lemon	1 teaspoon baking powder (gluten-free if required)
½ cup plus 2 tablespoons sugar	3 extra large eggs
1½ cups almond meal	1¼ cups frozen raspberries (not thawed)
⅔ cup fine polenta (not instant), or fine cornmeal	1 x 8-inch square cake pan

○ Preheat the oven to 350°F, and lightly grease the pan with a dab of olive oil.

○ Beat the oil with the finely grated lemon zest (you'll need the juice later), then add the sugar and mix together. This can be done in a freestanding mixer or by hand with a wooden spoon, or you can blitz all the ingredients, bar the raspberries, in a food processor.

○ In a separate bowl, combine the almond meal, polenta, baking soda, and baking powder and fork together to mix well. Add a spoonful to the oil and sugar mixture, beating all the while, then add 1 egg, followed by about a third of the almond and polenta mixture, and so forth, until all the eggs and the almond and polenta mixture are used up and you have a smooth, sunny, yellow batter.

○ Whether you've mixed the batter with a processor, freestanding mixer, or bowl and wooden spoon, now fold in the frozen raspberries by hand and then spoon and smooth the mixture into the prepared pan. Bake for 40 minutes, by which time the cake will start to come away from the edges of the pan, be brown on top, and a cake tester will come out clean with all but a few golden crumbs (this is meant to be a damp cake).

○ The minute the cake is out of the oven, pour or brush the lemon juice on top and leave until warm (rather than fresh-from-the-oven hot) before eating it.

STORE NOTE	FREEZE NOTE
Store in an airtight container in a cool place for up to 2 days, or in refrigerator for up to 5 days. In hot weather, keep in refrigerator.	Leftovers can be frozen, in an airtight container, for up to 3 months. Thaw overnight in refrigerator, or for 2–3 hours at room temperature.

Licorice and black currant chocolate cake

Any recipe with licorice is essentially a divisive one, but I've written of my licorice-love before, and know there are many more of my persuasion out there. Besides, while my No-Churn Black Currant Ice Cream with Licorice Ripple on **p.336** is definitely a no-go area for any but the true believer, this cake is gentle enough to lure in those who profess initial caution. The chocolate seems to soften the licorice's dark intensity, and the sharp black currant is a fitting foil and traditional partner; indeed, the inspiration for this cake came from a lifelong love of the black currant and licorice candies I ate in my childhood. And it is worth getting the black currants for the top of the cake: they are more than just decorative. I had to pick mine out of a bag of frozen mixed berries, then let them thaw, but it was worth it.

I use Lakrids' Fine Liquorice Powder, but if you're using raw licorice powder, then reduce the amounts to 3 teaspoons in the cake and ¾ teaspoon in the frosting. The point is, the licorice should not hit you over the head, but become subtly present in the "follow," blooming after the bite. With the quantities below, professed licorice-haters actually liked the cake; licorice-lovers, of course, adored it.

By the way, although this cake is dairy-free, by all means substitute reduced fat milk if that isn't a consideration. As for the chocolate, if it has a minimum of 70% cocoa solids it should be, in effect, dairy-free but may still contain some traces of milk. So if this is a concern, do check the labeling on the package to be sure.

CUTS INTO 8–12 SLICES

FOR THE CAKE:

1½ cups all-purpose flour

1⅓ cups sugar

¾ cup unsweetened cocoa powder

2 teaspoons baking powder

1 teaspoon baking soda

4 teaspoons fine licorice powder (see Intro)

¾ cup almond milk

¾ cup vegetable oil, plus extra for greasing

2 extra large eggs

1 cup hot water, from a recently boiled kettle

¾ cup best-quality black currant preserves

FOR THE FROSTING:

2 tablespoons hot water, from a recently boiled kettle

1 teaspoon fine licorice powder (see Intro)

¼ cup golden or light corn syrup; oil the cup before measuring

4 ounces bittersweet chocolate (preferably min. 70% cocoa solids), very finely chopped (see Intro)

TO DECORATE:

1–1¼ cups black currants (optional; see Intro)

2 x 8-inch round cake pans

- Preheat the oven to 350°F. Prepare your cake pans by greasing with oil and lining with parchment paper.

- Measure the flour, sugar, cocoa, baking powder, baking soda, and licorice powder into a large mixing bowl, and fork to combine, breaking up any lumps.

- Whisk the milk, oil, and eggs in a measuring cup. Add these wet ingredients to the dry ones and, still whisking – or move to a wooden spoon if you prefer – beat to mix. Now beat in the boiling water and, when all is combined, pour equally into the 2 pans. It is a very liquid batter and a tight fit, but don't let that alarm you.

- Carefully put the cakes in the oven and bake for about 25 minutes, by which time they should be coming away from the edges of the pans, feel firm to the touch, and a cake tester should come out clean. A few crumbs may still adhere, as this is a desirably damp cake, but you shouldn't have any actual batter on the cake tester.

- When they're done, stand the cakes in their pans on a wire rack for 10 minutes, then unmold them carefully – they should slip out easily, but they are tender, so be gentle – onto the wire rack, peel away the parchment paper, and leave to cool.

- Once the cakes are cool, put 1 cake, flat-side up, on a plate. Spread with the black currant preserves and top with the other cake, flat-side down.

- To make the frosting, put the hot water and licorice powder in a small saucepan and whisk to mix, so that the powder dissolves, then add the golden syrup and bring to a boil. The second it starts bubbling, turn off the heat (but leave the pan on the stove) and add the finely chopped chocolate. Swirl the pan, making sure the chocolate is covered and is starting to melt, and leave for a scant minute, then whisk until you have a glossy frosting. Pour this onto the center of the top of the cake and, using a small spatula, ease it to the edges, letting some bits drip a little down the sides. If you want, top with black currants, making sure that – if they're frozen – they are completely thawed and drained. And if you do want to add the black currants or any other sort of decoration, move fast as the frosting sets quickly!

STORE NOTE	FREEZE NOTE
Store in an airtight container (or under a cake dome) at cool room temperature for up to 5 days.	The cake can be made ahead and frozen, without frosting. When cool, very carefully wrap cake layers in a double layer of plastic wrap and a layer of aluminum foil. Freeze for up to 3 months. To thaw, unwrap and place on a wire rack for 2–3 hours.

Dark and sumptuous chocolate cake

This cake. It confounds me. It delights me. I almost want to leave it there.

But I should explain: I never ever thought I would be in raptures about the joyfulness of a – yes – vegan chocolate cake. This isn't the voice of prejudice but was – "was" being the operative word – the conclusion of experience.

It's true that I first made a version of it – the recipe kindly given to me by Caroline Stearns, my technical guru in the kitchen – when I was giving a supper for a vegan friend, but I now make this as my chocolate cake of choice for people where dietary restrictions are *not* an issue, and I don't even need to explain it's vegan. No need to offer explanations: you just need to offer the cake. On top of everything else, it's incredibly simple to make.

My version has coconut oil in the cake, and coconut butter in the frosting, but of course you can use vegetable oil in the cake, and vegan margarine for the frosting if you prefer. The combination stipulated in the ingredients list, however, creates a cake and frosting of such depth and fudginess that I never veer from it, even though I know the shopping list is a tiny bit demanding. But once you've tasted it, you too must surely concur that a cake as good as this can be as demanding as it likes. Besides, it asks nothing of you in the kitchen beyond some simple stirring. You are not required to get a mixer out, or do any heavy lifting at all: this is a simple bowl-and-wooden-spoon number. Both the coconut oil and coconut butter need to stand out of the refrigerator for a good couple of hours before using. I often take them out the night before, as then they are easier to measure out.

Please check the labeling on the chocolate you buy. It needs, whatever your concerns, to be bittersweet (minimum 70% cocoa solids for my taste), but if you need this to be absolutely dairy-free or vegan, make sure it says so on the package.

I hate the worthy association that comes with vegan cakes, and celebrate this one by scattering rose petals and chopped pistachios over it.

FOR THE FROSTING:

¼ cup cold water

5 tablespoons coconut butter (this is not the same as oil)

¼ cup dark brown sugar

1½ teaspoons instant espresso

1½ tablespoons unsweetened cocoa powder

6 ounces bittersweet chocolate (preferably min. 70% cocoa solids, see Intro), finely chopped

FOR THE CAKE:

1½ cups all-purpose flour

1½ teaspoons baking soda

½ teaspoon fine sea salt

1½ teaspoons instant espresso powder

¾ cup unsweetened cocoa powder

1½ cups dark brown sugar

1½ cups hot water, from a recently boiled kettle

6 tablespoons coconut oil

1½ teaspoons apple cider vinegar or white wine vinegar

1 tablespoon edible rose petals

1 tablespoon chopped pistachios

1 x 8-inch round springform cake pan

○ Start with the frosting, though first preheat the oven to 350°F and put in a baking sheet at the same time. Put all of the frosting ingredients except the chopped chocolate into a heavy-based saucepan and bring to a boil, making sure everything's dissolved. Turn off the heat – but leave the pan on the stove – then quickly add the finely chopped chocolate and swirl the pan so that it is all underwater, so to speak. Leave for a scant minute, then whisk until you have a darkly glossy frosting, and leave to cool. I find this takes exactly the amount of time the cake takes to make, cook, and cool. But do give the frosting a stir with a spatula every now and again.

○ Line the bottom of your springform cake pan (you will need a good, leakproof one as this is a very wet batter) with parchment paper.

○ Put the flour, baking soda, salt, and instant espresso and cocoa in a bowl and fork to mix.

○ Mix together the sugar, water, coconut oil, and vinegar until the coconut oil has melted, and stir into the dry ingredients, then pour into the prepared pan and bake for 35 minutes. Though do check at the 30-minute mark to see if it is already done. When it's ready, the cake will be coming away from the edges of the pan and a cake tester will come out clean, apart from a few crumbs. This is a fudgy cake and you don't want to overdo it.

○ Once the cake is cooked, transfer the pan to a wire rack and let the cake cool in its pan.

○ Turn to your frosting, and give it a good stir with a spatula to check it is at the right consistency. It needs to be runny enough to cover the cake, but thick enough to stay (mostly) on the top. So pour over the unmolded cake, and use a spatula to ease the frosting to the edges, if needed. If you wish to decorate, now is the time to do it. In which case, sprinkle joyously with rose petals and chopped pistachios or anything else that your heart desires; otherwise, leave it gleaming darkly and, indeed, sumptuously. Leave to stand for 30 minutes for the frosting to set before slicing into the cake.

STORE NOTE	FREEZE NOTE
Store in an airtight container (or under a cake dome) at room temperature for up to 5 days.	The cake can be made ahead and frozen, without frosting. When cool, carefully wrap cake in a double layer of plastic wrap and a layer of aluminum foil. Freeze for up to 3 months. To thaw, unwrap and place on a serving plate at room temperature for 3–4 hours.

Thyme and lemon bundt cake

I love thyme and sprinkle it wantonly in my cooking, but I wanted a cake that relied on it as a leading ingredient, not merely as a decorative flourish. Besides, with a rosemary loaf cake under my belt (in *Feast*), I had no doubt that it would work. And it does. Don't be alarmed at the amount of thyme in the cake batter, as it doesn't overwhelm. It charms.

I've specified buttermilk in the ingredients list, but you can use runny plain yogurt in its stead. Or, easier still, make your own buttermilk – my fallback position – by adding 1 tablespoon of lemon juice (since you will have lemons at hand for this recipe; otherwise you can use white wine vinegar or apple cider vinegar instead) to 1 cup reduced fat milk and letting it stand for 20 minutes before you need it, stirring before use.

Now, a cautionary word: even when the cake looks bronzed and ready, you need to make sure that it's cooked through around the funnel. Otherwise, not only will it be the devil to unmold, but you will also find the cake disappointingly undercooked (however brown it looks on the surface) once you slice into it.

If you don't have a bundt pan, then you can make this in an 8-inch square cake pan (approx. 2¼ inches deep). It makes quite a high cake, almost the full height of the pan, and takes between 1 hour to 1 hour 20 minutes at the oven temperature below (and check that it is cooked all the way through to the center before removing it from the oven).

CUTS INTO 10–14 SLICES

3 cups all-purpose flour	3 extra large eggs
¾ teaspoon baking powder	1 cup buttermilk (see Intro)
¾ teaspoon baking soda	1¼ cups confectioners' sugar
1 stick plus 5 tablespoons (13 tablespoons) soft unsalted butter	non-stick cooking spray (or vegetable oil and all-purpose flour) for greasing
2 unwaxed lemons	
small bunch fresh thyme	1 x 10-cup bundt pan or 8-inch square cake pan approx. 2¼ inches deep
1¼ cups sugar	

° Preheat the oven to 325°F, slipping in a baking sheet at the same time. Spray the inside of your bundt pan with non-stick cooking spray, or brush on a paste made of 2 teaspoons of all-purpose flour mixed with 2 teaspoons of oil, making sure you get into all the crevices of the pan. Leave the bundt pan upside down over a piece

of newspaper or parchment paper while you get on with making the cake batter. (And keep this piece of paper once you've put the batter in the pan, as it'll come in handy for the glacé icing part.)

○ Combine the flour, baking powder, and baking soda in a bowl, and fork to mix.

○ Put the butter in the bowl of a freestanding mixer or a regular mixing bowl, grate in the zest of both lemons, and beat until creamy.

○ Strip ¼ cup of thyme leaves from the sprigs, and add along with the sugar, and beat again until you have a light fluffy mixture.

○ Now, one by one, beat in the eggs and, after the last one, slow down your mixing and add a third of the flour mixture, followed by a third of the buttermilk, and so on until both the flour mixture and buttermilk are used up.

○ Finally, beat in the juice of 1 of the lemons and transfer this mixture to the prepared bundt pan. Place on the baking sheet in the oven and bake for 1¼ hours, though start checking after 1 hour. Don't be alarmed if it looks like there's too much batter for the bundt pan: all shall be well, and all manner of things shall be well. In other words, the cake will rise but then sink back down comfortably.

○ When a cake tester comes out clean, remove the cake to a wire rack and leave in its pan for 15 minutes before carefully unmolding. This is always a tense moment, but if the pan's been sprayed or greased adequately, and the cake is fully baked, you should have no problem. Besides, it's that moment of breathless tension which makes the dramatic unmolding and unveiling all the more gratifying.

○ When the cake is cool, slip the piece of newspaper or parchment paper under the wire rack, then sift the confectioners' sugar into a bowl and beat in the juice of the remaining lemon until you have a glaze that is thin enough to run down the cake – I reckon on 2½–3 tablespoons – but thick enough to act as a tangy glue for the thyme leaves you are about to sprinkle on top. Or you can pour this directly over the cake on its serving plate. Duly pour the sherbetty glaze over the cake, and immediately scatter with thyme leaves and the odd sprig or two. How many you add is entirely up to you, but I tend to strew with abandon.

STORE NOTE	FREEZE NOTE
Store in an airtight container in a cool place for up to 5 days.	This cake can be frozen, without icing, for up to 3 months. Wrap cake in a double layer of plastic wrap and a layer of aluminum foil. To thaw, unwrap and place on a wire rack at room temperature for about 5 hours.

Pumpkin bundt cake

I love the Thanksgiving feel of a pumpkin cake, even if the pumpkin does come out of a can. The first time I made this, I didn't frost it, just dusted the cake with confectioners' sugar and served it alongside a bag of frozen mixed berries that I'd thawed, stirring a little finely grated orange zest into the fruits as I tipped them, still frozen, into their bowl. Then, I felt I really had to do something with the half can of pumpkin I had left over, and so came up with the No-Churn Brandied Pumpkin Ice Cream (**p.334**), which goes especially well here should you choose to serve the bundt while it still has a little residual warmth about it. But don't feel bad if you want to eat this as a coffee-or-tea-accompanying cake; in which case, ice it as below.

Yes, this is the second of three bundt cakes for your delectation, but it seems to me that if you own such a pan (and I am in possession of one that creates a cake that looks like a cross between an old-fashioned mother-of-the-bride hat and a Catherine wheel) you will want to get as much use out of it as possible.

However, if you don't have a bundt pan, use an 8-inch square cake pan (approx. 2¼ inches deep) instead. This makes quite a high cake, almost the full height of the pan, and will need 45–55 minutes' baking time at the oven temperature below (and check it is cooked all the way through to the center before removing it from the oven).

CUTS INTO 10–14 SLICES

1½ cups light brown sugar

1 cup vegetable oil

zest and juice of 1 orange, preferably unwaxed

3 extra large eggs

2⅔ cups all-purpose flour

2 teaspoons baking soda

2 teaspoons ground cinnamon

½ teaspoon ground allspice

1¼ cups pure pumpkin purée (from a 15-ounce can – save the rest for the No-Churn Brandied Pumpkin Ice Cream on p.334)

non-stick cooking spray (or vegetable oil and all-purpose flour) for greasing

FOR THE GLACÉ ICING:

2 cups confectioners' sugar

2½–3 tablespoons orange juice (using orange from above)

small square bittersweet chocolate for grating

1 x 10-cup bundt pan or 1 x 8-inch square cake pan approx. 2¼ inches deep (see Intro)

- Preheat the oven to 350°F. Spray your bundt pan with non-stick cooking spray, or make a paste by mixing 2 teaspoons of oil and 2 teaspoons of flour and brush it all over the insides of the pan, making sure you get into all of the crevices. Leave upside down on a piece of newspaper or parchment paper to drain off any excess oil while you prepare the cake.

- In the bowl of a freestanding mixer (although you could do this by hand), beat together the sugar, oil, the finely grated zest of half the orange, and 2 tablespoons of its juice until smoothly combined. You'll need to stop and scrape down the bowl once or twice.

- Add the eggs, beating again.

- Measure the flour, baking soda, and spices into another bowl, forking everything together lightly so that it's all mixed well.

- Then beat the pumpkin purée into the egg mixture, before finally adding the flour and spices and folding to combine. Once you have a smooth cake batter, carefully fill your oiled bundt pan with this mixture.

- Bake for 45–55 minutes, though I always start checking at 40. The cake should be coming away from the edges of the pan and a cake tester will come out clean. Remove to a wire rack, leaving the cake to cool in its pan for 15 minutes.

- Gently prise the cake away from the pan with your fingers, paying particular attention to the part around the funnel, then turn out the cake onto the wire rack and leave to cool completely.

- To ice the bundt, stand it on the plate of your choice, then sift the confectioners' sugar into a bowl and gradually whisk in the orange juice, beginning to slow down after the second tablespoon, just to make sure you get the consistency you want. Once you have a smooth icing that's thick enough to stick to the cake, but with just enough runniness to drip down the sides a little, start spooning it over the top of the cake, letting it move naturally on its own: it will run down the architectural grooves of the cake, rather beautifully of its own accord; don't worry if it drips a little onto the plate as — for me, anyway — this adds to its charm. Sometimes, if I have a little icing left over, I can't stop myself doing a bit of a frenzied Jackson Pollock (as you can see from the photo).

- Grate the chocolate on top, to finish: even a small square gives you too much, but it's no great sacrifice to eat what you don't use.

STORE NOTE	FREEZE NOTE
Store in an airtight container in a cool place for up to 1 week.	Freeze, without icing, for up to 3 months. Wrap the cake in a double layer of plastic wrap and a layer of aluminum foil. To thaw, unwrap and place on a wire rack at room temperature for about 5 hours.

Cider and 5-spice bundt cake

Most of the time I refer to this as my Cider and 5-Spice Gingerbread, but I changed the name out of concern for those who expect a little more gingeriness from their gingerbead (although anyone is free to boost the amount of ginger at will). But, actually, the tender crumb has the lightness of a cake rather than the damp heaviness (gorgeous though that is) of a gingerbread. Besides, I felt it only proper to accord the magnificently aromatic 5-spice seasoning its star role. I have since found that there are many variants of 5-spice powder out there. While generally it is a mixture of star anise, cloves, cinnamon, Sichuan pepper, and fennel seeds, I also love the versions that have licorice and dried mandarin peel. But what I've found is that all types work, even the one or two brands that erroneously add garlic: a couple of people have made it with this version, and both vouch that the garlic is not detectable. Still, when you're shopping, it's best to check the ingredients label and go for one without garlic if you can.

If you want to intensify the ginger element, without doing a lot more peeling and grating (or don't want to use alcohol), then use 1 cup ginger beer in place of the cider.

Either way, this is wonderful enough plain as it is, though I have something of a *faiblesse* for the gleaming accompaniment of the Smoky Salted Caramel Sauce on **p.342**, as you can see from the picture.

One last note: if you don't have a bundt pan, you can make this in an 8-inch square cake pan (approx. 2¼ inches deep), in which case it will need 50–55 minutes' baking, or until a cake tester comes out clean and the cake is firm to the touch. Let the cake cool in the pan, before unmolding and wrapping (see overleaf).

CUTS INTO 10–14 SLICES

1 cup hard cider, preferably dry or at least not sweet

¾ cup vegetable oil

½ cup soft dark brown sugar

1 cup molasses

3 extra large eggs

1¼-inch piece fresh ginger, peeled and finely grated (2 teaspoons)

2 cups all-purpose flour

2 teaspoons baking powder

¼ teaspoon baking soda

½ teaspoon freshly grated nutmeg

2½ teaspoons Chinese 5-spice powder

1½ teaspoons ground cinnamon

non-stick cooking spray or vegetable oil for greasing

1 x 10-cup bundt pan or 1 x 8-inch square cake pan approx. 2¼ inches deep (see Intro)

- Open the cider so that it loses its fizz. Preheat the oven to 325°F, and grease your bundt pan with non-stick cooking spray, or simply oil it, and leave the pan upside down on a piece of newspaper or parchment paper while you get on with the batter.

- Measure the oil, brown sugar, and (always lightly oil the receptacle for the molasses first and it will slide out easily) molasses into a bowl.

- Pour in the cider and crack in the eggs, add the ginger, and beat till smooth. While I use a freestanding mixer to make this cake, it's simple enough by hand: in which case, beat the eggs together first before adding to the other ingredients.

- In another bowl measure out the flour, baking powder, baking soda, nutmeg, 5-spice, and cinnamon, and fork through to combine.

- Gently tip the dry ingredients into the wet molasses mixture, beating as you go to make a smooth batter. Scrape the sides and the bottom of the bowl well to make sure there aren't any pockets of flour.

- Pour the dark and aromatic batter into the prepared pan: it will be very runny, but don't be alarmed. Place in the oven to bake for 45–50 minutes, but start checking after 40. When the cake's ready, it will start to come away from the sides of the pan and a cake tester should come out clean; that's to say, not wet, but with some crumbs adhering to it. Transfer the bundt to a wire rack for about 30 minutes, then use your fingers to help prise the cake away from the edges of the pan, most particularly around the funnel, and turn out. Leave to cool completely before wrapping, first in parchment paper and then aluminum foil, as it tastes best if eaten the next day. I don't always manage this.

STORE NOTE	FREEZE NOTE
The cake can be kept loosely wrapped in its parchment and foil, in an airtight container at cool room temperature, for up to 1 week.	The fully cooled cake can be tightly wrapped in a double layer of plastic wrap and a layer of aluminum foil and then frozen for up to 3 months. To thaw, unwrap and place on a wire rack and leave at room temperature for about 5 hours.

Matcha cake with cherry juice icing

I've had an *idée fixe* in my head for some time now about the making of a matcha cake. And ever since I saw a picture of a recipe for doughnuts with cherry juice glaze, I knew the latter had to play some part in my culinary life. You will have noticed that I have (subtly, I hope) a bit of a green-and-pink theme dancing through the book, so I suppose it was inevitable that these two – the matcha cake and the cherry juice glacé icing – would need to be realized together. I love the evocation of Japanese cherry blossom alongside the equally Japanese matcha – and I am childishly delighted that a cake so beautifully vibrant, so magically tinted, can be achieved without food coloring. Please don't think for one moment that this is the product of the Concept Kitchen. It tastes as exquisite as I'd dreamt it could, or it wouldn't have found its way to these pages.

Good-quality matcha, that greenest of green tea powders, is expensive, but I've found other uses for it so, once bought, it does have more play in your kitchen (see **pp.338** and **348**). Think of it as a culinary investment. My favorite matcha for this is Premium Izu Matcha by Tealux, which is not cheap but by no means among the most costly. I don't recommend buying a lesser variety, for the simple reason that it will still be expensive, and will neither taste as good nor be as green as the real thing. There's no point doing all this and ending up with something dusty and khaki. Yes, this is a luxury cake, and must be savored as such.

I find that making a chiffon-style cake – in which the eggs are separated and the whipped whites folded into the batter – makes for a softer texture, which is much needed here, as the matcha powder would dry out a regular sponge. However, you can be left with a slight indentation at the top of the cake, as it rises more on cooking, inevitably to fall. If the indentation is minimal, you can reduce the icing to 2 cups confectioners' sugar mixed with 3 tablespoons of cherry juice (bought in a bottle, not arduously squeezed by hand, I should add), but otherwise proceed as below. Should cherry juice (not acerola, which is yellow) elude you, try pomegranate juice. And if that fad hasn't hit where you are, then push a few raspberries through a strainer and mix the red juice with a little water.

One final note. Strictly speaking, chiffon cakes should not be made in non-stick and ungreased pans (which impede their rise), but I have only non-stick cake pans, and all the times I've made this, I have had no trouble.

CUTS INTO 12–14 DELICATE SLICES

1 tablespoon Izu Matcha (see Intro)

1/3 cup hot water, from a recently boiled kettle

3 extra large eggs, separated

½ cup plus 1 tablespoon superfine sugar

¼ cup vegetable oil

¾ cup all-purpose flour

1 teaspoon baking powder

2¼ cups confectioners' sugar

¼ cup pure organic cherry juice (not acerola)

1 x 8-inch springform cake pan (preferably not non-stick)

- Preheat the oven to 350°F. Line the base of your springform pan with parchment paper, but don't grease the pan.

- Put the matcha powder in a small bowl and whisk in the hot water until smooth. Leave to cool slightly.

- Put the egg whites in a separate bowl and whisk to floppy peaks. Still whisking, add 3 tablespoons of the superfine sugar and combine, then set aside for a moment.

- Put the egg yolks and remaining superfine sugar in another bowl and whisk until pale. Whisk in the matcha liquid followed by the oil. Sift over and fold in the flour and baking powder.

- Add a dollop of the egg white mixture and fold in, then follow up with the remainder. Gently pour the mixture into the springform cake pan and bake for 25–30 minutes, until a cake tester comes out clean. Do not even think of opening the oven door before 20 minutes to check, as it could make the cake deflate.

- Let the cake cool completely in its pan, sitting on a wire rack. The cake will shrink back slightly as it cools. Run a spatula around the edge of the cake and unspring from the pan. Put a plate on the top of the cake, flip it over, then remove the base of the pan, peel away the parchment paper, and carefully sit the cake, bottom-side down, on a plate or cake stand.

- Once the cake is ready to ice, sift the confectioners' sugar into a bowl and whisk in the cherry juice a little at a time to make an opaque but still runny glacé icing. The cake may have a slight dip on top and this amount of icing allows for this, though it does mean it will pool out pinkly as you cut the cake (I find this rather pretty). Ice the top of the cake and let the icing run down the sides a little. Leave for up to 1 hour to set: it will still be a little runny, but any longer and it starts to lose its gleam.

STORE NOTE	FREEZE NOTE
Store in an airtight container in a cool place for 2–3 days.	The fully cooled, un-iced cake can be frozen, tightly wrapped in a double layer of plastic wrap and a layer of aluminum foil, for up to 1 month. You may find it easier to leave the cake on the springform pan base when freezing. To thaw, unwrap (carefully remove cake from the pan base if left on) and place on a wire rack at room temperature for about 3 hours.

Date and marmalade Christmas cake

This cake tastes like Christmas pudding – a very, very good Christmas pudding – the sort the Quakers (as I'm fond of quoting) once magnificently condemned as "the invention of the scarlet whore of Babylon." It's molasses-rich, damp, and so heady, it doesn't even need the traditional alcohol in it. It also happens to be gluten- and dairy-free, and is a last-minute cake, so very useful if you haven't got round to making that family recipe that needs to be baked ahead and fed with brandy for 6 months.

I like to use a wonderful home-made marmalade (thanks to Helio Fenerich, who also supplied me with the Italian Veal Shank Stew on **p.185**), which is good and bitter and rather soft set, and it's a miracle I can keep it long enough to use in this cake. But there are many good marmalades out there. Just bear in mind that the dates have their own rich and fudgy sweetness (on top of all the other dried fruit) so don't go for anything too jam-like: Frank Cooper's Original Oxford Marmalade or Wilkin & Sons "Tawny" Orange would be my choice; in other words, go for a marmalade with depth, and one that provides that *frisson* of bitterness.

And while I adore the deep caramelly taste of medjool dates (the fruit of the biblical kings), you can use dried dates – the sort styled "ready to eat" – in their stead.

One final thing: the finely chopped almonds came, as did the almond meal, from a bag – any chopped nuts would do, but that nubbly texture, among all the plump-soaked fruit, is most desirable.

CUTS INTO APPROX. 14 SLICES

1 cup strong black tea

18 ounces medjool dates

¾ cup natural color candied cherries

1 cup dried cranberries

1 cup golden raisins

¾ cup plus 1 tablespoon dark brown sugar

¾ cup plus 3 tablespoons coconut oil (15 tablespoons)

2 teaspoons ground cinnamon

2 teaspoons ground ginger

½ teaspoon ground cloves

scant 1 cup good-quality marmalade (see Intro), plus more to brush on the cake

2 cups almond meal

¾ cup chopped almonds

3 extra large eggs, beaten

1 x 8-inch springform cake pan

- Preheat the oven to 300°F. Using your springform cake pan as a template, cut out a parchment paper circle for the bottom, and then make a lining for the sides of the pan that is about 2¼ inches higher than the height of the pan itself. Do this by making a very long rectangular strip of parchment paper, then fold the long bottom edge in by about ¾ inch, as if turning up a hem, then take a pair of scissors and snip into this hem at intervals as if to make a rough frill. Curl this around the inside of the pan, with the frilly edge flat on the bottom, and then sit your parchment circle on top of the frilled bit to hold it in place.

- Make your tea: I just pour 1 cup boiling water over a tea bag, let it steep, and make sure I take out the bag before adding the tea to the pan. Remove the pits from the dates, and snip each date into 4 pieces, using scissors. Halve the candied cherries, also using scissors. Of course, you can use a knife if you prefer.

- Get out a saucepan that will take all the ingredients, including the tea, and put everything in it except for the almond meal, almonds, and eggs. Place on the heat, stirring to mix, and stir every now and again until it comes to a boil. Then turn down the heat and let it simmer for 10 minutes, stirring frequently. The stirring not only helps the dates break up and "dissolve," but it also keeps the heat even and stops the mixture burning on the bottom of the pan. After 10 minutes, take the pan off the heat and let the batter stand for 30 minutes; an hour wouldn't matter.

- Stir in the almond meal and chopped almonds, followed by the beaten eggs, and when it's all combined – though frankly I could eat the batter just like this – pour it into the prepared pan and even out the top with a spatula, then bake for 1½–1¾ hours. The sides will be coming away from the pan, and the cake, while squidgy, should leave only a slight stickiness (rather than any actual batter) on a cake tester.

- Remove to a wire rack, brush with about 3 tablespoons of marmalade, and let the cake cool in its pan (if your marmalade is firm, you may need to warm it a bit first to make it brushable – 20–30 seconds in the microwave, or warmed through in a small saucepan should do). Leave for a day before eating. I like to brush a little more bitter marmalade on top again, before slicing and serving. Obviously, you must feel free to decorate further and more seasonally if you wish.

MAKE AHEAD NOTE	STORE NOTE
The cake can be made 1 week ahead. Wrap the cooled cake in a double layer of parchment paper and a layer of aluminum foil. Store in an airtight container in a cool place.	Once cut, store the cake – still wrapped in parchment paper and foil – in an airtight container for up to 1 month.

Gluten-free apple and blackberry pie

Generally, my way of tackling gluten-free baking is simply to exclude flour altogether – as various recipes both here and on my website testify – because, unless you are a celiac or are cooking for a celiac, I don't really see the point of trying to come up with substitutes, which all too often are lesser choices rather than equal alternatives. However, I was cooking for a late-diagnosed celiac, and one who felt sorely deprived of pie, and clearly this was a sad state of affairs that I couldn't let stand. After an amount of research, I found my pie pastry in *The How Can It Be Gluten Free Cookbook*, published by the estimable America's Test Kitchen. I did have to quash my qualms about xanthan gum (which, despite its name, is a powder) and I'm glad I did: this pastry is indeed no lesser choice – you'd have to tell people it was gluten-free in order for them to realize – and is a public service on behalf of pie-deprived celiacs everywhere.

I love the look of a pie baked in one of those old-fashioned looking cast iron skillets – and I wouldn't want to cook without them generally – but you can just as easily use a pie dish, though go for a metal rather than ceramic one. Although this recipe makes enough dough to line and cover a 9-inch pan or dish, I am faced with the choice, in my kitchen, between an 8-inch or 10-inch diameter pan, so I use the former.

Should you want to make this dairy-free, then use 1 cup of coconut oil (when solid) as butter, replace the sour cream with soy or coconut yogurt, and put the pan or dish, once lined with pastry dough, in the refrigerator for 5 minutes before adding the fruit.

FOR THE FRUIT FILLING:

1 tablespoon unsalted butter

4 cups Granny Smith apples, peeled, cored, and sliced or chopped

2 tablespoons sugar

½ teaspoon ground cinnamon

2 cups blackberries

¹⁄₈ teaspoon xanthan gum

FOR THE PIE DOUGH:

1 stick plus 5 tablespoons (13 tablespoons) cold unsalted butter

¹⁄₃ cup ice-cold water

3 tablespoons sour cream

1 tablespoon rice vinegar

2¼ cups plus 2 tablespoons gluten-free all-purpose flour

1 tablespoon sugar

1 teaspoon salt

½ teaspoon xanthan gum

TO BAKE:

1 egg white, lightly whisked (till just frothy)

½ teaspoon sugar

1 x 8- or 10-inch pie dish or cast iron skillet

○ Start with the filling. Melt the butter in a wide, heavy-based saucepan, then add the sliced or chopped apples, sugar, and cinnamon, turning everything about in the pan, and cooking for about 3 minutes or until the apples soften and make a caramelly liquid in the bottom of the pan. Add the blackberries, stir gently, then take off the heat, mix in the xanthan gum, and leave to cool.

○ Now for the pie dough. Cut the cold butter into ¹⁄₈-inch cubes and place on a plate in the freezer for 15 minutes while you get on with the rest of the ingredients.

○ Mix the water, sour cream, and rice vinegar together in a small pitcher or bowl.

○ Tip the gluten-free flour, sugar, salt, and xanthan gum into a food processor and blitz quickly to combine.

○ When the butter's had its 15 minutes of fame in the freezer, add it to the flour mixture in the processor and give about 10 pulses, until the butter is the size of large peas.

○ Pour in half the sour cream mixture and pulse till incorporated. About 3–5 pulses should do it: the mixture will be crumbly and quite fine.

○ Pour in the remaining sour cream mixture and process until the dough just begins to come together, clumping around the blades.

○ Tip out the dough and form into 2 equal-sized balls, then flatten each into discs, wrap in plastic wrap, and put in the refrigerator for 40 minutes to rest. Preheat the oven to 400°F, and slip in a baking sheet to heat up at the same time.

- When the discs of dough have had their time to rest in the refrigerator, take 1 of the discs and roll out between 2 pieces of parchment paper. It is important not to add any flour to the dough during the rolling process.

- Roll out the dough so that it is big enough to line the bottom and sides of your dish or pan, with about 1½ inches of overhang. Take off the top layer of parchment paper, then turn the dough upside down over your dish and carefully peel off the remaining paper.

- Ease the dough into your dish, pressing it into the sides. Take out the remaining disc of dough and roll out in the same way. Then tip the apple and blackberry mixture into the pie crust and dampen the lip of the crust with a little of the frothy egg white. Peel away the top layer of paper off the top crust and flip it over the top of the filled pie, discarding the last remaining layer of paper.

- Cut around the overhang of pie dough with a knife and then seal the edge by either crimping or pressing it down with the tines of a fork. Cut a few slits in the center of the pie for steam to escape, then paint the top with the egg white and sprinkle with the sugar.

- Bake for 30–40 minutes, or until the crust is cooked and golden. Remove from the oven and let the pie sit for 15–30 minutes before slicing.

MAKE AHEAD NOTE	STORE NOTE	FREEZE NOTE
Pie dough can be made 2 days ahead. Wrap in plastic wrap and store in refrigerator, and let it stand at room temperature for 20–30 minutes before rolling. Very chilled dough may need to stand for 30 minutes at room temperature before rolling.	Store in refrigerator in an airtight container or loosely covered with plastic wrap or foil for up to 5 days.	Pie dough can be frozen: wrap discs of dough tightly in plastic wrap and put in a resealable bag or wrap in aluminum foil. Freeze for up to 3 months and thaw overnight in refrigerator.
Filling can be made 1 day ahead. Once cool, transfer to an airtight container or covered bowl and store in refrigerator until needed.	Best reheated before serving. Reheat portions in an oven preheated to 300°F for 20–30 minutes.	Freeze leftover portions in airtight containers. Thaw overnight in refrigerator and reheat as in Store Note.
Pie can be assembled 3–4 hours ahead of baking, but brush with egg white just before baking. The pie will keep warm for up to 1 hour after baking if left in a warm place.		

Bitter orange tart

Since my Seville Orange Tart in *How To Eat*, I've never stopped feeling the urgent need to use Seville oranges for their short season between December and February (as you will see elsewhere in this book), but that bitter orange taste is too good to forsake during the long months that Seville oranges are not about. Then I simply try to recreate their floral sharpness by using regular orange and lime juices in something approximating a 2:1 ratio. And although I am not someone who uses the freezer as one great, efficiently stacked culinary filing cabinet, I do try and make little packages of the zest and juice of 4 Seville oranges just for this; then when I run out, I use the eating orange and lime combo.

This is more than a simplified revision of the *How To Eat* recipe: it uses a crushed gingersnap-and-butter base in place of home-made pie dough, and is even more acerbically – and excitingly – sharp than its predecessor. I love its cheek-squeaky, sherbetty bitterness, but I serve a small pot of good honey alongside, and urge everyone (to the point of irritation) to drizzle some over as they eat.

I have to say, that when Seville oranges *are* in season, this tart looks like a disc of winter sunshine on the plate – and tastes like it, too. I love it particularly after the Asian-Flavored Short Ribs or Italian Veal Shank Stew (**pp.179** and **185**), but don't want to restrict its application in any way. I must also add that the curd is just as fabulous spread over toasted crumpets or on a sliced pullman loaf.

FOR THE BASE:

9 ounces gingersnaps (approx. 2¼ cups crumbs)

5 tablespoons soft unsalted butter

FOR THE CURD FILLING:

3 extra large eggs

2 egg yolks

½ cup superfine sugar

zest and juice of 4 Seville oranges (scant 1 cup

juice) or use ¼ cup lime juice (from 2–3 limes) and ½ cup plus 1 tablespoon orange juice (from 1 large or 2 medium oranges)

1¼ sticks (10 tablespoons) soft unsalted butter, cut into ½-inch cubes

TO SERVE:

good honey

1 x 10-inch loose-bottomed, shallow tart pan (approx. 2 inches deep)

- Blitz the gingersnaps in a food processor until they are crumbs, then add the butter and process again, patiently waiting until it begins to clump and look like damp, dark sand. If you don't have a food processor, put the gingersnaps in a resealable plastic bag, and bash with a rolling pin or similar heavy implement, even if it has to be one with less comedy value. Melt the butter, and transfer the crumbs to a bowl. Mix in the melted butter until the crumbs are evenly coated.

- Tip into your tart pan, and carefully spread the cookie base all around the pan and up the sides; you can do this with your hands or the back of a spoon.

- Put the pan in the refrigerator, to allow the cookie base to harden, for at least 1 hour – although it may take up to 2 hours if your refrigerator is stacked. I often find it easier to get the base done in advance, so it's coolly ready and waiting, in which case, I do it up to 2 days ahead.

- Once your base is set firm you can get on with your curd filling. In a heavy-based saucepan – off the heat – whisk together the eggs (both the whole eggs and the yolks) and sugar, making sure you incorporate them well.

- Add the zest (grate gently so you don't get the pith, too) and juice from the oranges along with the cubes of butter, then put the pan over a medium heat and cook, stirring constantly; I use a small flat whisk for this.

- This thickening process will take about 5–7 minutes, but do take it off the heat regularly during this time, while you carry on whisking, to prevent it from getting too hot. Once the curd has thickened, take it off the heat, keep whisking for about 30 seconds, and carry on doing so as you pour it straight into a pitcher (it makes about 2¼ cups). Then place a piece of dampened parchment paper on top of the filling (this will stop it forming a skin), and let it cool in the refrigerator for about 30 minutes.

- Once the filling has cooled, but not set solid, pour and scrape it into your crumb-lined pan and spread it out evenly.

- Let the tart set further in the refrigerator for at least 4 hours (or overnight), and up to 2 days, before unmolding. This is best done while it is still cold – so don't take it out of the refrigerator for more than 5–10 minutes before you want to cut it. Then serve in slices, with a little pot of honey for people to drizzle over as they wish.

MAKE AHEAD NOTE	STORE NOTE
Base can be made 2–3 days in advance and stored in refrigerator until needed, covered loosely with plastic wrap. Once firm, the base (in its pan) can also be wrapped tightly in a double layer of plastic wrap and a layer of aluminum foil and frozen for up to 1 month. Thaw in refrigerator for 2–3 hours before filling. Curd can be made 2 days ahead. Fill the tart and refrigerate for about 4 hours, until the curd has become firmer, then tent loosely with foil, trying not to touch the surface of the tart.	Leftovers can be stored in refrigerator for 2 days. The tart base will soften gradually as the tart stands.

Salted chocolate tart

I have always avoided making chocolate tarts, not out of laziness (I love a bit of pastry-making, in the right mood), but because I have never really felt that the crust served the chocolate, or was worth the effort here. This is my simple solution: make a base out of chocolate cookies. And the filling is just as easy to make, too. Not that you'd know from the taste. I never lie about how effortless something is to make, but no one will believe me on this one. I think the hit of salt is crucial: it subtly counters the richness of all the chocolate, so even if you don't normally go in for the sweet-salt combo, don't be tempted to leave it out. Halve the amount of salt, if you must. I am having a bit of a smoked salt moment (see the Smoky Salted Caramel Sauce on **p.342**) and urge you to try the flakes in general and, in particular, here.

CUTS INTO 14 SLICES

FOR THE BASE:

28 Oreo cookies

2 ounces bittersweet chocolate (preferably min. 70% cocoa solids)

3 tablespoons soft unsalted butter

½ teaspoon smoked sea salt flakes (see Intro)

1 x 10-inch deep-sided (approx. 2 inches deep), loose-bottomed tart pan

○ Snap the cookies into pieces and drop them into the bowl of a food processor. Do likewise with the chocolate, then blitz them together until you have crumbs. Add the butter and salt, and blitz again until the mixture starts to clump together. If you're doing this by hand, bash the cookies in a resealable bag until they form crumbs, finely chop the chocolate, and melt the butter, then mix everything, along with the salt, in a large bowl with a wooden spoon or your hands encased in disposable vinyl gloves.

○ Press into your tart pan and pat down on the bottom and up the sides of the pan with your hands or the back of a spoon, so that the base and sides are evenly lined and smooth. Put into the refrigerator to chill and harden for at least 1 hour, or 2 hours if your refrigerator is stacked. I wouldn't keep it for longer than a day like this as the Oreo crust tends to get too crumbly.

FOR THE FILLING:

4 ounces bittersweet chocolate (preferably min. 70% cocoa solids)

3 tablespoons cornstarch

¼ cup whole milk

2 cups heavy cream

7 tablespoons unsweetened cocoa powder, sifted

2 teaspoons instant espresso powder or strong instant coffee powder

⅓ cup sugar

1 teaspoon vanilla paste or extract

2 teaspoons extra-virgin olive oil

¾ teaspoon smoked sea salt flakes

○ Finely chop the chocolate. Put the cornstarch into a cup and whisk in the milk until smooth.

○ Pour the cream into a heavy-based saucepan into which all the ingredients can fit and be stirred without splashing out of the pan, then add the finely chopped rubble of chocolate, the sifted cocoa (or just sift it straight in), espresso or instant coffee powder, sugar, vanilla paste or extract, olive oil, and smoked salt. Place over a medium to low heat and whisk gently – I use a very small whisk for this, as I'm not aiming to get air in the mixture, I'm just trying to banish any lumpiness – as the cream heats and the chocolate starts melting.

○ Off the heat, whisk in the cornstarch and milk mixture until it, too, is smoothly incorporated, and put the pan back on a low heat. With a wooden spoon, keep stirring until the mixture thickens, which it will do around the 10-minute mark, but be prepared for it to take a few minutes more or less. Take the pan off the heat every so often, still stirring, so that everything melds together, without the cream coming to a boil. When ready, it should be thick enough to coat the back of a wooden spoon, and if you run your finger through it (across the back of the spoon) the line should stay.

○ Pour into a large measuring cup (it should come to about the 2½-cup mark). Now run a piece of parchment paper under the cold tap, wring it out, and place the damp, crumpled piece right on top of the chocolate mixture, then put the measuring cup into the refrigerator for 15 minutes. The mixture will still be warm, but will be the right temperature to ooze into the base without melting it.

○ Pour and scrape the mixture into the cookie-lined tart pan and put back in the refrigerator overnight. Don't leave it longer than 24 hours, as the base will start to soften.

○ Take out of the refrigerator for 10 minutes before serving, but unmold straightaway. Sit the tart pan on top of a large can or jar and let the ring part fall away, then transfer the dramatically revealed tart to a plate or board. Leave the pan base on.

○ Slice modestly – this is rich and sweet, and people can always come back for more – and serve with crème fraîche; the sharpness is just right here. Leftovers will keep in the refrigerator for 4–5 days, but the base will soften and the sides crumble a bit. That will not detract from your eating pleasure too much, but I still like to give it its first outing at optimal stage!

MAKE AHEAD NOTE	STORE NOTE
Base can be made 1 day ahead. When firm, cover and keep refrigerated until needed. Tart/filling can be made 1 day ahead. Fill tart and refrigerate overnight, until set. Tent with aluminum foil, trying not to touch the surface of the tart.	Store the tart in refrigerator until needed. Leftovers will keep in refrigerator for 4–5 days. The base will soften gradually as the tart stands.

Honey pie

As anyone who follows me on Instagram (I'm @nigellalawson for anyone asking) knows, I have something of an obsession with The Four & Twenty Blackbirds Pie Shop in Brooklyn and nothing but gratitude for their mission to share the pie-love. It all started with their Salty Honey Pie, and this is my version of it. Nothing much is different – why mess with perfection? – but mine does have an easier-to-make pie crust, a dough for those with (apologies to Mel Brooks) Pie Anxiety. I've fiddled with the balance of ingredients in the filling – this latter point is hardly worth mentioning, but I feel any deviation from a recipe should be openly made. And, by the way, you shouldn't have to limit yourself to just one of their pies: luckily, *The Four & Twenty Blackbirds Pie Book* exists to put that right. I find the saltiness here tempers the rich, honeyed sweetness, but if you prefer to embrace its intensity head on, reduce the salt in the filling to 1 teaspoon. But in either case, it's essential you use sea salt flakes, not pouring salt.

Pie-pedants will insist it is, in fact, a tart, since it doesn't have a top crust, but this is an American recipe, and if pastry is involved in America, it's a pie. OK? Anyway, why would you not want to glory in the chance to make something called Honey Pie?

Now, you know that I am not one for mean portions. So believe me when I say you must cut this into modest slices. Partly because it is very intense, and partly because it is just too annoying if people don't finish, and you could have had some slices left for when they've gone.

CUTS INTO 14 SLICES

FOR THE PIE DOUGH:

1½ cups all-purpose flour

½ teaspoon fine sea salt

½ cup light and mild olive oil

¼ cup whole milk

FOR THE PIE FILLING:

7 tablespoons soft unsalted butter

¾ cup sugar

1 tablespoon fine polenta (not instant) or cornmeal

2 teaspoons sea salt flakes

1 teaspoon vanilla paste or extract

¾ cup good honey

3 extra large eggs

2/3 cup heavy cream

2 teaspoons apple cider vinegar

TO SPRINKLE ON TOP:

¼ teaspoon sea salt flakes

1 x 10-inch deep-sided (approx. 2 inches deep), loose-bottomed tart pan

- First, mix the flour, salt, oil, and milk to form a rough, slightly damp, dough. You can do this by hand or at low speed in a freestanding mixer.

- Tip out into your tart pan, and press patiently over the base and a little up the sides of the pan. I find a mixture of fingers, knuckles, and the back of a spoon the easiest way to go. Put into the freezer for at least 1 hour. I tend to do this the day before, but in any event, you bake from frozen.

- Preheat the oven to 350°F and put in a baking sheet at the same time.

- Melt the butter in a medium saucepan. Take it off the heat and leave to stand for 5 minutes, then beat in the sugar, polenta or cornmeal, 2 teaspoons of sea salt flakes, and the vanilla paste or extract.

- When all the above ingredients are incorporated, stir in the honey – oiling the measuring cup you're using first – and beat in the eggs, followed by the cream and vinegar.

- Take the dough-lined tart pan out of the freezer and pour the honey mixture into the crust, then place on the baking sheet in the oven to bake for 45–50 minutes, turning it around after 30, at which time it will still seem very uncooked. When it's ready, it will be a burnished bronze on top, puffy at the edges, and set in a soft jelled way in the middle (and it carries on setting as it cools).

- Remove to a wire rack, sprinkle with the ¼ teaspoonful of sea salt flakes, and leave to cool – this will take about 2 hours. I like this best when properly cold.

- To unmold easily, sit the tart pan on top of a large jar or can and let the ring part fall away, then transfer the liberated pie to a plate or board. I manage to get the pie off the pan base easily, but if you feel safer leaving the metal base on, then do. Slice modestly – this is rich and sweet, and you will want leftovers for yourself – and serve with whipped cream or crème fraîche.

MAKE AHEAD NOTE	STORE NOTE
The crust can be made up to 1 month ahead. Once frozen, wrap the crust (in its pan) in a double layer of plastic wrap and a layer of aluminum foil. Bake directly from frozen.	Leftovers should be refrigerated as quickly as possible. Store in refrigerator, loosely covered with plastic wrap, for up to 3 days.

Lemon pavlova

Ever since my first pav in *How To Eat*, I have been something of a pavaholic. For me, acidity is key. I never understood why anyone would pile sweet fruit on top of something that is essentially – and dreamily – a cross between a marshmallow and a meringue. So naturally, a lemon pavlova made perfect sense. I had the idea – yes, really – from the actor Michael Sheen. This didn't come in the form of a personal tip, I should admit. I saw him create a great pile of lemony pavs on the British TV show *The Great Comic Relief Bake Off*, and it inspired me. *Diolch* Michael (if I may). (And that's "Thank You" in Welsh by the way.)

You will note there are a lot of sliced almonds required: that is because they are the topping of the pav and not mere decoration; the crunch they offer is essential.

I make this with a jar of store-bought lemon curd, but obviously I wouldn't stop you from making your own. Should you want, proceed as follows: whisk together 2 extra large eggs, the yolks from 2 more extra large eggs, and ¾ cup superfine sugar in a heavy-based saucepan (off the heat). Add the finely grated zest and juice of 2 unwaxed lemons and 7 tablespoons soft unsalted butter, cut into ½-inch cubes or teaspooned out into similar-sized blobs, and put the pan over a medium heat, stirring constantly with a little flat whisk, until thickened. This will take around 5–7 minutes, but keep taking it off the heat – stirring or whisking all the while – at regular intervals during this time. When thickened, pour and scrape into a cold bowl and let it cool, stirring occasionally.

I am childishly excited about this pavlova: a reminder that good ideas come unbidden, much as happiness does.

SERVES 8–12

6 egg whites (feel free to use unseasoned egg whites from a carton, if wished)	½ cup sliced almonds
1¾ cups plus 1 tablespoon superfine sugar	1¼ cups heavy cream
2½ teaspoons cornstarch	1⅓ cups jar lemon curd (see Intro)
2 unwaxed lemons	

- Preheat the oven to 350°F and line a baking sheet with parchment paper.

- Beat the egg whites until satiny peaks form, then beat in the sugar a spoonful at a time until the meringue is stiff and shiny.

- Sprinkle the cornstarch over the meringue, then grate in the zest – a fine microplane is best for this – of 1 lemon and add 2 teaspoons of lemon juice.

- Gently fold until everything is thoroughly mixed in. Mound onto the lined baking sheet in a fat circle approximately 10 inches in diameter, smoothing the sides and the top with a knife or spatula.

- Place in the oven, then immediately turn the temperature down to 300°F, and cook for 1 hour.

- Remove from the oven and leave to cool, but don't leave it anywhere cold as this will make it crack too quickly. If you think your kitchen is too cool, then leave the pavlova inside the oven with the door completely open. When you're ready to eat, turn the pavlova onto a large flat plate or board with the underside uppermost – I do this before I sit down to the meal in question and let it stand till dessert time. This is so the tender marshmallow belly of the pav melds with the soft topping.

- Toast the sliced almonds, by frying them in a dry pan over a medium to high heat until they have started to color. Shake the pan at regular intervals and don't let them burn. This doesn't take more than a minute or so. When they're done, remove to a cold plate so that they don't carry on cooking.

- Whip the cream until thick and airy but still with a soft voluptuousness about it, and set it aside for a moment.

- Put the lemon curd into a bowl and beat it with a wooden spoon or spatula to loosen it a little. Taste the lemon curd (if it's store-bought) and add some lemon zest and a spritz of juice if it's too sweet.

- With a light hand, a glad heart, and a spatula, spread the lemon curd on top of the meringue base. Now top with the whipped cream, peaking it rather as if it were a meringue topping. Sprinkle with the zest of the remaining lemon – you can grate this finely or coarsely as you wish – followed by the sliced almonds, and serve triumphantly.

MAKE AHEAD NOTE	STORE NOTE
Meringue base can be made 1 day ahead. Store in an airtight container until needed.	Leftovers can be stored in refrigerator, loosely covered with plastic wrap, for up to 1 day.
Curd can be made up to 3 days ahead. Cover and store in refrigerator until needed. Stir before using.	
Almonds can be toasted a week ahead. When cold, store in an airtight container at room temperature until needed.	
Assemble the pavlova about 1 hour ahead of serving.	

Old Rag Pie

Old Rag Pie is not the most glamorous name for something which, while being incredibly simple to make, will have you, and anyone who eats it, in raptures. The name is the English translation for the Greek *Patsavoropita*, created by bakeries as a way of using up old scraps of phyllo dough: the "old rags" indicated by the title. They'd just go along their counters, collect up all the bits, and turn them into this pie. For this reason, you don't need to worry about keeping your phyllo covered as you go, as is normally advised. It doesn't matter if it dries out a little as you make it, indeed this can even be desirable.

In Greece, there are two variants, one sweet, one savory, but this version is the brainchild of my friend Alex Andreou (a bona fide – if it's not too rude to go into Latin here – Greek from Mykonos, and the source of other recipes here, too) which merges the two, adding honey to salty feta, to create what I can best describe (in taste terms) as a Greek cheesecake.

I have made this with a variety of phyllo pastries, and I have found that some fresh doughs are too damp and too heavily sprinkled with flour to do the job well. However, frozen phyllo doesn't seem to suffer from the same problems, which is why I stipulate this, below. (The other benefit of using frozen phyllo is that – given that feta has such a long shelf life – you can keep all the ingredients to make this in your freezer, refrigerator, and pantry without an extra visit to the stores.) However, should you be lucky enough to have access to good-quality, authentic phyllo, then please use fresh. And if you plan to freeze the pie before baking it, then you will definitely have to start with fresh, not frozen phyllo for sure. Since the packages of frozen phyllo that I buy come in 10-ounce size, that is what I have used, but another 3–4 ounces or so wouldn't go amiss. So, if you can buy this in bigger packages, or are buying fresh by weight, go ahead, but don't break open a second package for it.

I'm afraid this Patsavoropita does make for an annoyingly difficult pan washing later, but when you eat this, you'll know it's worth it. Tip: use bio washing powder for clothes, or a dishwasher powder, rather than dishwashing liquid when you soak. Or you could eliminate the problem by using a good non-stick pan, which has entered my life rather late in the day. But in which case it's better to slip the pie out whole (it should be easy) and cut it on a wooden board instead.

7 tablespoons soft unsalted butter

10 ounces frozen phyllo dough, thawed (approx. 14 sheets)

8 ounces feta cheese (approx. 2 cups crumbled)

2 teaspoons grated Parmesan

2 teaspoons fresh thyme leaves or 1 teaspoon dried

2 extra large eggs

²⁄₃ cup whole milk

1 tablespoon sesame seeds

1 jar good honey (such as Greek thyme honey or orange blossom honey)

1 x 8-inch non-stick cake pan

○ Melt the butter in a small saucepan, then take it off the heat.

○ Line your cake pan with a layer of phyllo, making sure it comes up the sides; you will need to use more than one sheet. Then pour 1 tablespoon of melted butter over the pastry.

○ Using one third of the remaining phyllo sheets, tear and scrunch the sheets up and drop them loosely in the pan. Then crumble in half the feta, sprinkle with 1 teaspoon of Parmesan and just under ½ teaspoon of thyme leaves (or ¼ teaspoon of dried thyme), and pour a third of the remaining melted butter over the top.

○ Repeat, so that you use up all but a little of the butter and a small amount of thyme. For the last layer, you can use larger pieces of phyllo "rags" (as it's the top crust), filling the pan a little more tightly, but still scrunching them.

○ Fold the edges of overhanging phyllo over themselves, and pour the remaining butter on top. Using the sharp point of a knife, make 2 cuts down and 2 cuts across into the phyllo-packed pan, from edge to edge to create 9 sections. It's important that you don't use a blunt knife, as you don't want to drag the phyllo or press down on it.

○ Beat the eggs with the milk, then pour over the contents of the pan. Sprinkle the last bit of thyme along with the sesame seeds on top. Let it stand for at least 30 minutes in a cool place before baking. If 2 hours is easier for your timetable, then put it in the refrigerator. And you can do this in advance (see Make Ahead Note, right).

○ Heat the oven to 400°F, and bake the pie for 30 minutes. When it's ready, the phyllo will be golden and puffed up, and the inside set.

○ Let it stand for 10 minutes, then spoon 1 tablespoon of the honey over the top.

○ Cut into slices or slabs – using a serrated bread knife and sawing action to prevent squishing the phyllo on top too much, then pushing the knife down to cut through. Serve the pie directly from the pan and put the jar of honey, with a spoon in it (or you can pour it into a pitcher) on the table for people to add extra as they eat.

MAKE AHEAD NOTE	STORE NOTE	FREEZE NOTE
The pie can be made 1 day in advance and kept in refrigerator. Pie can also be frozen at this stage, in which case cook from frozen, as in Freeze Note.	The pie is best on the day it is made, but leftovers can be stored in refrigerator, on a plate covered with plastic wrap or in an airtight container, for up to 2 days. Slices can be reheated in an oven preheated to 300°F for 15–30 minutes, until piping hot. Cool for 5 minutes before serving (this will crisp up the phyllo again).	Wrap pan tightly in a double layer of plastic wrap and a layer of aluminum foil. Freeze for up to 1 month. To cook from frozen, unwrap the pan and put into a cold oven, then turn the oven on to 400°F and bake for 45–55 minutes. If the top browns too much (check at about 40 minutes), cover with aluminum foil. Make sure the pie is piping hot in the center before removing from oven. Leftovers can also be frozen, tightly wrapped in a double layer of plastic wrap and then put into a resealable bag or wrapped in aluminum foil, for up to 1 month. Thaw overnight in refrigerator and reheat as in Store Note.

Chocolate chip cookie dough pots

My children love a chocolate chip cookie so gooey on the inside that I can't really make the outside firm enough to let the cookies keep integrity of form. This, then, is the solution: a cookie dough you bake in a little dish, and then eat with a spoon, dolloped with ice cream or crème fraîche as desired. The recipe itself I've adapted from one I found on a favorite website, thekitchn.com, and very grateful I am, too.

If you don't own any ramekins, or similar, know that you could just use a pie dish; I used one that measures 8 inches in diameter at the base and 10 inches in diameter at the lip, and it needed 5 minutes' longer cooking time. But the ramekins give you a better goo-to-crust ratio, and that's what these are all about.

I know I blamed my children for them (what else are children for?), but don't think of these just as junior fare: any time you're having friends over for supper and don't know what to make for dessert, this is the answer.

SERVES 6

1 cup all-purpose flour

½ teaspoon fine sea salt

½ teaspoon baking soda

1 stick (8 tablespoons) soft unsalted butter

⅓ cup plus 1 tablespoon light brown sugar

1 teaspoon vanilla paste or extract

1 extra large egg

¾ cup small bittersweet chocolate chips

6 x ramekins approx. 3½ inches in diameter x 1¾ inches deep (approx. ¾–1 cup capacity)

- Preheat the oven to 350°F, and measure the flour, salt, and baking soda into a bowl, forking together to mix.

- With an electric mixer, or by hand, beat the butter and sugar until you have a light and creamy mixture, then add the vanilla paste or extract and the egg, beating again to incorporate.

- Gently fold in the flour mixture, then, once it's all mixed in, fold in the chocolate chips.

- Divide the dough between 6 ramekins (you will need about 4½ tablespoons of batter for each one). Using a small offset spatula (for ease) or the back of a teaspoon, spread the mixture to cover the bottom of the ramekins, and smooth the tops.

- Place the ramekins on a baking sheet and bake in the oven for 13–15 minutes. They will still be quite gooey inside, but the top will be set, and they should be golden brown at the edges and just beginning to come away from the sides of the ramekins.

- Leave to cool for 5–10 minutes before serving. You can spoon a scoop of ice cream on top of each one or serve with cream or crème fraîche on the side. They will set as they cool down, so don't dally now.

MAKE AHEAD NOTE	FREEZE NOTE
These can be made up to 6 hours ahead, then covered with plastic wrap and stored in refrigerator. Allow to come up to room temperature before baking.	Wrap each ramekin tightly in a double layer of plastic wrap and put in resealable bags or wrap each in a layer of aluminum foil. Freeze for up to 3 months. Bake directly from frozen, adding an extra 2 minutes to the baking time.

Nutella brownies

When I made these the first time, I put them on the table after supper and I have never seen a plateful of anything go down so fast. Naturally, I have been making them a lot ever since. As the ingredients – yes, all of them – are among my kitchen basics, I know I always have the wherewithal to make these, unplanned. Having said that, this is one of those recipes that is actually better the following day, not that it's likely you'll get a chance to find out.

MAKES 16 SQUARES

4 extra large eggs

pinch fine sea salt

1 cup Nutella

½ teaspoon confectioners' sugar

1 x 8-inch square cake pan

- Preheat your oven to 350°F. Line the base and sides of your cake pan with parchment paper.

- Break the eggs into a mixing bowl, then add the salt and beat, using a freestanding mixer with the whisk attachment or electric handheld whisk, until they have more than doubled in size and are pale, aerated, and mousselike; this will take about 5 minutes.

- Measure the Nutella into a microwave-safe measuring cup, filling it up to the 1 cup mark, and microwave for 1 minute on full power (750w). Or you can soften it in a heatproof bowl over (but not in) a saucepan of simmering water for 3–4 minutes, stirring occasionally, until warm and slightly runny.

- Stir the heated Nutella, then pour it in a continuous thin stream onto the eggs, whisking as you go, until all the Nutella is combined. This will knock the volume out of the eggs quite a bit, but don't worry about it.

- Pour this mixture into your prepared cake pan and bake for 17–20 minutes, by which time the top will be dry, and the middle tender but set in a slightly jelled fashion.

- Leave to cool completely in the pan; the mixture will shrink away from the sides a little as it does. Once cool, cut it into 16 squares, arrange them on a plate, and dust with a little confectioners' sugar pressed through a fine tea strainer.

STORE NOTE	FREEZE NOTE
Store in an airtight container in a cool place for up to 5 days or in refrigerator for up to 1 week. In hot weather, store in refrigerator.	Stack the squares in an airtight container with parchment paper in between the layers. Freeze for up to 3 months. To thaw, put squares on a wire rack and leave at room temperature for about 1 hour, or thaw overnight in refrigerator.

Flourless peanut butter chocolate chip cookies

I can't seem to stop making these, and as I make them, so they get eaten. Luckily, they are extraordinarily easy to throw together. And, incidentally, they are gluten- and dairy-free. Do check the ingredients list on the peanut butter if you do absolutely need this to be gluten-free (were you to be baking them for a celiac, for example) as brands vary. I'm afraid health-food-store-type natural peanut butter (the sort I like on my toast) doesn't work here.

These do soften if left overnight – though there are those who actively prefer them this way – and are crisper when freshly cooked, though they will be fine from any other point of view in an airtight container for up to a week. Good luck with that.

¾ cup plus 1 tablespoon creamy peanut butter, such as Skippy

½ cup light brown sugar

½ teaspoon baking soda

pinch fine sea salt

1 extra large egg

1 teaspoon vanilla paste or extract

¼ cup small bittersweet chocolate chips (if necessary check they are free from gluten and dairy)

- Preheat the oven to 350°F.

- In a bowl, beat together the peanut butter, brown sugar, baking soda, and salt.

- Beat in the egg and vanilla extract, but not too vigorously: just to mix them; gently does it.

- Stir or fold in the chocolate chips, then line 1 or 2 baking sheets with parchment paper.

- Scoop out heaped tablespoonfuls of the cookie dough onto the lined sheets, placing them about 2 inches apart, then bake for 10 minutes, until they're slightly darker around the edges. They will look undercooked but will be the perfect texture once cooled (if you can wait that long).

- At any rate, leave them on the baking sheets for 10 minutes, as they will be very fragile. Then transfer gently to a wire rack to cool. This takes another 10 minutes; I tend to cave in after 5.

MAKE AHEAD NOTE	STORE NOTE	FREEZE NOTE
Form the dough into mounds and freeze on a baking sheet lined with parchment paper. Once solid, transfer to a resealable bag and freeze for up to 3 months. Bake directly from frozen, adding 1 minute to the baking time.	Store in an airtight container at cool room temperature for up to 1 week.	Put baked cookies in a resealable bag, or stack in an airtight container with parchment paper between the layers. Freeze for up to 3 months. Thaw on a wire rack for about 1 hour.

Triple chocolate buckwheat cookies

For those of you not yet familiar with the term procrastibaking, this is a prime example of the genre, and while I have certainly pioneered the practice, the brilliant coinage is one Aya Reina's – I feel it deserves wider circulation, and many congratulations. I was in the middle of the photo shoot for this book when I first made these – I was putting off typing up some recipe changes (admin holds not the greatest lure for me) – and was suddenly gripped by an urgent need to make these cookies. (There's not a book of mine when I haven't taken a detour from my shoot list to go rogue and introduce a hitherto unplanned recipe.) The recipe itself is adapted from londonbakes.com, which in turn is an adaptation from the book *Chocolate Magic* by Kate Shirazi: this is the story of cooking.

I've fiddled with amounts a bit, only because I wanted a little less sugar and a lot more chocolate, but the star here is the buckwheat, not only because it makes these cookies gluten-free, but mainly because I feel it brings its own nutty flavor and unique texture, creating a cookie that has softness and a shortbread bite, as well as a subtle smokiness. Those who like a truly chewy cookie might find these a little cakey, but I like chewiness in a cookie and yet find constant excuses to make these. They are meltingly good, and entirely sui generis.

Buckwheat flour – rather more exotically *farine de sarrasin* in French – is in itself always gluten-free, but (as with oats) it is often contaminated by the presence of gluten, depending on the factories in which it is produced. So if you are making these because you need them to be gluten-free, rather than just going for the flavor of the flour, make sure the package is labeled as such before you start.

MAKES APPROX. 25 COOKIES

2/3 cup small bittersweet chocolate chips

5 ounces bittersweet chocolate (preferably min. 70% cocoa solids)

¾ cup plus 2 tablespoons buckwheat flour

3 tablespoons unsweetened cocoa powder

½ teaspoon baking soda

½ teaspoon fine sea salt

4 tablespoons soft unsalted butter

½ cup plus 2 tablespoons soft dark brown sugar

1 teaspoon vanilla paste or extract

2 extra large eggs, fridge-cold

○ Clatter the chocolate chips out into a flattish dish and put this in the refrigerator while you get on with making the batter. It wouldn't hurt to sit them in the freezer, either. I do this so that the chips don't melt too much while baking, leaving you with nuggets of intense chocolatiness.

○ Preheat the oven to 350°F and line a couple of baking sheets (or 1 if baking in 2 batches) with parchment paper.

○ Roughly chop the bittersweet chocolate, and melt it either in a suitable bowl in the microwave or over a saucepan of simmering water. Set aside to cool a little.

○ In another bowl, mix together the buckwheat flour, cocoa, baking soda, and salt, and fork to make sure everything's well combined.

○ In yet another bowl (I use my freestanding mixer here, but a bowl and a hand-held whisk or, indeed, wooden spoon and elbow grease would work, too), cream together the butter and sugar with the vanilla extract until a dark caramel color and fluffy, using a spatula to scrape down the sides of the bowl if necessary. Beat in the cooled, melted chocolate then the fridge-cold eggs (I find this means one doesn't then have to refrigerate the dough before baking) one by one, and when both are absorbed into the butter and sugar mixture, scrape down the sides of the bowl again, turn the speed down, and carefully beat in the dry ingredients.

○ Using a wooden spoon or a spatula, fold in the cold chocolate chips, then dollop heaping tablespoonsful of the dough onto a lined baking sheet, leaving about 2½ inches between each one. Put the bowl with the remaining cookie dough in the refrigerator while the first batch is underway.

○ Bake for 9–10 minutes, by which time the cookies will be just set at the edges, but otherwise seem undercooked, then remove the sheet from the oven and let the cookies sit on the warm tray for another 10 minutes before transferring them to a wire rack to cool.

○ When the sheet is cool, or you have another one lined and ready to go, take the bowl of dough out of the refrigerator and proceed as before.

MAKE AHEAD NOTE	STORE NOTE	FREEZE NOTE
The cookie dough can be made ahead, then covered and stored in refrigerator for up to 3 days. If the dough is too firm to scoop into tablespoons, let it stand at room temperature for 20 minutes.	Store in an airtight container in a cool place for up to 5 days.	Form the dough into mounds and freeze on a baking sheet lined with parchment paper. Once solid, transfer to a resealable bag and freeze for up to 3 months. Bake directly from frozen, adding 1 minute to the baking time. Baked cookies can also be frozen in resealable plastic bags for up to 3 months. Thaw on a wire rack at room temperature for about 1 hour.

Seed-studded Anzac cookies

Anzac cookies, purportedly sent to those serving in the Australian and New Zealand Army Corps during the First World War, significantly contained no ingredients that could spoil on the long voyage. Although I think it is important to remember Anzac Day in the proper fashion each 25 April (this was the date of the first Anzac landing at Gallipoli in 1915), I don't feel it is necessary to make the cookies as hard, dry, and durable as they needed to be then. So, I have taken liberties and added pumpkin seeds, sunflower seeds, and sesame seeds, which might not last a long-distance journey without refrigeration, but make for a much more beguilingly textured cookie. They are like less stodgy oat bars in cookie form.

Now, there are those who like their Anzac cookies crisp, and those – like me – who like them on the chewier side (I also like mine made with sprouted oats). To accommodate both tastes, I have baked those you see in the picture overleaf in 3 different ways. On the left, the crispest cookie, baked with regular oats, for 12 minutes; in the middle, cookies made with sprouted oats and baked for 12 minutes; and on the right, my cookies of choice, using sprouted oats and baked for 10 minutes. However, don't get hung up on the sprouted oat issue. A far more decisive factor is the baking time. Those with hotter ovens than me may find the range closer to 8–10 minutes than 10–12.

7 tablespoons soft unsalted butter	¾ cup shredded, unsweetened coconut
½ cup light brown sugar	1 cup sprouted or quick cooking oats (not instant)
2 tablespoons golden or light corn syrup	
½ teaspoon baking soda	3 tablespoons shelled pumpkin seeds
2 tablespoons hot water, from a recently boiled kettle	3 tablespoons sunflower seeds
	3 tablespoons sesame seeds
¾ cup plus 2 tablespoons all-purpose flour	

○ Preheat the oven to 350°F and line 2 large baking sheets with parchment paper (or use 1 if baking in batches).

○ In a decent-sized saucepan, big enough to hold all of the ingredients, melt the butter, sugar, and golden syrup together, then take off the heat.

○ In a bowl, dissolve the baking soda in the hot water, then add to the butter mixture in the saucepan.

○ Now add the remaining ingredients to the saucepan and combine well.

○ Scoop heaping tablespoons of the mixture onto the lined baking sheets, leaving about 1 inch between these dollops to allow room for the cookies to spread as they bake, then slightly flatten them with a spatula or the back of a spoon.

○ Bake for 8–10 minutes (or a little longer if you want them wholly crisp) until golden brown, swapping the baking sheets over and rotating them halfway through baking. When baked, the cookies will still feel slightly soft, but will harden to a desirable chewiness once cooled.

○ Remove from the oven and let the cookies stand on their sheets for 5 minutes, before using a wide cranked spatula to transfer them to a wire rack to cool.

STORE NOTE	FREEZE NOTE
Store in an airtight container at cool room temperature for up to 1 week. The crisper version of the cookies will soften slightly over time.	Put baked cookies into a resealable bag, or stack in an airtight container with parchment paper between the layers, and freeze for up to 3 months. Thaw individual cookies on a wire rack for about 1 hour before eating.

No-churn brandied pumpkin ice cream

I have made no-churn ice creams ever since *How To Eat*, but it's fair to say that the No-Churn Coffee Ice Cream in *Nigellissima* marked the beginning of my flirtation with condensed milk as a simplifying ingredient in lazy ice cream making. There are people too pure for this kind of dalliance but, while I respect them, I am not among them.

The genesis of this particular recipe is the Pumpkin Bundt Cake on **p.289** or, rather, the fact that having made it, I had a small amount of pumpkin purée left over. I paired it with half a can of condensed milk, added cream, fresh nutmeg, and a splosh or two of brandy and, *eccoci*, a gorgeously spiced and – strange though it sounds – warm-flavored ice cream. Eat it with its mothercake or the Cider and 5-Spice Bundt Cake on **p.293**, or be radical, and cast it in the role of brandy butter alongside your Christmas pudding. Those who celebrate Thanksgiving should need little encouragement to bring it out alongside a warm apple or, obviously, pumpkin pie, and it is a damn fine accompaniment to pecan pie, too.

MAKES APPROX. 1 QUART

½ cup pure pumpkin purée (from a can – use the leftover purée from the Pumpkin Bundt Cake on p.289)

½ x 14-ounce can (²/₃ cup) condensed milk

1¼ cups heavy cream

1 teaspoon freshly grated nutmeg

3 tablespoons brandy

2 x 1-pint (2 cup) empty ice cream containers or airtight containers (or 1 x 1-quart tub or airtight container)

- Combine the pumpkin purée and condensed milk in a bowl, and stir to mix.

- Whisk the cream in a bowl until it reaches soft peaks, then whisk in condensed milk mixture and continue whisking until thick again.

- Grate the nutmeg over the ice cream and whisk in the brandy as you pour it in a slow trickle.

- Decant into your airtight container or containers and freeze overnight. Take it out of the freezer for 10 minutes to soften before serving.

MAKE AHEAD NOTE	STORE NOTE
The ice cream can be made and frozen up to 1 week ahead.	Leftover ice cream should be returned to freezer as quickly as possible, and is best eaten within 1 month.

No-churn black currant ice cream with licorice ripple

As with the Licorice and Black Currant Chocolate Cake on **p.280**, this ice cream is inspired by my favorite hard candy. And in ice cream form, these flavors – the fresh sharpness of the currants gorgeously countered by the almost dizzyingly pungent hit of the licorice – are particularly compelling, as both are conveyed through the smooth, soothing, melting medium. This is not one for licorice-loathers, however. Especially given that I go for the uncompromising rasp of salty licorice syrup here and, indeed, anywhere I can find an excuse for it.

I keep an old 1 quart ice cream container (it measures 7 x 6 x 3 inches) for this, as you need a surface area not provided by the 1-pint cylindrical ice cream containers I normally prefer. Obviously, any similarly dimensioned airtight container would do.

Black currants are often fiendishly hard to come by, but you might be able to find them frozen. Usually I am reduced to picking them out of a package of frozen mixed berries by hand. If you can't get up to 1½ cups, use 1 cup black currants and increase the lemon juice to 3 tablespoons.

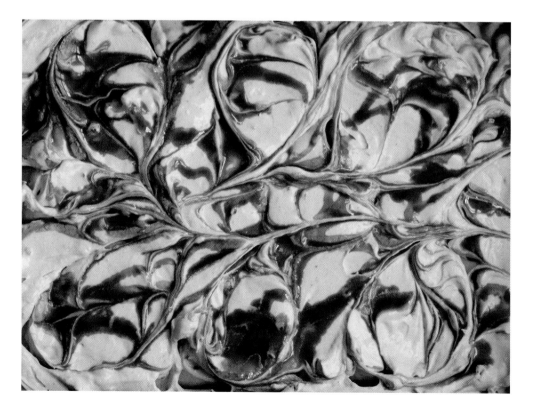

1½ cups frozen or fresh black currants

2 tablespoons lemon juice

½ x 14-ounce can (²/₃ cup) condensed milk

1¼ cups heavy cream

3 teaspoons salty licorice syrup

1 x 1-quart empty ice cream container (approx. 7 x 6 x 3 inches) or similar-sized airtight container

- Put the black currants into a small saucepan (do not thaw them, if using frozen) with the lemon juice, put on a lid, and cook over a medium heat for 5 minutes, by which time you should have a runny, deep-tinted liquid bobbled with berries. Pour into the bowl you're going to mix the ice cream in and use a fork to mash to a textured purée; it's good to have bits of sharp berries in the smooth ice cream later. Leave to cool.

- Stir the condensed milk into the cold currant purée. In a separate bowl whisk the cream to soft peaks, then whisk in the condensed milk mixture and continue whisking until thick. Pour half of this mixture into your container. Now dip a pointy teaspoon into the licorice syrup and drizzle it over the ice cream mix, either zigzagging or just in stripes across, refueling when your teaspoon's empty with a further ½ teaspoonful.

- Top with the remaining half of the ice cream mix, and do the same again with the licorice syrup. Now, get a skewer and squiggle through – making the sort of shapes in the ice cream you might make in the air were you holding a sparkler – so that the glossy licorice ripples through the pink cream and you end up with an edible example of Florentine marbling.

- Put on the lid and freeze overnight, until set. Take it out of the freezer 10–15 minutes before serving, to allow it to soften. And do I have to tell you to bring the jar of licorice syrup to the table to pour more over as you eat?

MAKE AHEAD NOTE	STORE NOTE
The ice cream can be made and frozen up to 1 week ahead.	Leftover ice cream should be returned to freezer as quickly as possible, and is best eaten within 1 month.

No-churn matcha ice cream

I love matcha ice cream, and this version gives me particular pleasure. Yes, it's ridiculously easy to make, which is gratifying, but more glorious — and important — is the perfect balance between the sophisticated bitterness of the matcha powder and the uncompromisingly childish sweetness of the condensed milk. You would never imagine such an uncouth ingredient could be a factor in the exquisite outcome here.

I first made this during the photo shoot for this book, as a spontaneously on-the-spot recipe, simply because I had the matcha still out on the counter from the making of the Matcha Cake (**p.295**) and I have to say it has emerged as one of my absolute favorite recipes.

Should you ever be making the Molten Chocolate Babycakes from *How To Be A Domestic Goddess*, I urge you to serve this alongside.

MAKES APPROX. 1 QUART

1 ¼ cups heavy cream

½ x 14-ounce can (²/₃ cup) condensed milk

2 tablespoons Izu Matcha green tea powder (see Intro to Matcha Cake on p.295)

2 x 1-pint empty ice cream or airtight containers (or 1 x 1-quart tub or airtight container)

° Whisk the cream to soft peaks, then whisk in the condensed milk.

° Then whisk in the green tea powder until you have a whipped green cream.

° Decant into your airtight container or containers and freeze overnight.

° Take the ice cream out of the freezer to soften for 10 minutes before serving.

MAKE AHEAD NOTE	STORE NOTE
The ice cream can be made and frozen up to 1 week ahead.	Leftover ice cream should be returned to freezer as quickly as possible, and is best eaten within 1 month.

No-churn white miso ice cream

This is a domino-effect leftover story. I had some pumpkin purée left from the bundt cake on **p.289**, so I made the Brandied Pumpkin Ice Cream (**p.334**). That left me with half a can of condensed milk open, so I made this. I am afraid this is how I operate. Still, I should also say, in my defense, I have always wanted to make a simple, no-churn version of a white miso ice cream, along these lines, ever since having the real thing at The Shiori, a tiny Kaiseki restaurant in London that I would much prefer to keep my secret, but won't.

The idea of a miso ice cream may sound strange, but think of salted caramel, only subtler and deeper at the same time. (And if it's actual salted caramel ice cream you want, see nigella.com for my No-Churn Salted Caramel Bourbon Ice Cream.) I like it with a skinny drizzle of salty licorice syrup over it, but perhaps a softer introduction would be to try it with a thick drip of golden syrup. But it's wonderful plain, with a wafer or in a cone, or dolloped alongside the Cider and 5-Spice Bundt Cake (**p.293**) while it's still warm, or the Gluten-Free Apple and Blackberry Pie on **p.302**.

MAKES APPROX. 1 QUART

7 tablespoons sweet white miso

½ x 14-ounce can (²⁄₃ cup) condensed milk

1¼ cups heavy cream

2 x 1-pint empty ice cream tubs or airtight containers (or 1 x 1-quart tub or airtight container)

○ Combine the miso paste and condensed milk in a bowl, and stir to mix and loosen. In a separate bowl whisk the cream to soft peaks, then whisk in the condensed milk mixture and continue whisking until thick.

○ Decant into your airtight container or containers and freeze overnight.

○ Take the ice cream out of the freezer to soften for 10 minutes before serving.

MAKE AHEAD NOTE	STORE NOTE
The ice cream can be made and frozen up to 1 week ahead.	Leftover ice cream should be returned to freezer as quickly as possible, and is best eaten within 1 month.

Smoky salted caramel sauce

I first made this sauce for *Stylist* magazine, as part of what became almost an entire issue (I was guest editor) given over to the allure of salted caramel. I have never stopped making it. I don't care if the hipster crowd feel that salted caramel is no longer cool and new. Food is either good or it isn't, and while fashion relies on quick-change, taste — if it is authentic, rather than faddish — endures.

I have made a small adjustment to my original recipe. I have since come across Maldon smoked sea salt flakes, and they take this to another level of delectability. But any good soft flaked sea salt will do. It is all about that unholy trinity of fat, sugar, salt. Look, I'm not asking you to live off it!

Tip: one Christmas, I turned this into a Salted Caramel Brandy Butter, by beating 2 tablespoons of this sauce (when cold) along with 2 tablespoons of brandy into 10 tablespoons soft, unsalted butter. It was a very good Christmas.

SERVES 6, AS A SAUCE FOR CAKE OR ICE CREAM

5 tablespoons unsalted butter	3 tablespoons golden or light corn syrup
¼ cup light brown sugar	½ cup heavy cream
¼ cup sugar	2 teaspoons smoked sea salt flakes, or to taste

° Melt the butter, sugars, and syrup in a small, heavy-based saucepan and let it simmer for 3 minutes, swirling the pan every now and then.

° Add the cream and the smoked salt and swirl again, then give it a stir with a wooden spoon, and taste. Go cautiously so that you don't burn your tongue, and see if you want to add more salt, before letting it cook for another minute, then pour into a pitcher to serve.

MAKE AHEAD NOTE	STORE NOTE	FREEZE NOTE
The sauce can be made ahead and stored in an airtight container in refrigerator for 1 week. Remove the sauce from refrigerator about 1 hour before serving, until it has come up to room temperature, or warm it very gently in a saucepan.	Leftover sauce should be refrigerated as quickly as possible and stored in an airtight container in refrigerator, where it will keep for up to 1 week from the day of making. Do not reheat the sauce more than once.	The sauce can also be frozen for up to 3 months. Thaw the sauce overnight in refrigerator before serving. Thawed sauce should be used within 1 week.

BEGINNINGS

I am not going to keep you long: no one wants to be engaged in vigorous conversation first thing in the morning. But this chapter has been a delight for me and has changed the way I think about my breakfast: I now look forward to it. We all know that breakfast is supposed to be the most important meal of the day, but it has always been the one time I actually have to force myself to eat. Because of this, I have generally had one breakfast – egg on toast – which I repeated, automaton-like, just because I knew I had to eat something, and didn't want to think about it. In other words, for a brief hour in the morning, I turned into one of those alien people who aren't thinking about food all the time. Luckily, these recipes have saved me. True, I still often decide the night before (much like, when I worked in an office, I took out the clothes for the next day when I went to bed) to remove the burden of decision-making on the morning itself. But what I am left with is the joy of anticipation, the pleasure of eating, and the feeling that the new day is to be celebrated.

I have chosen to finish the book with this appropriately named chapter, rather than start with it, because I feel that out of endings come new beginnings, and the recipes that follow are my kitchen *carpe diem*.

Matcha latte

When I first read about these, I confess I thought them a ridiculous fad. Now, I am a total convert. Yes matcha is expensive, but making these at home is nothing compared to what you'd pay at a coffee shop. And there is a reason the beautiful green matcha powder costs a lot: the tea is tended carefully, grown under cover (to boost its green color, and keep it tender) and harvested by hand, for a start. There are too many unproven health claims made in its name, though it is certainly rich in antioxidants and high in L-Theanine levels, and L-Theanine – a water-soluble amino acid which has been found to help with anxiety and promote "relaxed alertness" – works in conjunction with the tea's caffeine content to improve cognition. So, all in all, a good start to the day, I'd say.

Being a regular tea drinker on the whole, I find this is the perfect tea for a non-coffee-drinker who wants something with froth and get-up-and-go. And the amount of milk certainly keeps one full (I think of it as a meal of a drink). I like mine made with oat milk (and I buy one especially made for baristas, as it froths fantastically) but otherwise do use almond milk (and, if you're a sugar-taker, which I'm not, sweetened almond milk) or other milk of your choice.

Matcha powder varies tremendously in taste and price but try to use a good quality one.

SERVES 1

1½ teaspoons matcha powder, plus more
if you're making a pattern on top

2 tablespoons hot water, from a recently boiled
kettle

¾ cup milk of your choice

° Spoon the matcha powder into a mug, add the hot water, and combine using a frothing mixer, such as an Aerolatte.

° Warm the milk in the microwave for 1½ minutes, or in a saucepan on the stove, till steaming hot, then remove and froth until it has almost doubled in volume.

° Pour half the milk into the matcha paste and combine, using the frother, then top with the rest of the milk. If you want to feel like a barista in your own home, buy a pack of stencils made just for this purpose (they saw me coming) and place the one of your choice on top of the mug as you dust the cut-out parts with matcha powder.

Rhubarb and ginger compote

I haven't written a book yet without a recipe for rhubarb ("like a sharp-tongued best friend, who makes everything more interesting" in the words of the *Los Angeles Times* food writer Russ Parsons) and I am not about to start now.

Here, the rhubarb's sharpness is given extra pep by copious amounts of ginger and, dolloped on to yogurt in the morning with a sprinkling of chopped pistachios, is a beautiful, uplifting, and invigorating start to the day. In January in the UK it is possible to buy tender indoor-grown forced rhubarb which is the most glorious pink color but look out for the younger more tender stalks in spring when the season starts.

---

1 ¾ pounds rhubarb (trimmed weight)

2-inch piece fresh ginger, peeled

1 cup sugar

○ Preheat the oven to 375°F. Chop up the rhubarb: thin stalks should be cut into 2-inch sticks; fat stems should be cut into 1-inch chunks. The point here is just to make sure that all the rhubarb cooks evenly. Put into an ovenproof dish or roasting pan in which the rhubarb can sit in one layer; I use one measuring approx. 12 x 10 x 2 inches.

○ Cut the peeled ginger into thin-ish slices lengthways, then cut these slices in half across. Add to the rhubarb and, using your hands, toss to mix. Now add the sugar and gently mix in: you may prefer to use spatulas for this, but I don't mind getting my hands sticky. With clean hands, cover with a sheet of aluminum foil, making sure the edges are sealed tightly, and put in the oven for 45 minutes. It may be wise to check at 30 minutes and turn the mixture gently to help all the sugar dissolve, and I mean gently: you don't want to break up the rhubarb and risk turning it into mush. Certainly, I like the rhubarb pieces to be discrete entities.

○ After 45 minutes, or when the rhubarb is tender, but still holding its shape, and the sugar has turned to a pink syrup with the rhubarb's juices, take out of the oven, remove the aluminum foil lid, and let it stand for 5–10 minutes to cool a little, and then scoop gently into a large strainer suspended over a bowl or a wide-necked pitcher. Pour the pink liquid into a saucepan and put on the stove over a high heat to reduce. You could always do this using the pan you've just cooked the rhubarb in, if it can go onto direct heat. Let it simmer briskly until reduced by half. If you're doing this in a saucepan, this will take about 5–7 minutes, and it'll be a lot quicker in an oven pan. You can go in and check for taste and viscosity.

○ When the puce syrup's reduced, pour it into a pitcher or bowl to cool a little – if you want warmth rather than heat from the ginger, pick out the strips of ginger from the rhubarb at this point – and then pour over the rhubarb. Leave the dish of rhubarb to cool completely for about 2 hours, before covering and putting in the refrigerator until the morning, or for up to 5 days, or portion up for the freezer for further future breakfasts.

STORE NOTE	FREEZE NOTE
Cooled compote will keep, covered, in refrigerator for up to 5 days.	Can be frozen for up to 3 months. Thaw overnight in refrigerator.

Spiced apple and blueberry compote

I love an old-fashioned dish of apple compote: it strikes that all-important balance between soothing and astringent, which makes it the perfect, edible wake-up call.

This fantastically hued blueberried version, with its warm spices, loses none of that desirable sharpness, but do add more maple syrup if you want a sweeter compote, and anyway, the sweetness of blueberries varies enormously. Should you want to eat this dolloped onto a bowl of tangy yogurt, you may want to drizzle a little extra maple syrup over, too.

MAKES APPROX. 2 CUPS, ENOUGH FOR 4–6 PORTIONS, DEPENDING ON WHAT IT'S SERVED WITH

4 large Granny Smith apples (approx. 1¾ pounds total), peeled and quartered

¾ cup blueberries

1 stick cinnamon

1 whole clove

¼ cup water

2 tablespoons maple syrup, or more to taste

- Chop the apple quarters into fairly small pieces and drop these into a heavy-based saucepan that comes with a tight-fitting lid.

- Add the blueberries, cinnamon stick, clove, and water, put the lid on, and place over a medium to low heat. In about 2–3 minutes, you can lift the lid up to check that the scant amount of water has come to a boil. Replace the lid, and let it cook for about 10–15 minutes, giving a vigorous stir every 3 minutes or so with a wooden spoon. This is just to make sure that nothing sticks to the bottom of the pan, and so that you can aid the delicious disintegration of the fruit.

- When everything is cooked and stirred to a purée (bar the odd speck) take the pan off the heat, add 2 tablespoons of maple syrup, and beat exuberantly with your wooden spoon, but don't break up the cinnamon stick. You should have a ridiculously magenta, spiced, and sharp compote in front of you. Taste to see if you want any more maple syrup, and add accordingly, then leave to cool.

STORE NOTE	FREEZE NOTE
Cooled compote will keep, covered, in refrigerator for up to 5 days.	Can be frozen for up to 3 months. Thaw overnight in refrigerator.

Avocado toast with quick-pickled breakfast radishes

Avocado toast is my favorite breakfast, lunch, tea, supper, and I know I am not alone in this. Crowned with some, appropriately named, breakfast radishes, it makes a breakfast that will see you through for hours on those days when you're frightened that lunch may be late. French breakfast radishes are long in shape, with their red fading to white at one end; these are much easier to cut into juliennes for pickling. But if an evening's quick pickling isn't for you, then just cut a radish or two in the morning and scatter the peppery crimson strips over your greenly luscious avocado.

SERVES 1–2

FOR THE PICKLED RADISHES:

6 ounces French breakfast radishes

½ cup rice vinegar

½ cup cold water

2 tablespoons sugar

2 teaspoons sea salt flakes or kosher salt

2½ teaspoons whole pink peppercorns

FOR THE AVOCADO TOAST:

½ teaspoon sea salt flakes or kosher salt, or to taste

2 teaspoons lime juice

1–2 slices bread of your choice

1 ripe avocado

¼ teaspoon crushed red pepper flakes

1–2 tablespoons chopped fresh dill

½-inch piece fresh ginger, peeled and grated (¾ teaspoon)

○ Cut off the beards and the stems of the radishes, and then slice into eighths lengthways (if they are very skinny, then quarters will do). Put into a small bowl.

○ Put the rice vinegar, water, sugar, salt, and peppercorns into a small saucepan and bring to a boil. Turn off the heat, and stir to make sure the sugar and salt are dissolved, then pour over the prepared radishes, patting them down with the back of a spoon for a minute or two until they are all submerged. Leave to cool, then put some in the refrigerator overnight for tomorrow's breakfast, before transferring the remainder to an airtight jar with a vinegar-proof lid and keeping for up to 1 month, and many future breakfasts.

○ Add the salt to the lime juice, and toast your bread. While it's cooling a little, fork the flesh of the avocado to a rough purée in a bowl with the ¼ teaspoon of red pepper flakes, 1 tablespoonful of chopped dill, and the freshly grated ginger, for extra pep. Now add the salt and lime juice, stirring it first, and fork to combine. Taste for seasoning. Spread the toast with the zingy avocado, top with radishes, pickled or otherwise, and sprinkle with some more red pepper flakes and dill to taste.

Breakfast banana bread with cardamom and cacao nibs

I positively will everyone in the house not to eat the bananas so that they overripen and I have an excuse to make this. I love all the variants of banana bread I have ever made – much more than I do bananas – but this one is on another level. The smoky bitterness that emanates from both the cardamom and cacao nibs offers a subtle foil to the natural and rich sweetness of the bananas. As this is for breakfast, it isn't terribly sweet, so feel free to up the sugar to 2¼ cups if you have a sweet tooth and want to indulge it. It is also excellent (and tastes sweeter) when toasted and spread with unsalted butter.

2 very ripe or overripe bananas (approx. ¾ cup mashed)	1 ¼ teaspoons baking powder
2 extra large eggs	1 teaspoon baking soda
¾ cup plain (runny) yogurt or buttermilk	2 teaspoons ground cardamom, or seeds from 1 tablespoon cardamom pods, ground
½ cup light and mild olive oil	½ cup cacao nibs
2 cups plus 2 tablespoons all-purpose flour	
1 cup light brown sugar	1 x 2-pound loaf pan approx. 9 x 6½ x 3 inches

- Preheat the oven to 350°F, and put a paper liner into your loaf pan (or line the bottom with parchment paper and grease the sides with a little vegetable oil).

- I do the whole thing using a freestanding mixer, but a bowl and an electric whisk, or a wooden spoon and plenty of elbow grease would be fine. Mash the bananas (and if you're not using a freestanding mixer, use a fork and a smallish bowl first, otherwise the flat paddle of a freestanding mixer will do) and beat in 1 egg at a time, followed by the yogurt or buttermilk, then the oil, and beat it all together. I measure the flour, sugar, baking powder, baking soda, and cardamom into a bowl, and whisk together, while this is going on.

- Slow the speed down while you add the dry ingredients, gradually, beating all the while, and then turn the speed slightly higher again, and beat for 1 minute until all the dry ingredients are incorporated. You may have to scrape the bowl down and give a short final beat if you notice any flour sticking to the edges of the bowl. Then, using a rubber spatula or wooden spoon, fold in the cacao nibs by hand and transfer the mixture to your prepared pan and thence to the oven for 1 hour (it is wise to start checking at 45 minutes) or until a cake tester comes out clean.

- Sit the loaf pan on a wire rack and leave the banana bread in the pan until cold. Slip it out, in its paper liner (or parchment paper), and wrap with more parchment and then aluminum foil and keep for a day – if you can – before eating.

STORE NOTE	FREEZE NOTE
Store in an airtight container in a cool place for up to 1 week.	Can be frozen for up to 3 months. Wrap cake in a double layer of plastic wrap and a layer of aluminum foil. To thaw, unwrap and put on a wire rack at room temperature for about 5 hours. Or wrap individual slices in plastic wrap and put into a resealable bag, and thaw by toasting on a low heat.

Breakfast bars 2.0

I have a breakfast bar recipe in an earlier book, but this is the new, improved version: gluten-free, dairy-free, and enough seeds to make you start sprouting. I've used no sugar, but before you start thinking this is virtuously sugar-free (which I could claim it to be), remember that the sweetness that comes from the dates is, in essence, sugar, though certainly it's unprocessed and full of fiber at the same time. There are a lot of ingredients, but you need a good mixture to give crunch and chew — and all manner of smugness-inducing nutrients — though you can fiddle about with them. You can, for example, use sunflower seeds in place of flax seeds, or half and half rather than all flax seeds, as below, and you can also use puffed rice (gluten-free if needed) or buckwheat flakes in place of cornflakes. In theory, cornflakes (and oats) should be gluten-free, but if crucial, make sure it's stipulated on the package.

If you can't get hold of medjool dates, then use 12 ounces pitted dried dates and up the water to 1⅔ cups. And they'll take about 10, rather than 5, minutes to cook until they're soft enough to mash to a purée.

Make these bars at the weekend, and you'll be set up for the week if you're someone who needs to grab-and-go in the morning. They come in pretty handy for that 4pm slump, too.

MAKES 16 BARS

9 ounces medjool dates	½ cup cacao nibs
2 teaspoons ground cinnamon	3 tablespoons chia seeds
1⅓ cups cold water	1 cup cornflakes (gluten-free if required)
⅔ cup goji berries	1 cup organic quick-cooking oats (not instant)
½ cup shelled pumpkin seeds	
1 cup brown flax seeds	1 x 8-inch square baking pan

○ Preheat the oven to 350°F, and line the bottom and sides of your pan with parchment paper. Pit the dates and tear them with your fingers into a small saucepan, add the cinnamon, cover with the water, bring to a boil, and let simmer briskly for 5 minutes. Turn off the heat, and beat with a fork until you have a rough purée.

○ Put all the remaining ingredients into a large bowl, add the date mixture, and mix until everything is combined. I wear a pair of disposable vinyl gloves for this.

○ Squodge into your prepared pan and bake in the oven for 30 minutes, until firm and set, and golden on top and darker around the edges. Leave to cool in the pan before cutting into pieces.

STORE NOTE	FREEZE NOTE
Store in an airtight container in a cool place or in refrigerator for up to 1 week.	Wrap bars individually in plastic wrap or aluminum foil and put in a resealable bag, or stack bars in an airtight container with parchment paper in between the layers. Freeze for up to 2 months. To thaw, put bars on a wire rack and leave at room temperature for about 2 hours.

Chai muffins

Taking tea in muffin form seems ideal for breakfast, and the warm spices of chai bring scented richness without heft. I've made these dairy-free, but if you want to, you can easily use reduced fat milk in place of the almond milk, below. And if you can't get the white spelt flour, which is magnificent in muffins, use 2 cups all-purpose flour and ²/₃ cup whole wheat (not bread) flour instead. I want to make it as easy as possible for you to make these, as this is a particularly splendid specimen of muffin.

Talking of which, it makes sense to steep the milk, leave it to cool, and measure out all the ingredients, putting the eggs by the side, the night before, so that you can shimmy into the kitchen in the morning and bake up a batch without adding a furrow to your brow.

¾ cup plus 2 tablespoons unsweetened almond milk

2 Chai teabags

1 teaspoon ground cinnamon

2⅔ cups white spelt flour

2½ teaspoons baking powder

¾ cup light brown sugar

½ cup raw almonds, roughly chopped

2 extra large eggs

⅔ cup vegetable oil

1 x 12-cup muffin pan

- Warm the almond milk with the contents of the 2 teabags (I just rip them open over the pan) and cinnamon – stirring to mix – and leave to cool.

- While the milk's cooling, preheat the oven to 400°F and line your muffin pan with paper liners.

- In a large bowl, measure out the flour, baking powder, sugar, and all but 2 tablespoons of the chopped almonds, and combine well.

- When the milk has cooled, add the eggs, and oil, then whisk well.

- Add the liquid ingredients to the dry ingredients, using a wooden spoon. Don't be too efficient about this: a slightly lumpy batter makes for lighter muffins.

- Divide the mixture between the muffin cups (it will fill them well), then sprinkle equally with the remaining almonds and bake in the oven for 20–25 minutes, or until a cake tester comes out clean and the muffins are slightly risen and pleasingly golden on top.

- Remove to a wire rack to cool for about 10 minutes before devouring.

STORE NOTE	FREEZE NOTE
Best eaten on day they are made, otherwise store in an airtight container for 1–2 days. Reheat in an oven preheated to 300°F for about 8 minutes. Best served warm.	Stack fully cooled muffins in an airtight container with parchment paper between the layers, or wrap individually in plastic wrap then put in a resealable bag. Freeze for up to 3 months. Thaw on a wire rack for about 1 hour. Reheat as in Store Note.

Buckwheat, banana, and carrot muffins

These may not be the most splendid muffins you have ever cast your eye on, but they will be some of the most delectable you ever bite into. The reason they keep their magnificence hidden is that buckwheat flour is gluten-free, and so the muffins do not rise much as they cook. But the important thing – and this is not always the case with gluten-free baking – is that they are lush and light. The banana, carrots, and almond meal keep the muffins wonderfully succulent, but it is the toasty nuttiness of the buckwheat that is the stand-out star here. On the subject of which, while buckwheat itself has no gluten, some flour manufacturers do warn of cross-contamination from other flours milled on site, so if it is a matter of urgency, do check that it says gluten-free on the package.

1 ripe banana	½ teaspoon baking soda
zest and juice of 1 unwaxed lemon	2 teaspoons gluten-free baking powder
⅓ cup light brown sugar	8 ounces carrots, peeled and grated
2 extra large eggs	1½ teaspoons sesame seeds
⅔ cup light and mild olive oil	
1 cup buckwheat flour	1 x 12-cup muffin pan
½ cup almond meal	

- Preheat the oven to 400°F and line your muffin pan with paper liners.

- Mash the banana in a large bowl with the finely grated zest and juice of the lemon, and then whisk in the sugar, eggs, and oil until smooth.

- In another bowl, large enough to take all the ingredients later, combine the buckwheat flour, almond meal, baking soda, and baking powder, and mix thoroughly with a fork.

- Now, pour the bowl of wet ingredients into the bowl of dry ingredients, add the grated carrots, and stir with a wooden spoon till everything's just combined.

- Using an ice cream scoop, or however you find this easiest, fill each muffin cup liner. This mixture will give you enough to fill each almost right to the top. Sprinkle with the sesame seeds and bake in the oven for 15–20 minutes.

- When the muffins are ready, a cake tester should come out clean. Remove the pan from the oven to a wire rack. I like to take the muffins out of the pan straightaway and sit them directly on the rack, but then 1) I've got asbestos hands and 2) I'm very impatient. I'll leave it to you to take them out when you feel comfortable handling them. I love these best warm, but the juiciness provided by the carrots and banana means they are also good cold.

STORE NOTE	FREEZE NOTE
Best eaten on day they are made, otherwise store in an airtight container in a cool place for up to 5 days. Reheat in an oven preheated to 300°F for 5–7 minutes.	Stack fully cooled muffins in an airtight container with parchment paper between the layers, or wrap individually in plastic wrap then put in a resealable bag. Freeze for up to 3 months. Thaw on a wire rack for about 1 hour. Reheat as in Store Note.

Pomegranate muesli

My maternal grandmother used to mix up her Bircher muesli every night so it would be ready for her breakfast tray in the morning. I loved watching her quiet absorption and practiced deftness as she went about this evening ritual, even if it did let me know it was bedtime. But I just couldn't get on with her muesli, and still can't: I cannot abide the shredded apple in the milk that traditionalists insist upon. I fear this is an extravagant muesli my grandmother would not approve of; she'd look particularly askance at the fact that I buy my pomegranate seeds in containers. But it makes me happy – and she'd want that.

I find oat milk optimal here, but feel free to use the milk of your choice, of course. And in theory, oats should be gluten-free, but if this is crucial, do check the packaging to be sure.

SERVES 1

¼ cup old-fashioned rolled or sprouted oats (not instant)	1–2 tablespoons chopped raw almonds or sliced almonds
⅔ cup milk of your choice, plus more as needed	2 tablespoons pomegranate seeds
2–3 soft dried apricots	honey, to dribble over on serving (optional)

◦ Measure the oats into a bowl and pour the milk over. Snip in the dried apricots: I find it easiest to use scissors and let the pieces drop into the bowl. Give it a good stir, then cover with plastic wrap and leave overnight in the refrigerator or in a cool place.

◦ The next morning, stir it again – you shouldn't need to add any more milk, as I make this quite runny to start off with – just to combine the swollen oats and fruit with the milk still left at the top, then stir in half the chopped almonds and pomegranate seeds, and sprinkle more of both on top, to taste. Those with a sweet tooth might want to drizzle some honey over.

Toasty olive oil granola

This is a pared-down — though most definitely luxurious — granola, in the sense that it has no dried fruit in it. Nor does it clump together, as it is markedly less sweet than standard versions. In other words, what it's not is the sort of granola that's like confectionery through the back door, and I very much prefer it.

I like this with almond milk and sometimes toss in a few fresh berries too — blackberries being my favorite here — though it is also good eaten with yogurt and blueberries. And I have been known to eat it by grabbed handfuls straight from the jar.

MAKES ENOUGH TO FILL 1 X 1.5 QUART JAR

3 cups quick-cooking rolled oats (not instant), preferably organic

2 teaspoons ground ginger

2 teaspoons ground cinnamon

1 teaspoon sea salt flakes or kosher salt

¾ cup raw almonds

½ cup sunflower seeds

½ cup pumpkin seeds

1/3 cup brown flax seeds

½ cup sliced almonds

3 tablespoons sesame seeds

½ cup extra-virgin olive oil

½ cup maple syrup

1 x half sheet pan

○ Preheat the oven to 300°F and line your baking sheet with parchment paper.

○ Tip the oats into a large bowl, add the spices and salt, and mix well (I use my hands for this).

○ Now add all the nuts and seeds, and mix well again.

○ In a measuring cup, combine the oil and maple syrup, then pour the mixture into the oats, nuts, and seeds and, with either a fork, or hands encased in disposable vinyl gloves, mix to combine. Tip onto the prepared baking sheet, and move it around so that it covers the pan evenly.

○ Put in the oven to toast gently for 30 minutes and then, with spoons or spatulas, turn it to help toast the underside as well. Put back in the oven for another 30 minutes, and then sit the pan on a wire rack until the granola's cold.

STORE NOTE

Store in a sealed jar or an airtight container for up to 1 month.

Maple pecan no-wait, no-cook oats

This features prominently in my notional breakfast schedule because it is pretty well instant and needs absolutely no forethought. It is, if not a life-saver, then certainly a good-mood-preserver, and much called upon when I have to bolt out of the door and need something I can make last minute. But it also gets creamier as it stands, so by all means, mix it up before you go to bed, if you want.

SERVES 1

$^2/_3$ cup plain yogurt

½ teaspoon ground cinnamon

4 teaspoons maple syrup

4 teaspoons fine oat bran

4 teaspoons crumbled pecans

- Tip the yogurt into a bowl and stir in the cinnamon, followed by 2 teaspoons of the maple syrup and then the 4 teaspoons of oat bran.

- In a little cup, mix the crumbled pecans with the 2 remaining teaspoons of maple syrup and spoon over the oat bowl. That's all, folks.

Chia seed pudding with blueberries and pumpkin seeds

Well, blow me down if I don't love chia seed pudding. It certainly took me by surprise, anyway. Chia seeds don't have any taste in themselves, which is why I scent the milk they're soaked in with cinnamon, rosewater, and orange flower water, thereby giving myself a taste of exotica at breakfast. The deal about chia seeds (apart from the fact that they are meant to be a Force for Good in the world, nutritionally speaking, about which I have no view) is the texture, and this is not for everyone. The pudding that emerges, once the seeds have swollen in the milk, is tapioca-like, for sure, but then, I liked frog spawn at school, too. Those who are hesitant about trying it should be reassured by the fact that its glorious (to me) glutinousness is tempered by the crunch of pumpkin seeds and the juicy brightness of berries.

SERVES 1

¾ cup almond milk

½ teaspoon ground cinnamon

½ teaspoon rosewater

½ teaspoon orange flower water

1½ teaspoons black or white chia seeds

⅓ cup blueberries

2 tablespoons shelled pumpkin seeds

1 x 1-cup preserving jar or other resealable jar

- Since the chia seeds need to be stirred frequently once they've gone into the milk, I find it best to make these in small preserving jars, so that I can shake 'em up easily, rather than uncovering plastic wrap, stirring, re-wrapping, and repeating this dull procedure regularly. So: fill your jar with milk, stir in the ground cinnamon (which will not be absorbed, but still float about the surface at this stage), then add the rosewater, orange flower water, and chia seeds, seal with the lid, and shake. And then shake 3 or 4 times over about 15 minutes or so before putting in the refrigerator to soak overnight.

- Open the lid, and give the now-glutinous pudding a stir, then top with blueberries and pumpkin seeds before eating. (This has the virtue of turning your breakfast into a portable feast.) Or decant the pudding into a bowl, and mix the seeds and berries more thoroughly.

Fried egg and kimchi taco

This is definitely *the* breakfast for the morning after the night before. I don't leave it for those obviously infrequent occasions, however. If I can find an excuse for getting *kimchi* – a Korean pickle that has fire and tang – into something, I will, and at 11am on a Saturday morning when I am happily (and with a clear head) mooching about the house in need of something that serves both as a late breakfast and an early lunch, I can often be found wolfing this down.

SERVES 1

1 soft corn tortilla	1 large egg
2 tablespoons vegetable oil	pinch sea salt flakes or kosher salt
½ fresh red chile, seeded (or not, as desired) and finely chopped	¼ cup kimchi

- Put a cast iron skillet or heavy-based frying pan of about 8 inches in diameter on the heat, and when hot, warm the tortilla in it: give it a minute on one side, then turn over and give it 30 seconds on the other, then remove to a waiting plate.

- Add the oil and half of your chopped chile, then once the chile has paled a little in the hot oil, crack in the egg, sprinkle the yolk with a pinch of sea salt flakes, and spoon the chile-flecked oil over until the white is set. Transfer to the middle of the waiting tortilla.

- Add the kimchi around the egg, and sprinkle both egg and kimchi with the remaining chile. I then like to pierce the yolk, smear it over the kimchi and tortilla, halve it to form a half-mooned sandwich – and apply to face.

Sweet potato, black bean, and avocado burrito

Since I am in the habit of having ready-baked sweet potatoes around the house, I never need to cook them especially to make this, but if you need to start from scratch, and want to make just enough for this, know that the ½ cup of sweet potato, below, is the mashed interior of a 6-ounce sweet potato baked for 1 hour in a 425°F oven, then left to cool. And while I've used canned beans here, were you to have any leftover Cuban Black Beans (see **p.214**), then obviously use those.

SERVES 2–4

2 burrito wraps

½ cup cold mashed sweet potato

2 tablespoons plain yogurt

1 teaspoon pimentón picante or paprika

1 teaspoon ground cumin

2 fat pinches sea salt flakes

1 cup (about ¾ x 15-ounce can) black beans, drained

2 small ripe tomatoes, roughly chopped

¼ cup chopped fresh cilantro, plus more for sprinkling

1 ripe avocado, halved, pitted, and sliced

⅓ cup grated Cheddar or other cheese of your choice

- Preheat the oven to 400°F.

- Place the 2 wraps in front of you. Mix – a fork is all you need for this – the mashed sweet potato with the yogurt, pimentón or paprika, cumin, and a good pinch of salt and spread this over the 2 wraps.

- In a bowl, mash the black beans slightly with the back of a fork, then add the chopped tomatoes, another pinch of salt, and the chopped cilantro and stir to mix. Divide this between the 2 sweet-potato-sticky wraps, then do the same with the sliced avocado, and top, equally, with the grated cheese. Transfer to a baking sheet and cook for 5 minutes. If the wraps won't fit together on the same sheet, either use two sheets, or cook one burrito at a time, sharing each one – eaten unrolled – in succession.

- Either eat rolled up as is proper with a burrito, or – and this makes them go further – cut into quarters and then eat as you might a pizza, curling the softer pointy end of the triangle over the crunchier flat end, for the perfect breakfast – indeed, any time – sandwich.

Oat pancakes with raspberries and honey

If you promise pancakes to an 8-year-old, these are decidedly not the pancakes they will have in mind, though this doesn't mean they aren't for the rest of us. Think of them rather like the oatcakes you might have with cheese, only in pancake form; as with regular fluffy pancakes, however, it is what you eat with them that creates the magic. Here, I've made a honey and raspberry syrup, and the mixture of the soft, oaty cakes, the honey, and the raspberries has a decidedly Scottish flavor. This leads me to think this could be good with a wee nip of whisky somewhere in the mix and, in deference to the great Hibernian dessert, Cranachan, a dollop of whipped cream.

The lack of flour means that they are gluten-free (though because of cross-contamination where they are made, you should look for oats that say as much on the package, if this is crucial). And while you can use regular whole milk, I much prefer oat milk, which richly enhances their flavor, as well as makes them dairy-free for those for whom that is a concern. Though in which case, banish all thought of whipped cream now.

½ cup honey	1 ½ teaspoons ground cinnamon
1 ¼ cups frozen (or fresh) raspberries	7 tablespoons oat milk or any other sort you wish
1 cup quick-cooking oats (not instant), preferably organic	1 egg
¼ teaspoon sea salt flakes or kosher salt	1 teaspoon vanilla paste or extract
1 teaspoon baking powder	1 teaspoon vegetable oil

- Warm the honey and raspberries in a small saucepan over a medium heat, stirring frequently, until the raspberries have thawed. This shouldn't take more than 3 minutes or so. Take the pan off the heat.

- Put the oats and salt in a blender or a food processor with the small bowl fitted, and process until you get the consistency of flour, a mealy flour to be sure, but it should still be fine-ground.

- Tip into a bowl and stir in the baking powder and cinnamon.

- In a measuring cup, whisk together the milk, egg, and vanilla, and then stir the wet mixture into the dry, until thoroughly combined. If the batter thickens too much, add more milk. And do not let this batter rest, as otherwise it will thicken too much.

- Pour ½ a teaspoon of oil onto a smooth, non-stick griddle (or large cast iron or heavy-based frying pan) and, with a piece of paper towel, smear it over the whole surface. Put the griddle on a medium heat and, when hot, add the batter, using a quarter-cup measure but only filling it two-thirds full. You should get 4 pancakes at a time, and they will need around 2 minutes a side. Generally, when cooking pancakes, you turn them over when you see bubbles coming to the uppermost side, and while that still holds true, the bubbles are rather understated here. So slip a spatula underneath a pancake after 2 minutes to see if the underside looks cooked, and then when it is, flip it, and the rest of the pancakes, over and cook for another 2 minutes. As always, do not press down on the pancakes as they cook, and do not flip them more than once. When you've cooked the first 4, pile them on a plate, and cover with a clean tea towel, then oil the pan again and proceed as before.

- Serve immediately – the oats carry on drinking up liquid, and the pancakes will dry on standing – with the warm raspberry honey poured on top.

Dutch baby

I've only ever eaten Dutch babies in the States, where they are brought out to you at the table with great pomp: great pancakes puffed up and golden, still in the cast iron skillets they were cooked in. Obviously, I had to make my own at home. Not being a restaurant, I don't want to be juggling with heavy pans, giving each person their own, so I've made mine a giant one for sharing; this ain't no baby, that's for sure. It's a wonderful thing to whip up when you have people for breakfast at the weekend: firstly, because it looks so magnificent, and secondly, because you don't have to stand at the stove like a short-order cook.

The "Dutch" of the title doesn't in fact refer to Holland, or anything to do with that country, but rather owes its name to the fact that this particular pancake comes from the German-American community known as the Pennsylvania Dutch and would originally have been served with melted butter, sugar, and lemon, and indeed they often still are.

This kind of baked pancake is really a feature of much Northern European cooking: the Swedes have their *ugnspannkaka* just as the British have Yorkshire Pudding. It takes an American, however, to decide to start making them for breakfast.

While you can, of course, serve this mega-pancake just sprinkled with sugar and lemon juice or, for a more diner taste, with a side order of bacon and maple syrup, I like it tumbled with berries and dusted with confectioners' sugar with a bowl of crème fraîche within arm's reach. I confess, I also add an ooze of maple syrup as I eat.

3 extra large eggs

1 tablespoon sugar

²⁄₃ cup whole milk

²⁄₃ cup all-purpose flour

1½ teaspoons vanilla paste or extract

pinch salt

freshly grated nutmeg

2 tablespoons unsalted butter

TO SERVE:

confectioners' sugar

berries

crème fraîche

maple syrup

1 x 10-inch cast iron skillet, or 1 x small roasting pan approx. 11 x 8 x 2 inches

○ Preheat the oven to 425°F, and straightaway put your pan into the oven to heat up while you prepare the batter.

○ Beat the eggs with the sugar in an electric mixer until light and frothy. Whisk in the milk, flour, vanilla, salt, and grated nutmeg, and beat until you have a smooth but thin batter.

○ Wearing a thick oven mitt, remove the pan from the oven and put the butter carefully into the hot pan and swirl it to melt, then quickly pour in the batter and return it to the oven.

○ Bake until puffed and golden brown, about 18–20 minutes.

○ Serve dusted with confectioners' sugar, and a tumble of berries, if the idea appeals; otherwise, see Intro.

MAKE AHEAD NOTE

The batter can be made the night before. Cover and refrigerate until needed. Whisk briefly before using.

French toast "soldiers" with maple syrup

I am not normally in favor of cutesiness, but something came over me at the photographic shoot for this book – perhaps more hysteria than whimsy – and I felt compelled to wash out the egg I'd cracked for the French toast, before painstakingly removing every bit of membrane and then filling the shell with maple syrup. In my everyday life, I simply pour the maple syrup into a pair of egg cups, then dunk in my French toast "soldiers". But certainly, the tableau I have created here better conveys the pun.

I like to use a thin slice of sour and dense bread from the Poilâne bakery (it really is *French* French toast), but any good solid sourdough (or other) would do. I would advise against using ready-sliced white bread, or anything aerated.

And I should add, this makes as good a midnight feast as it does a breakfast.

2 slices sourdough bread, crusts removed

1 egg, carefully broken to reserve the egg shell

2 tablespoons whole milk

1 teaspoon vanilla paste or extract

1 teaspoon butter

¼ teaspoon vegetable oil

maple syrup, to serve

° Cut each slice of sourdough bread into 2 sticks or "soldiers". This should give 4 sticks that can just about fit into your egg shell (or, more easily, into cups) filled with maple syrup.

° Whisk the egg, milk, and vanilla extract in a shallow dish that the "soldiers" will fit in. Soak the "soldiers" in this for 2 minutes a side, by which time they should be quite sodden but not falling to pieces, and there will be a little egg mixture left in the bottom of the dish.

° Heat the butter and oil in a cast iron skillet or a heavy-based, non-stick frying pan, and, once the butter has melted, cook the "soldiers" for 2 minutes a side over a medium heat. You want the eggy bread to color gently and become golden on either side, but not scorch too much.

° Once the "soldiers" have had their time, take them out of the pan and arrange them on a plate, with an egg cup ready.

° Rinse the egg shell before putting it in the egg cup and filling with maple syrup or, more sensibly, fill a couple of egg cups (or a little bowl) with maple syrup, as much or as little as you like. However you have served the maple syrup, dip the French toast sticks into it, and eat in solitary splendor, savoring the moment.

Baked French toast with plums and pecans

This is the French toast recipe you need if cooking for a crowd. I find it particularly easy, since you can prepare it all the night before, which seems a good move should you be having people for brunch or – more pertinent still – have them staying overnight and need to provide breakfast.

Actually, you *need* really to get started a whole day ahead, so that the bread has time to stale (though you can do this more quickly in a low oven). Yes, obviously it would make more sense to do this with stale brioche, but you are unlikely to have 1 pound of stale brioche, surely. I, being lazy, buy ready-sliced brioche for this, though do use proper brioche (or, indeed, challah), and cut it into thin-ish slices, no more than ½-inch thick.

CUTS INTO 12 SLABS

1 sliced brioche loaf (approx. 1 pound)

butter for greasing

2½ x 15-ounce cans plums in syrup

6 extra large eggs

¼ cup sugar

2 cups heavy cream

2 cups whole milk

½ teaspoon ground nutmeg

FOR THE STREUSEL TOPPING:

½ cup chopped pecans

2 teaspoons ground cinnamon

2 teaspoons soft unsalted butter

½ cup maple syrup

1 x ovenproof dish approx. 9 x 13 x 2 inches, or 1 x oval ovenproof dish approx. 13 x 9 inches

- Cut each slice of brioche in half, so that you have triangles, and place these on wire racks to dry out: this could take about 6 hours, or up to a day, depending on the weather; or put them on a wire rack or directly on the oven shelf in an oven preheated to 200°F for 15–20 minutes (turning halfway).

- When the bread's stale, lightly grease your ovenproof dish with butter, and drain the cans of plums in a strainer over a measuring cup or bowl. Remove any pits from the plums, and reserve the syrup. Tip the drained, pitted plums into the bottom of the dish. Arrange the staled brioche slices, overlapping, on top of the plums, and get on with the custard.

- Whisk together the eggs, sugar, cream, milk, and nutmeg and pour over the brioche slices, pressing the bread to help it soak up its rich drink. Cover with plastic wrap and leave in a cool place for up to 2 hours or in the refrigerator overnight. If you have time, let it come to room temperature before putting it in the oven.

- Preheat the oven to 350°F. Make the streusel topping by mixing the chopped pecans, cinnamon, and butter together in a bowl until you have a dark clumpy mess, and then dot this on top of the custard-soaked brioche slices. Bake in the oven for 45–50 minutes, by which time the top will be risen and bronze, and the custard set. If baking from fridge-cold, add an extra 10–15 minutes to the cooking time. When it's ready, remove from the oven and let it stand for 10–20 minutes before serving.

- Pour the plum syrup you've saved from the cans into a saucepan and boil until reduced to about 1 cup (this should take about 6–7 minutes). You might have to check a couple of times while it's bubbling away, so keep a heatproof measuring cup handy. When you've got your 1 cup, or thereabouts, add the maple syrup and warm through, then pour into the measuring cup or a couple of warmed smaller pitchers for serving.

MAKE AHEAD NOTE	STORE NOTE
Pudding can be assembled up to 1 day ahead. Cover and store in refrigerator (remove from refrigerator 1 hour before baking). Topping can be made 1 day ahead. Cover and store at cool room temperature. Syrup can be made 1 day ahead. Store in an airtight container or sealed jar in refrigerator. Can be warmed gently in a saucepan on a low heat before serving.	Cool leftovers, then cover and refrigerate within 2 hours of making. Will keep in refrigerator for up to 2 days. Eat cold, or reheat individual portions in the microwave in short bursts, following manufacturer's instructions.

Soda bread rolls with fennel seeds and cranberries

I recommend eating one of these for breakfast with lots of unsalted butter, which gives all the sweetness I need, but if you want a sweeter roll, add 3 tablespoons honey along with the yogurt and egg. Like any soda bread, these rolls are as good eaten with a slice of cheese as they are with butter and preserves, and the slightly more exotic scent of the fennel seeds and the bursts of tart flavor from the cranberries don't stop these from having the coziness of a – perhaps fictional – Irish parlor. And while they are not something I would whip up for an everyday breakfast, when I've got time on my hands I love to get said hands working a dough to conjure up a batch of these. A cursory glance at the recipe will show you how gratifyingly easy they are to make.

3 tablespoons unsalted butter

1 cup all-purpose flour

2/3 cup whole wheat (not bread) flour, plus more for cutting and sprinkling

1 teaspoon fine sea salt

1½ teaspoons baking powder

¾ teaspoon baking soda

¾ teaspoon ground allspice

2/3 cup runny plain yogurt or buttermilk

1 extra large egg

2/3 cup dried cranberries

2 teaspoons fennel seeds

○ Melt the butter and then leave it to cool a little. Preheat the oven to 425°F, and line a baking sheet with parchment paper.

○ In a large bowl, combine both flours, the salt, baking powder, baking soda, and ground allspice, and use a fork to mix well.

○ In a measuring cup, whisk the yogurt or buttermilk together with the egg, and then whisk in the cooled, melted butter.

○ Pour the wet ingredients over the bowl of dry ingredients, then add the dried cranberries and fennel seeds, and stir to mix with a wooden spoon. I then do the final bit of mixing with my hands once the dough seems to be coming together.

○ Turn the damp or sticky dough out onto a floury surface, and then cut the ball of dough in half, and then each half into 4 pieces, so that you have 8 bits in total. Shape each piece of dough into a rough ball and place on your lined baking sheet with some space between them.

○ Take a pair of scissors and snip a small "X" shape into the top of each one, then – using your fingers – sprinkle a little whole wheat flour over each roll.

○ Bake in the oven for 15 minutes, or until the rolls are brown and sound hollow when tapped underneath. Let them cool for about 10 minutes before you eat them.

MAKE AHEAD NOTE	STORE NOTE	FREEZE NOTE
Dough can be prepared up to 3 months ahead and frozen. Shape dough into rolls, put on lined baking sheet, and, once solid, transfer to resealable plastic bag and into freezer. Bake from frozen, sprinkling with a little whole wheat flour, and add 2 minutes to baking time.	Rolls are best eaten on day they are made. Store leftovers in an airtight container for 1–2 days. Reheat in oven preheated to 300°F for 8–10 minutes, or split rolls in half and toast under preheated broiler.	Baked rolls can be frozen in resealable bags for up to 3 months. Thaw on wire rack for about 2 hours and reheat as in Store Note.

Oven-baked egg hash

I include this here, as nothing says "weekend breakfast" better than an egg hash, but you will no doubt find yourself rustling it up for suppers just as gladly. Yes, there is a bit of chopping involved, but since you don't have to peel the potatoes, this doesn't take too much time or effort. In fact, the whole brunch dish is wonderfully undemanding, though I'm glad to say, also irrefutably rewarding.

3 tablespoons olive oil

1¾ pounds waxy potatoes

1 red onion, peeled and roughly chopped

2 teaspoons cumin seeds

2 teaspoons black mustard seeds

2 red peppers, seeded and cut into roughly 1½-inch squares

1 teaspoon sea salt flakes

6 eggs

TO SERVE:

Simple Salsa on p.120 or bottled hot sauce

chopped fresh red chiles

- Preheat the oven to 425°F. Pour the oil into a large bowl. Cut each potato into ½-inch slices, then quarter each slice, and drop these slices, as you go, into the bowl.

- Add the chopped onion, along with the cumin seeds, mustard seeds, chopped peppers, and salt, and toss everything together patiently until evenly coated in oily seeds, then tip out onto a large baking pan (I use a half sheet one) in a single layer.

- Bake for 35–40 minutes, or until everything is cooked through and the potatoes are beginning to crisp.

- Take the pan out of the oven and crack one of the eggs into a cup or small bowl, then push the potatoes aside to make a little gap and slip the egg straight into it. Proceed likewise with the remaining eggs, making sure they're evenly spaced on the pan.

- Bung it back into the oven for 5 minutes, until the whites of the eggs are set and the yolks still slightly runny. Then eat immediately, serving a small dish of chopped red chiles and either a bottle of hot sauce or – for preference – the salsa on **p.120** alongside.

MAKE AHEAD NOTE

The potatoes can be cut 1 day ahead. Submerge in a bowl of cold water, cover, and refrigerate. Drain and thoroughly pat dry before using.

INDEX